ANDRÉ BRETON

ANDRÉ BRETON

MAGUS OF SURREALISM

Anna Balakian

NEW YORK
OXFORD UNIVERSITY PRESS
1971

To Elisa
and to Aube

ACKNOWLEDGMENTS

In the penumbra that envelops a writer of recognized stature immediately after his death, the difficulties surrounding the search for data are at their greatest. The absence of the writer as a living source and the curtain that descends on the written documentation as it becomes a pawn in legal stipulations, raise a wall between the critic and his subject. The idea of doing this semi-biographical book on André Breton was conceived some two years before the poet's death; it was to have been supported by answers to a long series of questions I was prepared to ask Breton; a tentative appointment had been set for a summer season at Saint-Cirq La Popie. Death intervened. Some of the questions will forever remain unanswered. But a number of clarifications resulted from the generous co-operation I received from those most intimately linked with Breton at various stages of his life: wife, daughter, former wives, son-in-law, friends, disciples, associates, all opened their memories to me, and to them I extend my gratitude.

First, my thanks go to Breton's only child, Aube, and her husband, Yves Elléouët, whose hospitality I enjoyed shortly after Breton's death; of the twenty-four hours that I stayed under their roof in Saché, we spent all of the waking hours in dialogue about André Breton. Equally sympathetic to my search through the memory of others were his widow, Elisa, and his two previous wives, Simone Kahn (now Mme Michel Collinet) and Jacqueline Lamba. Through all their collective testimony and the documents that each possessed and cherished I was able to reconstruct the total gamut of the development of André Breton's career.

Mme Collinet opened her library as well as her reminiscences to me, made available a copy of the first edition of *Les Champs magnétiques* in which Breton had marked in his own handwriting the passages that were his part of this first collaboration in automatic writing with Philippe Soupault. She also revealed carefully preserved manuscripts of André

Breton's earliest and most crucial writings: the labored First Manifesto, the freewheeling *Poisson soluble,* the heavily worked-over poems of *Clair de Terre* of which the many variants and revisions dispel any notion one might have had that they were the product of automatic writing. Mme Collinet supplied me with photographs of Breton and his companions in the 1920's and illustrations from famous artists, which were available only in limited de luxe copies. She is indeed a devoted curator.

Jacqueline Lamba illuminated Breton's middle years and shed light on his habits of work and his situation in the period of transition from Marseilles to self-exile in New York. An artist herself, she rendered vivid the personality of Breton, and the information contained in a letter she wrote to me about the way Breton worked on his poems should prove of lasting interest to students of the genesis of poetry. I am grateful for her honesty, enthusiasm, and warmth.

Mme Elisa Breton made rare editions accessible to me, she provided me with extremely valuable data surrounding the writing of *Arcane 17,* and has received me generously and freely in the studio that still bears so indelibly the mark and the presence of André Breton at 42 rue Fontaine. Her kind-hearted spontaneity and sincerity established easy communication between us. She let illustrative material from her precious rare editions be photographed and permitted me to quote freely from Breton's writings. Her co-operation at every stage of my work was a source of constant encouragement to me.

The earliest of Breton's surviving friends, Philippe Soupault, granted me two interviews, which were invaluable to my work, and he gave me clues that led to the discovery of the important role of Dr. Pierre Janet in the formation of André Breton's philosophy of surrealism. I appreciated immensely his stimulating conversations. My thanks go to other of Breton's friends and associates who talked to me or wrote to me: to Michel Leiris and Marcel Jean for their illuminating remarks about André Breton; to René Nelli and Georges Henein who cleared up some obscurities for me; to Mme Françoise Selz who made available to me the correspondence of Breton with her late brother, the critic and editor, Léon Pierre-Quint. Jean Schuster, the executor of the Breton estate and most intimate friend of the writer at the time of his death, had the kindness and generosity to invite me to what turned out to be some of the final meetings of Breton's surrealist followers at the Café de la Promenade de Venus, where thanks to the group of disciples and admirers, too numerous to mention here, a sense of the ambience of the last years of Breton's life was conveyed to me. I extend my affectionate thanks to those spontaneously generous writers and artists who scouted around Paris to procure for me Breton pamphlets and surrealist tracts and magazines in April 1967 when I met them.

A number of Breton's erstwhile friends whom I found in New York were equally co-operative. First and foremost, the late Marcel Duchamp, who a short time before his own death shared with me some of his memories of Breton and expressed his candid impressions of the man and the writer. Others who communicated with me about Breton were Edouard Roditi, the first extensive translator of Breton's poetry into English, Charles Henri Ford, poet and editor of *View*, Lewis Galantière, who wrote me a long and fruitful letter about his association with Breton at the Voice of America, art critic and scholar, Meyer Schapiro, who was Breton's only French-speaking neighbor for a while in Greenwich Village, Robert Motherwell, one of the few American artists of the time who recognized Breton's contribution to the art world, and Nicolas Calas, art critic and writer, whose association with Breton and the surrealist movement was among the most enduring.

Through all these dynamic people I was able to reconstruct almost a total continuity in the life that had just ended. There was not a single dull person, one might justifiably conclude, in the successive and cumulative entourage of André Breton.

I thank Dr. Michel Lanoote for his devoted and expert services as amateur photographer in supplying me with reproductions of the several rare frontispieces and cover designs to Breton's works that were made available to me. My appreciation goes to copy-editors Phoebe Hoss and Janet Hobhouse for their careful reading and scrutiny of my manuscript and their pertinent and intelligent editorial assistance.

Two successive grants from the Research Fund of the Graduate School of Arts and Sciences of New York University facilitated the completion of this book. The first permitted me to make a quick trip to Paris shortly after Breton's death—a significant moment for the gleaning of impressions and the acquisition of testimonials and journalistic comments relating to him. The later grant provided me with services for the typing of the manuscript.

Grateful acknowledgment is made to Editions Gallimard for permission to quote from works by André Breton.

Author's translations of passages from *Nadja* are made with the courtesy of Grove Press which owns translation rights for that work.

CONTENTS

PHOTO SECTION FOLLOWS P. 116

ANDRÉ BRETON

INTRODUCTION

Three French writers in the first half of the twentieth century revealed a particularly keen awareness of the need to realign the creative arts in relation to the apocalyptic changes that took place in their time with respect to notions of the significance of human life. André Gide, André Malraux, and André Breton, widely divergent in many respects, have this in common: an acute desire to redetermine the relationships between life experience and art experience.

André Gide, the oldest of the three Andrés, confronted the disintegrating social mores. He called upon a renascent paganism to purge Christian society of its system of morality; he proposed a revaluation of the sensual pleasure of physical life, and a reassessment of concepts of sin and virtue.

André Malraux associated literary expression with political action and revised the image of the literary hero. In his writings it is through action that man reveals his aspiration toward a new humanism, and the liberation of the individual depends on the salvation of the collective self of society. The vestiges of that society's notion of the beautiful are the only eternity in which, according to Malraux, man can believe and trust. Such is the message of his Museums without Walls, which are his own emblems of the emblems of civilization. The works of these two writers are disseminated all over the world, translated into many languages, and have earned them wide recognition during their lifetimes.

The case of André Breton is somewhat different. He has breached the language barrier more slowly; and at his death not only had his works not yet been "collected," but many of the most significant of them were out of print and rarely translated. Yet André Breton was perhaps better known personally to the representative men of letters of his time than either Gide or Malraux. No writer, not even Mallarmé who was famed for his Tuesday evening receptions for writers and artists from all over Europe, had ever been so accessible to colleagues and aspiring artists and so inaccessible to

3

the general public. Never believing that one should consult the dead for their wisdom, nor caring like Gide to influence generations yet unborn, André Breton made immediate life his immediate concern; and it was to living men that he addressed his communication. According to Marcel Duchamp, his lifelong friend, Breton became the great catalyst for writers and artists who were looking for a new focus for the arts.* The list of Breton's friends is a list of the artists, the writers, the psychologists, and the sociologists who have left their imprint on the various facets of contemporary society: Picasso, Aragon, Éluard, Max Ernst, Salvador Dali, Alexander Calder, Matta, Yves Tanguy, Toyen, Jorge Guillén, Octavio Paz, Léopold Sédar Senghor, Lawrence Durrell, Aimé Césaire, Jacques Lacan, Claude Lévi-Strauss—the list is endless. They all visited him at the rue Fontaine in the walk-up apartment that he occupied from 1922 until the day of his death, in the luminous enclosure behind the façade of a street specializing in burlesque and Parisian folklore, in gymnastic exercises for virility, and in sexual emblems. In his own living museum of arts and fetishes, which he collected and related actively to his philosophy of life, he received all those whose involvement in the basic problems of life he felt to be deep and intense.

Whereas André Gide's concern had been society, and André Malraux's, history, for Breton the broad inquiry into life, which we call "literature," was fundamentally related to his studies of medicine and psychology and to mathematical perceptions. Advances in these areas necessitated, as he saw early in life, basic revisions of notions of reality, eternity, life and death, chance, the dream, love, and the sacred; they required man to make a new adjustment to material existence, which in turn entailed a revision of the notion of the arts and their functions.

Surrealism, which was a creation of André Breton's mind, was nourished with his personality and verbal powers. For him it was not simply a literary movement or an artistic *cénacle*, but the crystallization of his notion of life, which galvanized abstract thought into living experience and promulgated personal adventure through language.

Previous studies of André Breton have been primarily thematic or personal in their approach.[1] The aim here is to view the work in its totality and continuity, with attention to the changes and fluctuations that the life and the thought of Breton have had on his writings as we follow him in the various stages of his life: from uncertain scholar and soldier between 1910 and 1920, to rebel and head of a literary coterie in the twenties, to poet, dreamer, lover, and social activist in the thirties, to philosopher and

* This was Duchamp's estimate of Breton as we reminisced about him a few weeks after Breton's death in the fall of 1966.

critic in exile in the forties during World War II and in the existentialist postwar era, and finally to mentor in the sixties to an ever-increasing number of young writers and artists. There could be much argument about the beliefs of André Breton; he has been challenged for apparent inconsistencies and for a certain candor in his faith in the possibility of human transformation.[2] In order for critical challenges to be viewed in context one must go directly to the work, as fully as possible, particularly in the case of a writer as controversial and many-faceted as André Breton.

As, paradoxically, this man, so audacious in his thoughts, was highly reticent about his private feelings and discreet about his traumas, even the biographical facts that his family and close friends can communicate are fragmentary. On the other hand, his writings are intrinsically part of his life experience. In reconstructing the circumstances that reveal the process of transformation of the experience into expression, I have used whatever testimony and insights I have been able to gather through conversations with Breton's friends, his three consecutive wives, his daughter, and his son-in-law. This data, together with my own three interviews with Breton in 1942, in 1952, and in 1964, and the autobiographical material in the interviews collected in *Entretiens* in 1952, have helped trace the development in his forty-seven active years as a writer and to clarify some of the ambiguities associated with his work and his intentions. Much, however, must remain obscure, to be illuminated only by future generations, for in his will Breton stipulated that his personal papers and correspondence must not be revealed until fifty years after his death.

In gathering the verbal documentation, I became aware of three different kinds of personal attitudes toward André Breton. The warm human character of a man of heart seems to be a prevailing impression among his close friends and members of his family: the tremendous passion for life; the power for love, which could turn so abruptly to hate when he felt friends were disloyal; the tenderness, the compassion for the downtrodden; the emotional approach to social injustices. Then there is the attitude of those who were young with him and can look back upon those days. For these comrades the stature attributed to the man is a figment of the reader's imagination; they see André Breton principally as "one of us," on a level with themselves, as much a product of the time as they, rebellious like so many others, a literary neophyte suffering the same turmoils as many others; someone they had fun with; one conspirator among many against the strictures of the Establishment. For these old friends Breton is part of a dynamic moment in the long-lasting crisis of Western culture; they view him more as a spokesman than as a prophet and are rather astonished that he should be singled out and studied as an individual writer rather than as a member of a group. The "he" is so closely linked in their minds with the "we" that even their recollections are of a collective nature and do not throw much light on the distinct personality of the man, André Breton.

The third category of witness consists of those who looked up to him as a mentor, who were considerably younger than he, who sought him out at a crucial hour in their own ideological development and received from him the nod of approval; for these he was virtually a god in the respect, admiration, and devotion they lavished on him. He was the giant of the age, towering over other literary or humanistic leaders, the great force for revitalization not only of literary concepts but of the very function of modern man in a society in transition.

We are still too close to the passage of André Breton to appraise definitively his contributions to literature and society; and although his concepts and his crusade appear extremely relevant to an increasingly larger group than in the 1920's, the duration of that relevancy is not predictable. Within the context of the life and the work I have sorted out what has so far seemed most meaningful and has prevailed as a constant among variables, in order to gauge the stature of the writer and the man, André Breton.

I

THE MAN
AND HIS
BACKGROUND

"Surely he was born at the end of a long river, in
some port of the ocean for his eyes to have had
that grey brilliance and his voice to have acquired the resonance of shells when he said:
'the sea.'"
—Aragon

André Breton was born in Tinchebray, a small town in Normandy. The
birthplace of a human being is important if he remains there through his
formative years, or if it tells us something of his ethnic origin. In the case
of Breton it is inconsequential, since it was a totally arbitrary place of
birth, from which his parents moved while he was still too young to have
stored even the dimmest remembrances. He had no Norman blood and
none of those personality traits of strict rationalism, economy, and fond-
ness for dialectic disciplines which make good lawyers and good merchants
and are the known stereotypes of Normandy. His parents settled in Lorient,
which corresponds much more to Breton's ethnic background. Lorient is
a fishing port on the Atlantic Ocean within the limits of the old province
of Brittany. The derivation of its inhabitants is Celtic, and they have
affinities with the Irish. Great Britain's Gaelic heritage was linked with
continental Brittany's in medieval times by a common body of myths and
legends, steeped in the type of apocryphal interpretations of Christian
dogma that can be seen in the Arthurian legends, whose characters flour-
ished on both shores of the Channel. Breton's daughter Aube pointed out
that besides the Breton ancestry there was also a Lorraine streak in their
family. The absence of further detail is significant in itself—evidence of

the small importance Breton attached to genealogy. The only way he liked to think of himself was as a man of the North, and he identified with the spiritual lineage of men like Chateaubriand, the Gothic writers, the German illuminists such as Novalis, Achim von Arnim, and Goethe himself. He attributed to the North in him his propensity for the Gothic notion of beauty, his fascination with the effects of dreams and with the powers of imagination. He wanted to renew Chateaubriand's unsuccessful effort to veer the French poetic inspiration away from Latin sources and to replenish French literature with Nordic myths and Celtic representations of the sacred and the marvelous. Malcolm de Chazal, himself an untypical Frenchman from the island of Mauritius, identified cogently this presence of the North in André Breton when he said in a letter that Breton seemed more German than French, "of the metal of the Novalises and Rilkes—with a mind like a dart pointed to the orient." [1] He added, as a generalization of his observation of Breton: "a true mind cannot belong to a physical nation; it leaves that kind of thing to regional minds." Indeed, Breton was to adopt a position of non-nationalism in both the arts and in politics throughout his life. This, despite the fact that linguistically he was, unlike most of his French contemporaries, essentially monolingual; and although he much admired English and German literatures, his competence in those languages was, to his own embarrassment and apparent regret, quite minimal. There is of course another way to explain this monolingualism. Breton was primarily a poet with the poet's regard for the sacredness of the language in which he wrote; like many another poet, he may have felt that any attempt to master another tongue might corrupt his native syntax and his sense of the connotations of words.

Breton's appearance belied the stereotyped image we carry of the Frenchman. Heavy-boned, possessing a thick crop of hair and a large brow, he gave an impression of majesty and great stature.* The often quoted description of Adrienne Monnier, whose bookstore, La Maison des Amis des livres, the young Breton frequently visited in his early years in Paris, contains the mingling of the physical and the spiritual that has marked most accounts of Breton's striking appearance, and that inspired so many of his artist friends to do portraits of him. Under her eyes passed a parade of the ascending literary generation, but she discerned in Breton something that she characterized as "hieratic." Although she was more at ease with some of the other young men who came to her bookstore, she saw in

---

* Only when his friend, Philippe Soupault, pointed out to me that Breton was no taller than Soupault himself, a man of moderate height, did I realize that the towering appearance was due more accurately to personality than to physique.

Breton a godlike quality that drew others to him magnetically and yet preserved a distance between him and his companions.

> He was beautiful, not of an angelic beauty, but archangelic. I open a parenthesis: angels are gracious and archangels serious. Angels smile all the time, they are all smile, their work is nice, while archangels have in general heavy duties: people to chase from paradise, dragons to kill etc. . . . The face was massive, well drawn, he wore his hair rather long and thrown back with an air of nobility; he had an absent look in respect to the world and even toward himself. Breton did not smile, but he laughed sometimes, a brief and sardonic laughter which surged as he spoke without disturbing his features, as in the case of women mindful of their beauty.[2]

Adrienne Monnier mentioned the timidity of his manner, the determination of his chin suggesting the potential for violence, the sensuality of the lip. She saw in him a person of high concentration, "who would singularly mingle duty and pleasure, in fact imbricate them."

From all accounts Breton possessed none of the easy vivaciousness and facile wit that we associate with the French temperament. His movements were deliberate, his words measured; his wit was dry, and his laughter did not bubble up easily, but like a clap of thunder it was unexpected and sometimes devastating. He was not the flexible *roseau pensant*—archetype of French philosophy—but an oak of the legendary magic forest of Brocéliande, straight, unbending, dark, towering.

When asked about the immediate family background, Aube and her husband Yves Elléouët (also of Breton stock) stated the significant facts: that as a child Breton felt close to his father, a small businessman, and to his grandfather. He was the only child of only children and had a sharp antagonism toward his mother, who was extremely straightlaced. These facts bear scrutiny. If extreme attachment to the mother can produce an Oedipus complex, effeminate attitudes, and even sexual inversion—that is, alienation from women friends because they cannot compete with the maternal ideal—the opposite situation may explain the pronounced virility of Breton, his physical and spiritual idealization of the many women whom he loved and who contributed to the ideal image of woman as a miracle of creation, which is the salient feature of his love poetry. That other women could be so much more attractive, radiant, warm than the mother whom he shunned and who did not live into his maturity, was a source of constant wonder to Breton, which he injects into his writings.

Another factor in his work derives from his relationship with his mother.

His daughter believes that the total absence of the scatological from the vocabulary of a man who made sexual breakthroughs and revolutionary assaults on the prudish character of bourgeois morality, may well be due to the fact that his mother brought him up with puritanical reticence and trained him to avoid certain vocabulary in daily conversation under threat of extreme punishment—often carried out. Although as a rebellious young man Breton broke away from many rules and restrictions for the sake of rebellion itself, the word *merde* in his second surrealist manifesto is a solitary explosion and does not recur. Breton texts can be singled out from most other surrealist writing on this internal evidence: that whereas scatological vocabulary abounds in many surrealist works, it is avoided by Breton even in his most sexually motivated poetry and his most rabid social and political vituperations. It is because of this purity of language and of a certain revulsion against the exhibitionism of fellow surrealists that he has been attacked for priggishness and puritanism—a paradoxical puritanism that creates a disparity between radicalism of thought, a certain conservatism of language, and an unerring personal probity.

His father's economic situation was also significant in the formation and orientation of André Breton and was a determining factor in his life. The word "bourgeois" has many variations of meaning in reference to the French social structure and embraces a broad economic spectrum. Like Breton, Proust and Gide belonged to the bourgeoisie, but there was an economic gulf between those financially independent sons of wealthy families and the salaried or self-employed, frugal families from which Breton and a number of his surrealist colleagues emerged. Philippe Soupault, Pierre Naville, and Jacques Baron, who came from prosperous families, helped whenever possible those of their friends who were compelled to earn their daily bread. For these, preserving spiritual independence in the face of economic dependence was to entail a constant series of compromises with their desire for personal autonomy. Many of the rifts between Breton and his friends were due to their eventual accommodations to dire economic necessity, accommodations which Breton judged to be artistic defaults. His own lifelong proclamation of *nonslavery to life* arises as a reaction to the economic constriction into which he was born. He was to rebel against the idea that contemporary society still subjected the workingman to a nine-to-five schedule: "I am obliged to accept the idea of work as a material necessity. . . . If the sinister obligations of life impose it on me, be it so, but to ask me to believe in it, to revere mine or someone else's never. . . . It is not worth living if one has to work." [3] He was thinking in terms of his own modest background when he deplored that the daily routine clipped man's intellectual wing, the free play of his imagination, his personal liberty of thought and movement, which for Breton were the most treasured human assets.

It is one thing for Proust to devote his life to the free practice of his art and the study of his own mind, or for the equally independent Gide to proclaim himself, thanks to his private means, a champion of the pursuit of gratuitous occupations, and to identify freedom with a constant attitude of *availability* to each new enterprise. In fact *disponibilité* is the enviable asset of the rich—a futile advantage for those without talent, a blessing for those who like Gide utilized their leisure fruitfully. Yet Gide wondered sometimes whether future generations would hold it against him that he never knew what it was to have to earn a living. Breton's availability to spiritual adventure will seem the more poignant when we realize at what cost, with what difficulties and renunciations of material necessities, he achieved his partial emancipation from the economic demands of society. He was to admire Gide immensely in his early youth not for the personal moral defiances that made Gide at fifty an idol of the younger generation, but for the series of characters he created who embodied an uncompromising enthusiasm for total freedom: the sensualist Ménalque in *Les Nourritures terrestres*, the uncommitted character of Edouard in *Les Faux-monnayeurs*, and particularly the impetuous, gratuitously free Lafcadio of *Les Caves du vatican*. Son of a white-collar worker and sometime glassblower, Breton could ill afford *disponibilité*, which was to be the moving factor in his life; and his parents, grimly conscious of the economic realities of life, were typical of their class in planning for their son the path of security through education; it was the pattern by which hosts of other literary figures of the generation after Gide's, emanating from the small bourgeoisie, had eventually reached literature—via the Ecole Normale or the Faculty of Medicine of the University of Paris. Whereas an earlier generation of literary men had for the most part started as teaching candidates, a number of the surrealists were instructed in medical and scientific disciplines, which were less directly within the humanistic frame of reference. The Faculty of Medicine was to be the common ground of Breton, Aragon, and Soupault; while not far away, at the Faculty of Letters, another doctoral candidate, René Crevel, was to find the nucleus of his own surrealist attitude in doing research for a thesis on Diderot.

One more aspect of Breton's family background is noteworthy as a factor in the development of his personality. He began life with the solitude and the introspection that are often the lot of an only child; the emotional involvement entailed by the family unit becomes a larger burden when there are no siblings with whom to share it. He was to sense early in life the dangers of becoming *fils à papa*; hence his categorical repudiation of the institution of the family, which was to be so often a target for derision in his writings. Protest against family ties was nothing new when Breton appeared on the scene as a writer. Before him Gide had launched his famous cry: *"Familles, je vous hais."* But if Breton claimed the liberty of the individual from the constriction of ties based primarily on social mores, he was to become neither a recluse nor a vagabond. He replaced the inherited loyalties by those of his choice. In his prevailing devotion to his father, in his deep attachment to his own only child, and in the family way of living he maintained in the last twenty years of his life in his marriage with his last wife, Elisa, he conciliated two apparently contradictory notions—of liberty and of attachment—in his definition of love as a *free union.*

His writings were to lack commentaries on family relations, in sharp contrast with the works of writers like Proust and Mauriac who made of their gallery of aunts, brothers, cousins, etc., the fruitful substance of their psychological study of the intricacies of human relationships within the family circle. Breton's work is totally devoid of this element. However, the fraternal needs of the *enfant unique* were to direct him toward a lifelong search for enduring friendships. The list of Breton's chosen brothers—to be equaled in later life by his indulgent, paternal affection for his many disciples—may well stem from the insufficiency of companions within the family structure. Among these brother substitutes were to be Théodore Fraenkel, his earliest Lycée friend, who opened many intellectual avenues to him; the subversive Jacques Vaché, who communicated his audacities to the then timid and fascinated medical student; his surrealist comrades, Soupault, Aragon, Eluard, Desnos, Crevel; and the most faithful of his friends, Benjamin Péret. The greater the satisfaction derived from such friendships, the deeper were to be the traumatic disappointments as the series of fraternal associations brought in their wake a series of dissolutions.

Besides the family relationships that helped shape the temperament of André Breton, there is also a strong ecological influence: the haunting presence of the sea in his background is as dominant as the sense of the North. It is Lorient, and not Tinchebray, that looms significant. Years later Aragon, in his quixotic account of the youthful adventures he shared with Breton, describes his companion in the context of this fundamental imprint of the sea:

> Surely he was born at the end of a long river, in some port of the Ocean for his eyes to have had that grey brilliance and his voice to have acquired the resonance of shells when he said: "the sea." Somewhere in his childhood slumbered docks at low tide of a heavy summer evening, and on the rippleless waters of pools, the sailboats that refuse to leave before the rising of the breeze.[4]

Lorient left in the mind of the child André teeming images of the ocean, of shells, of fish, of sun alternating with mist and rain, of estuaries, of fascinating stones (on which the sea has wrought its crystallizing metamorphoses). The luminous and unpredictable phenomena of nature, which impressed him in his earliest childhood, will motivate his writing; not analysis of human associations and behavior, but the revelation of the convulsive character of nature will engross him. One brought up at the seashore can realize perhaps more than any other the enigmatic character that nature assumes in the mingling of water and land and in the unexpected changes of the skies. The child who grew up on the sands of Lorient will forever seek out shining stones, apocalyptic skylights, brilliant stars in unimpeded horizons, fluctuations from mobility to serenity, the glow of earth and water under the sun; he will catch this radiance in the title of his first collection of poems, *Clair de terre* ("Earthshine"). This exciting sense of the natural forces of the universe will surge spontaneously from his early writings; it will form a network of poetic metaphors that shape, rather than merely express, his sensibilities. The fish—for the child it is the prize, the Golden Fleece with which the humble fishermen-Argonauts return—becomes the bridge, the fascinating hyphen between land and water, and the astrological sign of André Breton, born on February 19, 1896.

These reflections on his background are based on information revealed in conversations with his family and friends. Other biographical details can be gleaned from his early work in automatic writing, which may be likened to what Proust called the play of involuntary memory. The memories that the subconscious unleashed in *Les Champs magnétiques* were more totally uninhibited than those triggered by Proust's cup of tea and piece of madeleine. There is in the case of Proust the artisan's inescapable effort to fit spontaneous recollections into patterns, to place them into the structure of the novel. Breton's first try at automatic writing is neither controlled nor directed, and the images that surge freely from the subconscious determine their own internal priorities. Their documentary value, therefore, as they relate to Breton's background and early childhood, is more authentic. The fact that Mme Simone Collinet, the first wife of André Breton, has preserved a copy of the first edition of *Les Champs magnétiques* marked to show which parts were the writing of Breton and which belonged to his collaborator, Philippe Soupault, makes it possible to glean significant details of the development of his personality; it is revealing of the limits and the vistas of the child. Going as far back as the time he sat on someone's knee and was told bedtime stories that did not put him to sleep, all the significant ingredients that shaped his character are inherent in the text. The first sentence focuses on his Catholic background and the frame of reference it inculcated in him: *carême* instead of *printemps* to designate the season, the first communion of little girls, the prayers, the incessant church bells—"how we have had enough of the sound of bells"; [5] its constrictions are equaled only by those of school, to which he goes on the third-class commuter's ticket; images of keys appear as symbols of a prison that obliterates the sun. There are also indefinite, prolonged vacations. The images of school are varied: the standard communal French school with its drafty classrooms, the mint candies the children chew, the play yard, the games. He plays hooky and dreads the pursuit of the truant officer, he is locked up for a misdemeanor, he receives zero for conduct and arranges for his parents to have company for dinner to avoid confrontation with them. On the other hand, he does well in his studies, and we see him coming down a great stairway on the day of the *distribution des prix,* his arms full of books won as prizes.

He is a well-brought-up little boy, who is fascinated by the picture of a revolutionary hero, General Hoche,[6] on a friend's bedroom wall—perhaps he identified his own "time of revolution" with that of the great French Revolution. He refers to his companionship with his grandfather, who takes him to the nearby inn run by a man called Tyran, the tobacconist, whose cigarette paper appears later in some of Breton's poems; there are references to the peasants, the fresh air, open horizons, blue fountains. His grandfather buys him penny candy and all sorts of other delights. Overflowing with bounties, he wishes he had a third hand.

There are clues to the formation of his imagination and sensibilities: he looks through his collection of notebooks, "The Great Cities of the World"; [7] he loves Paris above all, that Paris which was to be his home for the major part of his life, which was to offer him its coveted key—a prize he refused, as he refused all honors and official recognitions to the end of his life. We can also see poetry becoming a dominant factor early in his childhood as he chooses his first friend for the way the boy reads Chénier's "La Jeune Captive."

His outbursts of anger, which were to become a characteristic of his adult life, are already apparent in images of "the multiple splendors of anger." [8] His leadership is also evident in childhood games in the countryside where he is always the chief. Not rebellion but disdain guides his attitude toward the adult world: boredom colors the saddening pictures of the family conversations. Cynicism grows in him as he realizes that the greatness of God is pitched at the level of Mont Blanc, the highest point in space imaginable by the devout. His mother's lacework harbors the prim and the monotonous (he calls it *"inspiration dentelle"*), but though the tone is scornful, this image may well be the fountainhead of all the lace analogies of his later phantasmagoria.

But all is not vain, confusing, and boring in the visions of his childhood. There is the world of nature in juxtaposition with the world of men; and as in *Les Illuminations* of Rimbaud, nature is full of signs and excitement —not a place where the child can bury his solitude but a source of effervescence; nature's prodigious powers lay bare the meagerness of man's scope: "The grotto is fresh and you feel like running away; the water calls us, it is red and the smile is more open than the cracks which cover your house like plants, oh magnificent daytime tender like that extraordinary little hoop. The sea, which we love, does not accept men meager as we are." [9] The picture of the sea, the bells of the estuary, the sand in his ears, the animal bouquets of fish, lions, tigers, are a basis for his fascination with the rich creativity of the earth. These exhilarating visions, which were to shape his philosophical benignity, are already part of his working universe.

Whereas spontaneous memory in the case of Proust conjures up the specific details of his perspective of the world of adults, and the intimacies of incident and precise details of places, *Les Champs magnétiques* conveys the vitality of nature and the magic it exercised on the child who was to become a poet: a feeling of the presence of sorcerers in the air, whose caldrons "make the clouds boil," [10] the phosphorescence, the tides, the movements of stones, the iridescence of the earth.

II

THE

FORMATIVE

YEARS

"There is in your verse a striking talent"
—Apollinaire

The dialogues conducted by a series of interviewers and collected in 1952 in a volume called *Entretiens* are the only available autobiographical documents about André Breton. Unlike most literary men of the twentieth century, Breton was loath to reminisce; he was too busy with the life of the moment and found it more exciting to probe into the future than to relive the past. He rejected the memoir as a literary genre. Life experiences are cast off like worn-out garments, and events loom like trees denuded of their leaves. *Entretiens* is the story of a mind rather than of a life; and none of Breton's commentators has complained of the lack of intimate details and introspection because the substance of the mentally and sensually active life is the work itself, candidly laid before us, available but often as undecipherable as a cryptogram.

He tells us on the first page of *Entretiens* that his lucid life dates from 1913, the year he began his medical studies at the Sorbonne. Previously in 1907 he had arrived in Paris to attend the Lycée Chaptal, from which he graduated in 1912. Of this period we have no direct testimony from him. According to his first wife he was good in his studies, but it was his friend Théodore Fraenkel who ran off with the prizes. He vacillated between fourth and seventh in rank in the various courses he took, first only in his penmanship, which, extraordinarily, did not change during the entire course of his life, and in recitation to which he brought a rich voice and impeccable diction, enhanced no doubt by the fervor of his love of poetry. Breton was not a precocious poet, as was Rimbaud, to whom he was drawn early in his adolescence. There are no childhood poems; he may even have been what we call today a late-bloomer in view of the steadily rising grades we can observe in the Breton notebooks which Mme Collinet has meticulously kept, and by the end of his lycée career he had reached the rank of contender for the first prize in France's highly competitive educational system.

It was with great hopes that his parents, who continued to maintain their home in Lorient, enrolled him as a medical student at the University of Paris. But Breton tells us in *Entretiens* that his presence in the amphitheater or the laboratory was merely physical; his mind was elsewhere.[1] He was reading Rimbaud, Lautréamont, and the Symbolist poets; his imagination was even more kindled by the streets of Paris. As he relates in his early volume of essays, *Les Pas perdus*, "The street which I thought capable of yielding to my life its surprising detours, the street with its anxieties as it peered at me, was my true element; I found in it the wing of eventualities."[2] He returns later to the same thought in *Entretiens:* "It was there in the chance encounters of the streets, that . . . what was truly and profoundly related to my destiny was to be played out."[3] The role that Paris has played in French poetry dates back to François Villon; Baudelaire renewed the inspiration, and after him French poets of the twentieth century were to find in the streets of Paris inspiration for their lyricism, targets for their curiosity, and conductors of a highly charged reality; of these more recent poets Apollinaire was the first great *promeneur* as he strolled from one bank of the Seine to the other. *Alcools*, teeming with images of the Parisian labyrinth, appeared in 1913. Breton singles out 1913 as the time of his intellectual awakening. It was a great literary year, in which there appeared in addition to Apollinaire's collected poems, the first volumes of Proust, and Gide's controversial *Les Caves du vatican.*

Four poets had at this time great significance for Breton: Rimbaud, Lautréamont, Valéry, and Apollinaire. Rimbaud is the first poet in whom Breton perceives a concept of poetry that he can adopt and extend to all the arts, making of them, not an end but a means to an end. The artist does not write to fill the leisure of his fellow men; rather, his writings or paintings are the evidences, the offshoots of the search for the solutions of the problems of life itself. By means of Rimbaud's *Les Illuminations*, Breton is able to "enter into communication with [his] own most intimate self," for it is indeed one of those books that make us travel: "we must not confuse the books that we read while traveling with those that make us travel."[4]

Breton later elaborates on this function of art in two articles that have been collected in *Les Pas perdus:* "Why I Write," and a lecture he delivered in Barcelona in 1922. These two pieces in which he explains his earliest attitudes toward the purposes of the artist are significant because they pre-date the surrealist manifestoes and also explain attitudes that he acquired before his affiliations with the Dada movement.

Proceeding from Rimbaud's notion of poetry, Breton examines the broader definition of the poet offered by Apollinaire: that one could be a poet in any field of creativity; and in view of the vast progress made by the inventive qualities of engineers and scientists, Apollinaire had thought that the "literary" poet had demonstrated less creative spirit than the technologist and the physicist in modern times. But Breton was not fully satisfied with Apollinaire's definition, which seemed to stress the *object* of creativity rather than the spirit that moved the creator. In fact he found Apollinaire's determination of *l'esprit nouveau* rather simplistic and his vision leading to a dead end. The spirit of self-probing and self-mutilation, of which Rimbaud had given a moving example, touched Breton more profoundly. It is important to realize that Rimbaud's letters were published in 1912; they included the now famous letter to his teacher Paul Demeny, in which he allocated to the poet the position of seer and visionary; he also explained how the poet commits self-immolation in the process of self-recognition. Breton reads Rimbaud and Apollinaire simultaneously. For him they are for all practical purposes his and each other's contemporaries. In juxtaposing their work he recognizes the values of both, but in contrasting Apollinaire's vigorously optimistic convocation of all the poets of the world with Rimbaud's tortured and lonely descent into self, he also discerns great differences. From Rimbaud to his own generation he sees a series of partial failures in the utilization of the *terrain vague,* which not only poets but scientists, philosophers, and artists have forged. The work of Rimbaud was not finished in 1875, he says, for all Rimbaud did was to "express with a surprising vigor a concern which no doubt thousands of generations had not been able to avoid, and has given it a voice that still resounds in our ears," to resolve "the frightful duality" of man.[5] The alarm had been particularly poignant in the case of the poet-prodigy who stopped being a poet at twenty-one, and who had the audacity to proclaim, "We are not in this world." Breton also marveled, as he tells us in *Entretiens,* at Rimbaud's other audacity: to reject all kinds of professions as means of livelihood and, most of all, the profession of writer.

It was also during the second decade of the twentieth century that Paris took its first, limited look at the works of the nineteenth-century poet, Isidore Ducasse (1846–70), who had written under the flamboyant pseudonym of Count de Lautréamont. The Uruguayan-born Lautréamont's brief contribution to French literature had gone unheralded during his short life; he had in fact accomplished the Marquis de Sade's desire not to leave a trace of his life behind him. But the burning pages in which Lautréamont depicted the anger of his diabolical character, Maldoror, who thought he was something more than the son of man and woman [6] and rebelled against his mortality, were to get a hearty reception from the rising generation. If ever a man had sold his soul to the devil and written his anguish in blood, it was the twenty-five-year-old Ducasse, whose message to society was lethal and vindictive. Since no copies of *Les Chants de Maldoror* were accessible (it was no doubt from Apollinaire that Breton learned of the young man who had given the word *imagination* a new dimension), Breton sat in the Bibliothèque Nationale and copied Lautréamont's poetic prose.

Among living writers Breton was attracted on the one hand to Valéry, on the other to Apollinaire, two poets widely divergent in their forms of writing but having in common the ability to make of writing a gratuitous activity not connected in any way with gainful employment. In symbolism, of which Valéry's work was the last spark, Breton cherished its sense of ephemeral, unmaterialistic beauty, its detachment from the coarse preoccupations of men, its power to remain uncompromised by bourgeois values. Although he thought that the "beauty it honored is no longer ours" but "a veiled woman disappearing in the distance," [7] the fact that the Symbolists worshiped something unprofitable and sacrificed to it the easy life of professional novelists appealed to the young medical student who sat absentminded on the university benches.

From his elders—Paul Valéry, Francis Viélé-Griffin, and Jean Royère who was to be responsible for getting his first poem into print in *La Phalange*, and Pierre Reverdy whose magazine *Nord-Sud* was to provide his first substantial organ for expression—Breton sought a "sign" of approval, of encouragement. Visiting Viélé-Griffin in his luxurious apartment on the Quai de Passy, he admired not simply the musical verse of the American who wrote French poetry, but his courage to shy away from social honors. Of Valéry he admired particularly the early work: the portrait of M. Teste, the archetype of the artist who lives in a constant state of self-chastisement and rigorous self-discipline. Valéry taught André Breton to be hard toward himself, to acquire the mystique of self-discipline. Valéry answered the young man's questions, replied to his letters, which Breton carefully saved—until the day when Valéry sought and won membership in the Académie Française. Breton's disappointment was great. He could not bear the thought that the man he had identified as a pure and disinterested poet should have aspired to official honors. To chastise Valéry he sold to a collector the letters he had previously cherished—but not before making copies of them for his own files.

In a sense 1913 was the end of an era which had harbored the illusion of forty years of peace and prosperity for France. The year 1914 changed all that as it unleashed "the frightful adventure of the war." [8] It had been there all the time, as a wild beast lying asleep, and it now awakened to perpetrate its terror upon the world. Lautréamont's anger found new meaning for the young men whom war tore away, as Breton reflects, "from all their aspirations to precipitate them into a cloaca of blood, stupidity, and mud." [9]

The sense of commitment to problems of life rather than of literature, which had been the basis of Breton's predilection for certain writers and his rejection of others, came into sharper focus. Through Lautréamont's venomous words he took a vicarious vengeance upon the society that he saw preparing for war. The desire to go a few steps farther than Rimbaud and Lautréamont became a deep-seated urge: to erase the artificial barriers between men, to untie bound eyes and open clamped lips in a redefinition not only of poetry but of human liberty became an urgent, vital drive, a mission of rescue, one that could not be carried out alone or brooded upon in solitary retreat.

The time when Breton begins to search for his peers as well as for mentors coincides significantly with the moment of his recruitment into that collectivity which was so repulsive to him. The army experience that started for Breton as a medical assistant in 1915 was not a time for antiwar demonstrations but for rallying forces for future protest, and for healing troubled minds in army mental hospitals. He became even more disillusioned with his elders as revered authors like Maurice Barrès, Anatole France, Henri Bergson, Paul Claudel, and Charles Péguy supported the Republic in an overt display of nationalism. "Nationalism had never been my forte" he later explained in *Entretiens*.[10] This freedom from nationalism in its political sense was to remain throughout his life a constant element of his philosophy, and at the end of the war it was to orient him toward many subversive actions, attitudes, and reactions, which directed the surrealist movement toward a non-national concept of the world it aspired to transform.

It is during the war, when he is first assigned to the hospital in Nantes (not far from his parents' home in Lorient) and later to the psychiatric center of Saint-Dizier as the assistant to Dr. Raoul Leroy, that he combines his medical interests with his literary concerns—two channels of free mental activity within the maze of military constrictions. Among writers he honors most at this time is the alien Apollinaire who at the first sound of cannon had enlisted in the army of his adopted country. It is interesting to note the distinction Breton makes between the patriotism of Péguy or Claudel and that of Apollinaire. The former put their poetry as well as their persons at the service of war-torn France. They were expendable as much in their function as artists as in their role as soldiers. Poetic incantations such as Claudel's *"Tant que vous voudrez, mon capitaine"* were to come under attack a few years hence in surrealist writings, which alleged that they created an aura of enthusiasm, a chain reaction of military fervor for human sacrifice. Breton and his companions felt that verbal eloquence could be as provocative as cannon in the encouragement of the war spirit.

But Apollinaire's commitment to military duty was of a different nature. This illegitimate son of a Polish mother and an unknown father found national legitimacy and identification in serving as a soldier of France, but he did not engage in inflammatory oratory and did not put his pen to the service of his adopted country. Whatever poems came out of the war expressed his wonder at the technological miracles that emanated from the inventions for war: "a modern gaiety more profound and at the same time more tragic." [11] The intransigent Breton did not condemn him although he found his attitude "ridiculous." [12] Apollinaire's involvement of self in the war was quite distinct from the others' use of war rhetoric. Breton viewed him with a certain degree of indulgence and almost condescendingly called him "the last poet" in the professional sense of the word. Breton saw here and there in those meager volumes flares and illuminations, the gallantry of taking risks; the man did not quite measure up to the dream but nonetheless was a rallying point, sensitive to the modern evolution because of his contagious sense of liberty, suggesting with his flamboyant personality and condition as wounded poet a new kind of hero.

Breton, who has been reading Apollinaire since 1913, begins to write to him from Nantes in December 1915; * it is a correspondence between two poet-soldiers. In his neat handwriting the neophyte expresses his enthusiasm with emotional elegance, as he did in a number of other letters he wrote to literary men in his early twenties. The format is clever; the emphasis is not on himself but on the *other*; the questions are direct and relevant, tinged with some discreet flattery that compels an answer. His modesty of tone does not prevent him from slipping a poem

---

* Apollinaire's part of the correspondence, published in *La Revue des lettres modernes*, Nos. 104–7 (1964), helps to reconstruct the broad lines of the friendship.

or two in the letters. The poems draw immediate compliments from
Apollinaire—"There is in your verse a striking talent" [13]—and he feels
such an immediate affinity with the young "poet" that he invites him
to call at the hospital the day after he is to be trepanned. Thereafter,
according to what Breton remembers in *Entretiens*, he saw his wounded
friend almost daily until Apollinaire's death, which occurred two days
before the Armistice of November 1918.[14] However, the series of letters
from Apollinaire to Breton between 1916 and 1918 suggests that the
encounters were somewhat less frequent. In fact, the correspondence
reveals Apollinaire's increasingly pressing desire to see his young friend
more often. He tries to draw Breton out of his natural pessimism with
his own optimistic outlook which survives all the physical suffering of
the surgery and prolonged treatment. "Overcome your disgust, shake off
your *ennui*." [15] He also gives Breton some literary advice, warning him
against refinement of style, a habit Breton had acquired in his early imitation of Mallarmé. Breton communicates his adoration of Apollinaire to
his friends, and he introduces them to Apollinaire. Adrienne Monnier
observes: "I have never seen him [Apollinaire] but God knows if I had
heard Breton speak of him." [16] Later, when Apollinaire does visit her
bookstore, according to her Breton hangs on his every word, struck
speechless as if in a trance.

Apollinaire feels enough confidence in his young friend to ask him to
write an article about him: "I have thought of asking a favor of you.
I know no one who could speak of what I have done as well as you. If
you would care to write a fairly long article on this subject, I think that
the *Mercure de France* would publish it." [17]

But the fact remains that there is a marked difference between the
fervent praise in Breton's article on Apollinaire written in 1917 while the
poète assassiné was still living, and his more guarded references to
Apollinaire in the lecture he delivered in Barcelona in 1922.[18] One may
conclude that with his genuine love for the very human qualities of
Apollinaire and in his own role as protégé he would have been careful not
to hurt the latter's feelings. In 1917 Breton showed how thoroughly he had
read Apollinaire; in 1922 reservations about the man and the poet begin
to emerge.[19] However, the importance of Breton's contact with Apollinaire
is undeniable if for no other reason than that the latter introduced him to
the painters who later were to become his constant companions as they
had been Apollinaire's; if not also for the fact that through them he
linked in more specific terms than had Apollinaire the common metaphysical purposes of art and poetry. It was also Apollinaire, as we have
noted, who opened his eyes to the mysteries of the streets of Paris; he

restored love as a subject of poetry after its virtual disappearance since the romantic movement, communicated his lust for life in its vibrant immediacy and its illusion of eternal youth, and directed Breton toward the magic of old enchanters who might reveal the secrets of life itself. Apollinaire had written a poetic dialogue, which has remained little known and little appreciated, but which Breton read in his most impressionable years: *L'Enchanteur pourrissant,* in which Apollinaire situated the poet as a magician decaying in his tomb in a state of living death. He had heralded the resurrection of the old magician, symbolized as Merlin and as all that Merlin stood for. As one follows the career of André Breton, one senses that he identified intimately with the image Apollinaire created of the poet, and with the effort to reawaken the magician in the twentieth century. In inscribing a copy of *Alcools* from his hospital bed to the aspiring poet, Apollinaire had passed the torch, had given Breton a strong sense of literary mission, which one could detect despite his many disavowals of literary goals. He deftly emulated his elder in combining the spirit of personal adventure with an awareness of his destiny as a poet.

But what Apollinaire's contact did for Breton's literary career, another encounter in Nantes almost erased. He met a young soldier who was the very personification of the subversive, and who was to upset Breton's literary apple cart by making him feel that writing was a futile practice beside the urgent business of living.

Jacques Vaché was a year older than Breton. He had red hair and a face formed, as it were, to express his derision of humanity. Breton had found him on a soldier's bed during his rounds at the military hospital; wounded in mind more than in body, Vaché was, in his rebellion against society, the embodiment of Lautréamont and the Marquis de Sade combined, and in his escape through absinthe he brought back Alfred Jarry, whose *Ubu roi* had decapitated society more brutally and totally, albeit verbally, than had Marat, Robespierre, and Saint-Just put together. Although Breton was born too late to meet Jarry in person, he had a substitute image in Vaché—more fully Ubuesque even than Jarry, since Vaché's was a personal dedication to total protest unmitigated by any literary expression. His writings are limited to some war letters to Breton and his friends, which were carefully—one wonders how carefully—edited by Breton.

One can indeed ponder to what degree the image of Vaché was a figment of Breton's imagination. To be sure, there existed a soldier, dying as much from alcoholism and drug addiction as from war wounds. But

his audacities, moral and social, his fusion of promiscuity and purity, were
they not to some extent projections of Breton's own desires, which he
could display not overtly but only through an intermediary? It is hard to
imagine a man, as intellectually oriented as Breton, so fervently involved
in companionship with Jacques Vaché; certainly in the rest of his life
all his fraternal attachments were to be with literary men and artists or
other intellectuals. Was not Vaché an invention, a creative portrait like
Gide's Lafcadio, with whom he has so many similarities? Breton promoted
a legend around this rather ordinary youth who, seized with dissent, became the symbol of his generation, immortalized by his friend Breton. A
precursor of the Dada image, Vaché was to die just before Tristan
Tzara came onto Breton's horizon. In the two articles Breton devoted
to his friend Vaché, collected a few years later in *Les Pas perdus,* he
characterized his meeting with Vaché as a milestone in his emotional development. "In those days I was composing Mallarméan poems. I was going through one of the hardest moments of my life, I was beginning to see
that I would not be doing what I wanted. The war was dragging on." [20]
The restlessness of the soldier immobilized by wounds was no greater
than that of one attending the maimed in situations regulated by military
automatism: "Those who have not had to stand at attention cannot
imagine what it is at times to have the urge to move one's heels." [21] Vaché
taught Breton what the proper attitude was under the circumstances: not
sentimental self-pity but a devil-may-care and brittle detachment. Although
Breton never developed more than an acid sarcasm, this was to become a marked characteristic of his personality, noticed by almost everyone
who came in contact with him; it was an unusual and somewhat unexpected corollary to his intensity and sensitivity.

In 1916 Breton took life seriously, the war indignantly, religion
angrily, whereas Vaché laughed, scorned a scornful god, found the war
absurd rather than tragic, deflated Breton's effervescence by calling him
pohète, taught him the defense mechanism of humor, which he called
*umour.** Vaché represented Breton's alter ego. He had the nerve that
the strictly brought-up Breton could not yet muster. He confronted the
world's imbecilities not with anger or indignation but with violence. It
was through Vaché that the revolver became for Breton the emblem of
protest. Vaché was prepared to pull the trigger in the theater where
Apollinaire's *Les Mamelles de Tirésias* had its first performance in 1917,
for he wanted to intensify the disparity between the sound and the

---

* During the next world war Breton was to define this "black humor" and trace
the legacy of this particular kind of literary protest against the human condition in
an organized anthology, *Anthologie de l'humour noir.*

fury of the rear-guard with which he identified Apollinaire, who he thought marked an epoch, and the totally brave avant-garde which had not yet rallied its forces. Commenting on the events of that evening, Breton, who approved Vaché's attitude but restrained his revolver play, says in *Entretiens* "Never, as on that evening, had I yet measured the depth of the ditch that was going to separate the new generation from the one that preceded it." [22]

Impudent, volatile, unpredictable, Jacques Vaché is the incarnation rather than the spokesman of *l'esprit nouveau*. He pokes fun at the young doctor walking along the streets of Nantes with a volume of Rimbaud's works under his arm, and convinces him that he owes more to Vaché than to his literary saints, and that he "will never belong to anyone else so completely." [23]

Frustrated in his projects for a future that seems more uncertain every day, Breton learns from Vaché the electrifying satisfaction of living for the moment. And if Vaché's mockeries do not make him abandon writing, they modify his notion of the purposes of writing. Where Rimbaud taught Breton to write to discover the meaning of individual life, Vaché taught him the value of nonconformism, the conquest of solitude, the magic of human encounters. It was at this period of his life that he wrote: "one publishes to seek men and nothing more. Men, whom I am every day more curious to discover." [24]

If Vaché, or Breton's elaboration of the personality of Vaché, fortified Breton, he did not do as much for Vaché in exchange. He was aware of the deterioration in Vaché's mental health, but the friendship he offered Vaché apparently did not suffice to deter Vaché from suicide. Vaché was found dead of an overdose of drugs; he had taken forty grams of opium—whether deliberately or accidentally no one knew. He had left life ambiguously; for is not intention often the prey of accident, and is not chance a necessity of phenomena? For many years Breton was to ponder this clinical question in his philosophical dogma. Vaché's death, which occurred in January 1919, was as absurd as his life; his nihilism had reached its climax in total self-destruction; his behavior had been a prelude to Dada—Dada that Vaché was never to know, but which he enacted all by himself.

Breton lost Vaché and Apollinaire within two months of each other. From different poles they had prepared him as poet and as man for the new century. Apollinaire had sensed that the automobile he rode for the first time as a soldier in 1915 said good-bye not only to an epoch but to an entire world that would never be the same again.[25] With Vaché's death as well something died in Breton: the cavalier manner

of a life without tomorrows, the tongue-in-cheek practice of the dream
sequence of events enacted in broad daylight, the behavior of "gay terror-
ists" exempt from the judgment of society and living at the tempo of
a Charlie Chaplin film: "Ah, we died, both of us." [26]

As time passed and as references to Vaché became less frequent in the
writing and conversation of André Breton, the memory of the short but
stimulating companionship became enlarged into a dominating force,
which seemed to preserve for him the delicate balance between fervor
and dissent.

III

MEDICINE,
MAGIC,
AND MATHEMATICS

"If the mysterium which is in us, and which
we are ourselves, was to come to be known to
us, would we not find at the same time, the
'key to the great mystery?' As a matter of fact
man is not isolated in nature, he is part of it."
—Jacob Boehme

As a medical assistant at the hospital in Nantes, André Breton stayed
close to his literary saints, and as he walked from the hospital to the park,
his thoughts were possessed by *Les Illuminations* of Rimbaud. But at
the same time, the revelations he was getting in the field of the human
psyche were increasing, and despite his alleged inattention at the Faculty
of Medicine, his scientific orientation had been deeply determined. The
mental aberrations of the patients, their deliriums, the narrations of night-
mares in shellshock were the material of investigation in that human
laboratory in Nantes; they implemented the theoretical knowledge he had
gained at the university, and he got even more practical experience at the
psychiatric center of Saint-Dizier, where he was transferred in 1917 as
the assistant to Dr. Raoul Leroy. He recalls these experiences in
Entretiens: "I was able to try out experimentally on the patients the
processes of [psychoanalytical] investigation, make a recording for the
purpose of interpretation of dreams, of disassociations of involuntary
thought." [1] And he adds, these were to be the first materials of surrealism.

But who pointed out to him the connection between these pathological
states of the mind and the possibility of "recuperation of the original
powers of the mind," which was to become the fundamental objective of
surrealism? How did he come to the idea that in the shackles of victims

caught in states of aberration might be found the key to the "liberation of all constrictions: logical, moral, and others?"

Although there is much mention of Freud and his precursor Charcot in the debts that Breton acknowledges to psychoanalysis, Charcot was dead, and the surrealists honored him historically on the fiftieth anniversary of his death as the pioneer in the study of hysteria. And, in spite of Breton's admiration for Freud and his efforts to bring to Freud's attention the applications he had found for the interpretation of dreams on a poetic basis, Freud had a certain scientific detachment from the mystical implications of his method for the realm of the arts, as he admitted to Breton.[2] He was not the one to suggest the bridge between the pathological and the normal recesses of the mind as a path by which the notion of legend is ascertained in the normal realities of the human mind. Freud viewed myth and superstition as sociological phenomena rather than as links in the chain from ancient magic to modern medicine.

But there was another source nearer to André Breton, and written in the only language he read with ease: the works of Pierre Janet, professor of psychiatric medicine, and the intermediary between Charcot and the pure scientists on the one hand and Freud and the pragmatists of medicine on the other. Professor Janet had been the teacher of Jung, and his works were on the required reading list of medical students of Breton's vintage. The resemblance between Jung's notion of the collective self and the surrealists' concept of what Paul Eluard was to call *"Les Dessous d'une vie"* is due to the fact that they both derive from Pierre Janet, whose character as psychologist was quite different from Freud's. If we examine the monumental works of Janet, we come upon the very vocabulary that André Breton was to transform into a lexicon for surrealism, thereby attributing to words like "reality," "nature," "anguish," *"amour fou,"* "automatism," and "human liberty" meanings they had never had in literary writing.

It was Philippe Soupault, Breton's earliest literary collaborator, who mentioned Pierre Janet when, a few months after the death of André Breton, he related to me the circumstances under which they undertook *Les Champs magnétiques,* their first joint venture in automatic writing. The term came from Pierre Janet at the same time that the vision of magnetic fields was inspired by graphic displays of electric patterns of magnetism, and the work derived thus in its double connotation from the scientific rather than the literary frame of reference.

Among the works of Pierre Janet there is a thick volume called *L'Automatisme psychologique* (first edition 1889, ninth edition 1921, indicating how available the work was to students of psychology). Several things are striking in Janet's notion of automatic writing, which of course he uses as a channel of therapy, but in so doing, unlike Freud, he is constantly aware of its implications for the exploration of the normal mind.

First of all, Janet makes it clear that automatism does not mean "mechanism." Two centuries earlier La Mettrie, the materialist philosopher, had demonstrated the mechanical structure of animal response to sensory stimuli as an automatic chain pattern of cause and effect, discernible to the outside observer. Janet was considering something quite different, as he explained in no uncertain terms. He pointed out how unwilling philosophers had been to use the word in any other context, just as they were wary of the ambiguity of the French word "*conscience*" because of its self-contained philosophy that equates the physical reaction to outer stimuli with the moral sense involved in its interpretation. *Conscience* actually separates one man from the *other* (that is, from a consciousness other than his own); and if automatism of thought communication were to be viewed as stimuli-response on the same basis as the undeniable automatism of physical reflexes, the notion of *conscience* would be eliminated and man would be reduced to the level of the animal-machine.

As Dr. Pierre Janet had realized in his definition of psychic automatism, he must make it clear that "automatic" was not synonymous with "mechanical." He thought that, on the contrary, his notion of automatism could end a battle long waged between determinists and idealists, and could conciliate the two points of view by considering them not in antithesis but in correlation. If man on the whole can control his reactions to his environment, there is an area, a most primordial one, the most elementary and most difficult to unveil, in which volition plays no part, and of which he is not aware unless it interferes with his conscious thought. This intrusion occurs in the mentally ill, but it is of no use to the subject because he has lost at the same time his sense of awareness of the intervention. However, it could reveal to the observer clues to the patient's fears and desires. If the normal person cannot lift the self-censuring mechanism of reason that bars access to automatic thought, he can in a moment of inattentive writing squeeze out the data stored in the deep recesses of the mind. The simplest example that occurs to Janet is the automatic recall of the spelling of a word when rational memory has had a lapse. If the spelling cannot be rationally conjured up, a moment of inattentive writing may bring it out of the area of the automatic functioning of the mind. "Let the pen wander," he says, "automatically, on the page even as the medium interrogates his mind." [3]

This is the premise on which the surrealist notion of automatic writing is founded. Its corollary is automatic speaking as practiced by mediums. Janet, the man of science, accepts the notion of "medium" in the same manner as the surrealists. A medium does not conjure the spirit of the dead, but he is a human, with all the physical characteristics of the human condition. Without extrasensory perception and without divine or unnatural aid, he has developed the power to loosen the strictures of mental inhibition to let the spontaneous workings of the mind emerge into view. It is very clear from Professor Janet's discussion that the data thus unveiled by automatic writing or speaking does not appear in a verbal form that is grammatically irrational. What is irrational is the effect produced on the observer when the mind is, in the process, unburdened of the overwhelming armor of patterns that are called "rational" because of collective, social agreement. Accidental in the insane, this process can be induced, Janet thought, by the adept and is most efficacious *without the aid of exterior stimuli.* The inner movement must be even and uninterrupted. As Soupault described the circumstances of the writing of *Les Champs magnétiques,* this appears indeed to have been the case with the young friends, and nightfall brought the only interruption in the flow of automatic thought. This admonition against exterior stimuli in the interest of authenticity explains Breton's exasperation when in collective experimentation with the production of automatic texts he observed that his collaborators were using alcohol or drugs as stimuli. It also explains his seemingly naive admiration of women mediums such as Solange for their apparently effortless success in automatic speech.

Janet's definition of automatic writing also points up the distinction between surrealist automatic writing, in its strictly scientific context, and what Dadaists and later avant-garde writers have made the language of the absurd—that is, *where the language itself is irrational* in structure and content and is offered as symptomatic of man's abject condition as an automaton (animal-machine) deprived of his autonomy in a world reduced to automation. It was not through Dada but through his medical studies that Breton became acquainted with the phenomenon of automatic writing, and it is as a scientific device that he tried to practice it. In Janet's teachings, and in Breton's adoption of them, psychic automatism becomes a breach in the wall that had previously shut off some of the most fundamental areas of man's knowledge of self. It is a means to an end; it foretells the gradual lifting of *le grand interdit.* It is part of the process of making man divine, as it gives him access to the sub rosa functioning of his mind without outside aids or provocations; it is a gate to self-observation and therefore to insight, to an enlargement of the magnetic field of his reality; it can lead to the eventual abolition of the man-made frontiers between material and spiritual existence. And in the hope that it may eventually abolish all contradictions, Breton makes it a fundamental canon in his definition of surrealism in his First Manifesto.

To Janet the study of psychic automatism could lead to a new grasp of the relation between the conscious and the subconscious through the discovery of the common mental activity from which emerge both sense perceptions and concepts: "the study of elementary forms of this activity will be for us," he said, "the study of the elementary forms of sensibility and consciousness." [4] The doctor, the medium, replaced by the poet, in the enlarged sense already suggested by Baudelaire and Rimbaud, as investigators of the unknown, will make this same field of research the object of the arts, the discovery of what Breton was to call *vases communicants*.

Janet's medical study not only of mediums but of hysterics, whose incoherent convulsive movements permitted the study of automatism, arrived at a broadly philosophical conclusion, not distant from Hegel's unproved hypothesis that "All idea is image, an internal representation of an act"; and he concluded further that the representation of the act is thereupon the beginning of the action. This precludes abstraction.

As it developed in Breton's mind, surrealism was to be an effort to abolish all antinomies. It was to aspire to a certain unity of mind and soul —a hypothesis in Hegel's philosophic meditations that came close to being proved in the laboratory. The focal point in this concept of human life is the *image*, as Janet pointed out in brushing aside all abstraction that did not reach concretion. The purifying process of abstraction had been the basis of the previous poetic school, Symbolism. Where surrealism was to spell a new era in the arts was in its philosophical matrix, the shunning of the abstract for the concrete, denying the existence of a reality separate from *image* and the existence of thought separate from the word. And the cult of the image was to become central when the literary intuitions of such poets as Rimbaud and Mallarmé were confirmed by scientific observations.

But Dr. Janet did not give his readers (he addressed himself to young men) just a broad philosophical base; he pointed out the avenues of investigation. The medium would not be considered without her instrument: the crystal bowl and its mirror-like properties. It might seem extraordinary to have a long discussion of crystal bowls in the middle of a psychology lecture, but that is exactly what Janet did. It was neither a literary man nor a sociologist but a scientist who traced the history of divination from Egypt to Greek antiquity and on to the Middle Ages. As a supporting source he referred to F. W. Myers's *The Subliminal Consciousness, Sen-*

sory Automatism and Induced Hallucination (1892). Again, the distinction between the mystical and the scientific was that the latter aimed to give a natural base to the supernatural: "the mirror incompletely lit up plays the role of a visual stimulus; it presents an empty space and invites the imagination to fill the gap. There is nothing particularly incomprehensible in this." [5] Both crystal and mirror were to become basic images in surrealist research and poetry under the direction of André Breton.

Janet accepted the involuntary character of hallucinations as an indication of the partial dependence of man on what he called "necessity" as opposed to free will. Life is a constant interplay of these two forces. As Breton outgrew his initial preoccupation with pure automatism, he was to pursue a particularly engrossing game: to see how far objective necessity could be made to coincide with the desires of the human will. Would not indeed the cult of coincidence bring man closer to the dream of absolute liberty?

The unexpected and involuntary character of the images in the crystal bowl became for Janet the basic ingredient of what we call the marvelous. The surrealists were to agree: they were to consider as "marvelous" not the spontaneous image, accepted in fright and surprise, but the power to catalyze images like those induced by the crystal bowl into a chain reaction even as in automatic writing.

Instead of confining his investigations to the observation of patients, Janet encouraged his students to confirm his findings in the domain of the *insolite* by performing a certain amount of vivisection, as it were, on themselves. But he did not minimize the pitfalls. For instance, he pointed out the difficulty for those engaged in automatism of maintaining a state of attention and inattention at the same time. He also realized that certain beings were more easily disposed than others to mental automatism. Among the surrealists such was to be the case with René Crevel and Robert Desnos, whom Breton utilized in expert medical fashion until he realized the dangers inherent to their health in the experiment, as Janet had warned: "I have advised you to try yourselves the experiment; I shall add softly: don't abuse, for I am convinced that its perfect success is not favorable to good mental health." [6] Janet also pointed out the role of inducer in the case of hypnotism, which demonstrated the polarization and, therefore, the physical dependence of men on each other, containing, as he thought, broad sociological and political implications.

His voluminous study of hysterics in a work called *De l'Angoisse à l'extase* (to which Breton refers in *La Clé des champs*) takes case histories in detail, with the names of patients and their descriptions; they read like characters out of a novel. There is one called Nadia, age twenty-eight, a study in obsessions, particularly noteworthy because Nadia happened to have an unusual insight into her own condition—just as Breton's demented Nadja was to have twenty-five years after the subject Janet had examined, and whose case history Breton had certainly read since he knew the book well.

Janet quotes another patient as saying: "Men often ask of what use is piety? If they only knew how it teaches us to suffer, how it makes us find happiness there where nature found only anguish and despair." And Janet adds: "for All is in all," [7] again implying the abolition of antinomies; it remained for Breton to crystallize this concept into a poetry of *l'un dans l'autre* ("one in the other"). With this basic analogical process Breton will create in his own poetry a lacework of interrelations between sensory data and his reactions to them, a continuum, uninterrupted in the reciprocity of containments.

Janet called the ecstasy of his hysteric young women patients "*amour fou*," their vision "convulsive"; Breton was to appropriate these expressions and transform their medical senses into poetic ones. Janet, unlike Freud, did not stop at clinical analysis; he concluded his case histories with a magnificent poetic synthesis about the human condition: "All this teaches us that we are richer than we think, we have more ideas and sensations than we thought. Our mind is full of beautiful thoughts of which we have no knowledge, which should console us for all the mediocre thoughts that we recognize so easily." [8] He implies that forgetting some of the mediocrity might light a path of mental lucidity for the more significant thoughts. Was not Breton to say some years later, in belittling the function of memory in the question: "Who will be the Christopher Columbus of forgetfulness?"

Dr. Janet's target was the Cartesian standard of mental discipline that had so long prevailed in French education. The following lines are not from a surrealist manifesto, but they reveal the fascinating convergence of Breton's medical and literary activities: "To limit the life of man," said Janet, "to this clear and distinct thought process Descartes speaks about, is to suppress, in my opinion, three quarters of this human life and to leave aside what is most attractive, the shadows and the *clair-obscur*. It is one of the merits of contemporary psychology to have tried to know the mysterious side of thought." [9] He went on to point out the common ground of priests and scientists since the beginning of time: "One must render justice to those ancient believers of the Middle Ages, whom we have so often laughed at." [10]

Dr. Janet believed that in the mansions of the mind as of the physical world nothing is lost. Astronomy came out of astrology, chemistry out of alchemy, and psychology owed much, he thought, to spiritualists and hypnotists. The difference was one of purpose: modern science was seeking not the treasures that the occultists had tried to uncover, but the powers of mind cultivated in the search. This was indeed exactly the attitude maintained by Breton as he went from the study of psychiatry to the study of occultism: to explore these two rich avenues, not to cure the sick mind or to find gold, but to restore to the normal mind some of the autonomy it might claim in the absence of all gods.

> "Let it be clearly observed that surrealist re-
> search presents with alchemic research a re-
> markable analogy of objectives."
> —*La Clé des champs*

It was under the double aegis of science and literature that Breton was oriented toward occult traditions. Michel Carrouges, in his book *André Breton et les données fondamentales du surréalisme,* points out the details of the influence of hermetic philosophies and concludes that Breton took the Philosopher's Stone and its quest symbolically without engulfing himself in its mysticism. Another critic, Ferdinand Alquié in *Philosophie du surréalisme* cannot see any empathy on the part of Breton with the occult because, he points out, Breton as a matter of fact dissociated himself from all the spiritism and extraterrestrial interventions in human life implied in gnostic concepts.

The contradiction among the critics is due, in truth, to the ambivalence of occultism itself. Louis Ménard, the nineteenth-century Hellenist who had translated the work of Hermes Trismégiste from the Greek, had revealed the heart of the difficulty.[11] Whether Hermes emerges as a monist, believing in the unity of all existence, or as a dualist, breaking up existence into spiritual and material entities, depends largely on the inherent philosophy that has shaped the language into which he is translated. In French, which is built on Christian concepts and accepts the duality of the universe in its linguistic structure, hermetic concepts are denoted in terms of distinctions between spirit and matter because the words into which the original is translated are those that serve a dualistic philosophy. In his important study *L'Hermétisme,* A. J. Festugière notes the two separate interpretations to which hermeticism lends itself: it is deemed, on the one hand, that man can attain the absolute in directing his efforts toward escape from the material world; on the other, that he can reach the divine essence only in the contemplation of this world, which is penetrated with it.[12]

In indicating time and again that there exists a lineage of long duration, which links minds over and above national and ethnic frontiers—a lineage to which Breton can adhere much more willingly than to any national one —he himself fails to indicate the ambiguity. He includes in the great family of illuminists the thirteenth-century alchemist, Raymond Lulle, the fourteenth-century gnostic, Flamel, the eighteenth-century philosophers, Fabre d'Olivet and Louis Claude Saint-Martin, the nineteenth-century visionaries, Charles Fourier and Eliphas Lévi, scholars of hermeticism, such as Frazer and Fulcanelli, and a varied list of poets from Novalis to Baudelaire, Rimbaud, Goethe, Hugo, and more recently, Apollinaire, Jarry, and Raymond Roussel.

Judging from the dates of the appearance of the work of Abbé Constant, alias Eliphas Lévi, in 1860–1861, and from the apparent infiltration of his terminology into Rimbaud's writing, it is likely that Rimbaud read Lévi (and was impressed by his attempt to give a material basis to the spiritual), in contrast with Baudelaire who is known to have read a popularized form of the writings of the earlier illuminist, Swedenborg (who had spiritualized material reality). If, therefore, Swedenborg was the patron saint of Symbolism, Eliphas Lévi through Rimbaud and more directly through Breton was to become a philosophical mainspring of surrealism.

Although witnesses to Breton's early years, including his first wife, have said that his interest in hermetic literature came later than his other formative readings, he himself insists in *Entretiens* that hermeticism influenced his entire work. Indeed he speaks of High Magic in his First Manifesto, and his very organization of the surrealist coterie is modeled on the nature of affiliations in occult societies described by Eliphas Lévi. Every one of his works was to bear some imprint of this hermeticism; Lévi's version of the hermetic vision of the universe was to affect the structure of Breton's poetic analogies from *Les Champs magnétiques* to *La Clé des champs*.[13] But what interests us at the moment is to read over the young poet's shoulder the works that were to be the basic frame of reference of his poetry, his activities, his literary criticism, and his philosophy of life and love. Among these the work of Eliphas Lévi looms large.

Born Alphonse Louis Constant in 1810, Eliphas Lévi was a French priest; but when Abbé Constant was expelled from the Church for heresy, he adopted what is said to be the Hebrew equivalent of his name. His romantic adventures as well as the particularly materialist emphasis he gave to High Magic lent a personal heretical twist to heresy itself. Much had been written about spiritualism, animal magnetism, and somnambulism in the second part of the nineteenth century, but Eliphas Lévi's ideas were to be most compatible with twentieth-century scientific thought; the basic fact was that, unlike most hermeticists, Lévi was a materialist. He saw in science the basic magic and in the natural world all the possibilities of the marvelous that other mystics attributed to the supernatural. In fact, he banished mysticism from magic. He underlined the difference. Mysticism is based on faith, which Eliphas Lévi rejected in favor of knowledge. He stated that the ideal must be conceived as realizable if not yet realized within the limits of physical laws.

> Magic differs from mysticism because it judges nothing *a priori* until after it has established *a posteriori* the actual base of its judgments, that is to say, after having apprehended the cause by the effects contained in the energy of the cause itself, by means of the universal law of analogy. Hence in the occult sciences all is read, and theories are established only on the foundations of experience. . . . and the Magus admires nothing as certain in the domain of ideas save that which is demonstrated by realization.[14]

He shows that "cabala" means reception, and reception involves discovery, a lifting of veils instead of harboring mystery or willingness to leave things under cover. "Revelation" means in its very etymology a reveiling; in other words, every discovery of the powers of the universe catalyzes new mysteries which in turn require unveiling. It is indeed the path of the modern scientist, which Eliphas Lévi identifies with his concept, that is inherent in the core of surrealism and in the distinction that André Breton was to make between the "marvelous" and the "mysterious": the *insolite* in the case of the surrealist is in a dynamic state of gradual illumination, whereas in the case of the Symbolist the mystery is without outlet. As Breton was to say in observing this half-secrecy in the work of Raymond Roussel: "All occult literature teaches that this secret is not forever enclosed." [15]

Although the gnostic tradition is said to be a mosaic of Jewish, Christian, Babylonian, and Egyptian elements, Eliphas Lévi minimizes the Christian. According to him, the Apocalypse is of this world. He derives most directly from the monist Simon the Magus who interprets Plato not as a seeker of abstractions but as an equalizer of concept with essence, which is the synthesis of reality and reached not through logic but through intuition. It is also from Simon that Eliphas Lévi derives the notion of overcoming the antinomies: *la coincidentia oppositorium*, the coexistence of opposites, and the reversal of one into the other; strangely concurring with Janet's conclusions is Eliphas Lévi's statement: "Harmony consists of equilibrium, and equilibrium subsists by the analogy of contraries." Breton will spell out these "contraries" so that the poetic vision may unite even as the hermetic and the psychiatric, and will arrive at a new definition of analogy incorporating this concept of the mediation of disparate entities. In his search for the keys of the universe Breton will believe with Eliphas Lévi that: "Analogy yields all forces of Nature to the Magus; analogy is the quintessence of the Philosopher's Stone, the secret of perpetual motion . . . the key of the Great Arcanum." [16]

Among the antinomies, the major one that Lévi attacks is the antithesis between spiritual and material; to him it is merely a matter of degree of opacity or of light: "Spiritual and corporal are simply terms which express the degrees of unity or density in substance." [17] Man has in him the power to transform the opaque into the translucent; Eliphas Lévi defines this power as *imagination*. "To imagine is to see" (*Donner à voir* will reiterate the surrealists!), and to see is to crystallize, to render *diaphane* or "transparent"; that is, imagination is not the creator of illusion, but the illuminator of reality. "Imagination, in effect, is like the soul's eye; therein forms are outlined and preserved; thereby we behold the reflections of the invisible world; it is the glass of visions and the apparatus of magical life." [18] Eliphas Lévi, basically an optimist, presents a universe not cursed by the wrath of God, and man as inherently capable of creating himself, that is to say in a position to reach "the full and entire conquest of his faculties and his future." [19]

In this the power of speech is manifest: a thought tends to realization in speech: "to speak is to create." [20] That is indeed what Rimbaud meant by the alchemy of the Word and what Breton was to repeat during the development of surrealist aesthetics. The adept going a step from self-mastery can learn to detect the forces of the universe, according to Eliphas Lévi: "The crowd will believe that you are God." [21] Again the echo of Rimbaud, and the stipulation of Breton that man may finally appropriate to himself the powers he has for so long attributed to the gods.

Eliphas Lévi was to shape Breton's mind in as many ways as his scientific studies had; and in fact the bridge between modern psychologists and the magi as interpreted by the nineteenth-century illuminists is extraordinary. The nature of personal magnetism, the spontaneity of dream, the nature of sleep, the participation through dreams in the "universal life"—what psychologists were groping to determine as the depths of the universal ego. Eliphas Lévi indicated three levels of magnetism, all important to Breton: self-magnetization, which is the empowering of the will, awakening one's own lucidity; relationships with another; the inducement of sleep in another—that is, hypnosis and its dangers.

The attraction of one to another caused sympathy: "Man and things are magnetized like the suns by light and by electromagnetic chains of sympathies and affinities they intercommunicate from end to end of the world." [22] When this sympathy extends to a group and forms a magnetic chain, it produces faith "and draws a large number of wills in a given circle of active manifestations." [23] Eliphas Lévi appears to define the mystique of the formulation of a coterie, of the creation of the current of ideas among a collective whole. He also indicates that among the many who come into frequent contact with each other, one inevitably becomes the "head of the current," "and the strongest will is not slow to absorb the others." [24] Indeed, one man becomes the Magus, a focus, as Breton was to be in the surrealist movement. Lévi even suggested ways of forming the "magic chain" and called the printed word an "admirable instrument," an "extension of speech." [25]

Three other notions in the writings of Eliphas Lévi are highly pertinent to the shaping of Breton's mind: Eliphas Lévi's concepts of liberty, love, and death. In the wake of the French Revolution he did not accept "liberty, equality, and fraternity" as equal values. In his opinion liberty precluded equality, for he saw inequality in nature and felt that the tendency to level off the unequal was an attack on personal liberty, and that the defense of that threatened liberty would through strife eventually destroy all fraternity: "The watchword of the republic which is to come will be Humanity, Justice, Solidarity: such is the enigma of the modern sphynx, which must be divined or we perish." [26]

To what extent this notion impressed Breton can be seen in one of the earliest documents of the young surrealists in the Dada period of their affiliation. In playing one of their games of rating personalities and concepts, whereas his companions ranked the three mottoes of the French republic equally, Breton gave top rating to liberty and very low marks to equality and fraternity.[27] This example shows merely the early impression Lévi's writings had on his mind; for indeed the values of Breton were to change thereafter; and while he never wavered in his passionate love of liberty as a supreme value, he became an equally staunch champion of fraternity, not on a personal but on a "one world" basis.

A more permanent influence of occult philosophy was the importance attributed to woman by Eliphas Lévi and by Simon the Magus before him: she was given the role of prophet, with the sacerdotal power to intervene in tragic circumstances and to transform anguish into ecstasy. Woman, whose elements are fire and water in the hermetic cult, is said to be in closer contact with the motive-transforming agents of the universe. To love then is to be through her closer to magical power. But, warns Eliphas Lévi, "He alone can possess truly the pleasure of love who has conquered the love of pleasure." [28] We shall see how Breton and a number of the other surrealists were to fashion their philosophy of love, distinguishing between the amateurs of libertinage and those of love in the hermetic sense, in which the sexual act had a sacred significance; as in

Eliphas Lévi's words, "the creative principle is the ideal phallus," [29] so emblematically it plays an equally prominent role in surrealism.

Finally, the concept of Lucifer in occult philosophy is dissociated from evil and instead becomes a force for adventure and audacity—what Apollinaire identified as "pilgrim of perdition." It is not possible to understand the notion of "black" in Breton's writings without reference to Eliphas Lévi's definition of Lucifer. For how could black be illuminating, a source of sinless strength, and compatible with Breton's optimism in regard to man's destiny if it were associated with the Christian devil? Lucifer, the rebel, according to Eliphas Lévi's interpretation of hermeticism, is not evil; he is the angel who enlightens, who regenerates: "The black intelligence is the divination of the Mysteries of the Night, the attribution of reality to the forms of the invisible. It is belief in vague possibility." [30] In other words Lucifer is a source of hope, darkness is a facet of light, rebellion is an agent of salvation.

Eliphas Lévi invites his readers to overcome the greatest darkness of all, death, by envisaging life and death as a continuum even as the conciliation of all other antinomies, a metamorphosis to be viewed as a shedding of a garment, a movement of the molecules toward liberation. Breton's analogy of the movement was expressed in the First Manifesto by the image of a moving van in which alone he would want to be taken to the cemetery at his death.

Thus, at an early age, through his studies and readings, Breton discovered two channels of the mind; they were revealed to him by the scientist of today and the magicians of the past, whose concepts strangely coincided: that the mind is deeper than we think; that it is not a closed vessel but is linked in innumerable ways to other minds and to the universal network of nature; that awareness of this linkage need not be based on religious dogma; that there were many ways of strengthening the links, but only through self-knowledge could one gain knowledge of the exterior world. Through their many evidences of the basic unity of human existence and of the universe, science and ancient hermetic philosophy belied the present world of chaos and disruption, of gross disjunction and mutual incomprehensions. These ideas were the ammunitions with which Breton was to seek meaning in the modern world.

> "The alleged instinct for causality is
> nothing more than the fear of the unusual."
> —Nietzsche

At the very time when Eliphas Lévi was introducing a materialistic mysticism combining the opposite poles of spirituality and rationalism, the mathematician Alphonse Cournot was developing the theory of the calculation of probabilities. It upset the determinist hypothesis by pointing out that not all occurrences and actions were controlled or controllable by predetermined factors, and that even after eliminating extranatural agents as impulsive forces, one could find unpredictable and uncontrollable powers in the material universe which belied the automatic—that is, deterministic—character of organic and inorganic realities. In fact, determinist science, and by extension philosophy, accounted for only one side of the coin of natural law.

If the Newtonian law of gravity governs the fall of objects, and if the fall is a constant that can be grasped by the logical mind without a grain of doubt (by simple deduction, in the face of a single possible outcome), then any suggested deviation or other possibility would be in the realm of the supernatural, the metaphysical, or the unreal. However, as Cournot showed, and as the English scientist Robert Brown had defined in 1827, all is not that simple in the universe. There are movements in molecules as in animals whose course cannot be predetermined or submitted to generalization. What has been called the "Brownian movement" is the multiplicity of movements following from a single impulsion; they cannot be coded by a mathematical formula but can only be charted graphically by a range of possibilities and statistical probabilities. Brown's first experimentation was with particles in water; later examples included the erratic movements of flies, the arbitrary routes of taxi drivers, and the irregular pattern of the dice player who is called an "aleator" because his so-called good luck or bad luck is determined by accidental (or aleatory) factors, which with all the experience in the world one cannot reduce to a constant pattern.

Materialist determinism runs parallel to pagan fatalism or Christian jansenism in accepting the predetermined factor in physical as well as in mental activity. On the other hand, the mathematical law of probabilities presupposes an uncertainty of cause and a multiplicity of effects. It implies the independence of events from each other, the possibility of a plurality of relations, a surprise element inherent in the occurrence and the coincidences of events.

It follows that the relationship of events is not a closed circuit but a field of free associations, which makes of the notion of liberty not a haunting aspiration but a physical and a necessary reality. *In other words, contrary to the philosophical assumption that man's search for liberty involves a battle against the natural forces of the universe, man's autonomy within the limits of the universe is a natural attribute of his human and physical condition.* Chance, which we are in the habit of splitting into good luck and bad luck according to the eventual outcome of the particular movement, is more scientifically identified, without the element of affective impression, as the geometrical locus of coincidences.

Early in the twentieth century the physicist Jean Perrin of the Sorbonne had experimented with the Brownian movement of particles and submitted it to the laws of probability. The scientist, Pierre Vendryes, pursuing the work of Perrin in terms of the aleatory movements of a fly and the chance patterns of a taxicab cruising in the streets of Paris, was struck by the extraordinary parallel between his own studies of the applications of the laws of probability and the surrealist concept of objective chance. He concluded that "the use that a living being makes of his motor autonomy in total independence permits him to enter into relations of probabilities with his environment." [31] Observing at first hand Breton's attempt to seek a state of grace with objective chance, Vendryes noted its relevance to the mathematician's preoccupation with the mechanism of the laws of probability.

If, as Vendryes pointed out, occidental civilization had concluded for many centuries that scientific thought was by its very definition deterministic, and therefore tended to rob man of his liberty, then probabilistic interpretation of autonomy opens anew two fundamental questions: that of liberty and that of the intervention of chance in self-determination. "To give a place to chance in the domains of science is to insert at the same time an element of mystery." [32] Mathematics was then in step with psychiatry in the acceptance of mystery in the study of the material world, restoring the sense of the unwonted which, with the weakening of religious faith, had been destroyed in many modern men. "The existence, real and proved, of purely aleatory encounters in life, adds to this life an element of mystery and anxiety." [33]

But how can the knowledge of the laws of probability affect man's exercise of his liberty? It opens up the possibility of automatic action, just as the knowledge of the passive resources of automatic thought leads to the exercise of automatic writing. Both are, as the scientist proves, available although they remain in general unexploited. Man's established habits of thought and action have closed the doors on both. Exercise of the purely rational process of thought locks the storehouse of images and desires; regularization of the patterns of behavior precludes the action of chance upon our lives. In that sense it is the logical thought process that is *mechanical* as opposed to *automatic* or unpredictable; and the daily routine life is also mechanical and deterministic in barring the intervention of the automatic event upon the life pattern. Presumably life could be so totally patterned that the only intervening, unstructured accident would be death (since birth itself now enters into the deterministic structure); thus there is a suppression of all aleatory movements that were meant to be part of the natural human condition.

If surrealism was to be basically an effort to recuperate the natural rights that man has lost in an ever-tightening structure of society, Breton saw in the laws of probability an avenue for exploration both similar to and parallel with automatic writing.

Although, as we said earlier, "availability" was the common aim of Gide and Breton, they came to mean different things by it. Gide thought of availability to ideas and physical pleasures through freedom from social or doctrinal obligations. Breton was to be more acutely preoccupied with availability to chance. In the search for chance and its coincidences, which was to become under his guidance one of the primary activities of surrealism, the most formidable obstacle is the routine of life itself. The young Breton's opposition to earning a living arose therefore out of an antipathy not to work itself but to regular activity in the pursuit of economic security; it cut off, he thought, the most precious hours and years of a man's discovery of self. The alleged freedom that the slave Sisyphus enjoyed in the time of his descent from the mountain after pushing up the stone was not sufficient compensation for what he had lost; [34] the meager limits of that liberty were unacceptable to modern man in view of his knowledge of the wealth of experience available within and around him. The pattern of work must be as erratic as the pattern of leisure and directed to opening as many avenues as possible to the flow of chance.

It is in this light that we must view the walks that, under the leadership of Breton, the surrealists took across the length and breadth of Paris. What city other than Paris could have afforded so many aleatory interventions of sights and events to this automatic ambulation, logically, intentionally free of destination, as unpreconceived as the subject matter of automatic writing?

Destiny, under the influence of mathematics, was to assume a new definition: the coincidences of natural necessities of the physical world with the spontaneous necessities of man who leaves himself open to his inner motivations, guided only by intuition and desire. If, as we shall see, the manner of communication in truly surrealist writing is analogical rather than logical, the structure of the work, particularly that of André Breton, is Brownian: its climax is identified by the sparks of encounter and coincidence. The intervention of chance replaces for the modern man the intervention of the divine, as Breton discovered. Inevitably the preponderant accident is love, for what experience in human life outside of death itself is as uncontrolled and as dependent on the undependable, the unscheduled, and the undeterminable in all its aspects of time, place, and form as the love-encounter?

Before Breton's time, Mallarmé had given poetic dimensions to the theory of probability in his "Un Coup de dés jamais n'abolira le hasard." His poem supports the omnipotence of the multiple possibilities of chance as proof that man, with his volition—that is, *coup de dés*—cannot bring about any but the slightest deviations in the arbitrary character of chance. There is a stoical pessimism in the assertion of man's limited area of self-determination, in the acceptance of the most limited scope of human liberty. What Mallarmé did not seem to realize—not because he was not wise but because the applications of determination were not extensive in his time—is that man's ability to determine and control an ever increasing number of factors in his life leads not necessarily to more liberty but to conformity, which puts a certain liberty in a few hands and takes it totally away from others.

André Breton, arriving at a time of more complete determinism, recognized its social implications as well as its infringements on personal liberty, its pattern superimposed upon the natural free play of events. He chose the caprices of chance as more conducive to human freedom of action in terms of acceptance or rejection, than society's assumption of the power to control chance. Breton's rejection of social collectivism had a profoundly philosophical basis, deeply rooted in his early training. The way to survive in a social structure that allows man to become continually, the object of chance is to seek chance, to be not its victim but its beneficiary, to be accorded a larger number of possibilities for self-determination.

These concepts were at work in Breton's mind for some ten years before he wrote his First Manifesto of surrealism; the major preoccupation of the young man who loved poetry but was educated in scientific disciplines was how to put poetry *at the service of the great work of the rehabilitation of man in the modern world*. That is why the purely aesthetic canons of Apollinaire, as presented in his *L'Esprit nouveau et les poètes*, seemed to Breton to mark the end of an epoch rather than the beginning of a new one. That is why at the end of Apollinaire's life, Breton was disenchanted with the "modernism" of the writer although full of affection for the man himself. That is also why Rimbaud's silence after 1875, which was accepted by his admirers as a tragic but romantic drama, seemed grievous to Breton; Breton was distressed not because Rimbaud had abandoned literature to become an Ethiopian trader, but because he had not carried out

the promises of his famous letter to restore poetry to the seat of the ancient magi. That is also why Breton was most disappointed when Valéry
broke what he had believed to be a pregnant silence, but what had proved
to be only a passive suspension, to write *La Jeune Parque* and *Le
Cimetière marin*. He could, Breton thought, have written them just as well
twenty years earlier. Was the twentieth century a time for pretty alexan-
drine verse? For Breton, as he contemplated the abandonment of the routine life of a successful psychiatrist for the aleatory existence of a poet,
there was, as Zola had indicated some fifty years earlier, no room for the
poet-prototype as identified heretofore in modern society. The alternative
was to make poetry something far vaster and more urgently significant to
modern life: "the terrain where there is most chance of resolving the terrible difficulties of conscience." [35] His aim consisted not of creativity per se,
as suggested by Apollinaire, but of the discovery—through speech, through
human relationships, through the unleashing of automatic forces in the human psyche, and through the reception of the outer forces of the physical
world—of the possibilities to "change life" as Rimbaud had wished and
to "transform the world" as Karl Marx had proposed. Breton felt that
neither could be accomplished by itself, but the change of personal life
and consequently the transformation of the social structure were dependent on the reshaping of the human mind—*entendement*, as he called it
in his later writings. That was to be the objective of the poet and his only
legitimate subject.

Automatism, magnetism, the keys to the marvelous, the sacralization of
the earth, the sanctification of sexuality, and the quest for objective chance
constitute the basic frame of reference necessary for the discussion and
situation of the literary writings of André Breton, and they have a direct
bearing on his personal life, the writing and the life inextricably melded
one in the other. The work was not a fruit of the tree but its sap, its
seminal content. The work shaped the life as the life made possible the
work, and each piece of writing was an erotic act:

"Sow your children in the woods." [36]

IV

THE YOUNG
POET
IN PARIS

"As they lived in the fresh air of the Boulevards
of Paris they felt no need to go to the country."
—Aragon

Breton explains in *Entretiens* that the soldiers of World War I were not immediately discharged at the end of hostilities. There was a gradual return to civilian life, and as he tells us Breton was not discharged from the army until September 1919. But in the meantime since his return from Nantes, his medical services, supplemented by additional training in the outskirts of Paris, had given him sufficient freedom to attend literary gatherings at the terrace of the Café de Flore, or to read Lautréamont in the Bibliothèque Nationale, or to browse in the bookstore of Adrienne Monnier and meet other medico-literary young men such as Aragon, or to visit Apollinaire in his apartment at 202 Boulevard St. Germain where he avidly read Sade, whom Apollinaire had unearthed in the *Enfer* of the Bibliothèque Nationale.

The demobilization was gradual, says Breton, as a precautionary measure against the anger of youths returning from what they considered a total waste of life, and returning in a state of regimentation which had left them stunned. The readjustment was slow: "As far as I am concerned, delivered from the military yoke, I was determined to evade all other restrictions, come what may." [1]

Breton had learned from his friend Jacques Vaché the most flamboyant application of the Brownian movement to daily living. Throughout his brief life, which ended early in 1919, Vaché had pursued the unpredictable, the totally arbitrary existence. Breton was disillusioned by both war and medicine, neither of which had, he thought, come to grips with life or led to a better understanding of the human condition; his first attitude after the cessation of the war was one of negation and nihilism. Vaché's sense of the uselessness of everything and in consequence his stance of total disobedience and insubordination seemed to Breton the only effective position for a young man to take. The frightful adventure of war was over, and its devastation of minds and places could be stomached only through the Vaché attitude: the reduction of everything to absurdity and derision. *Umour*, spelled according to Vaché, was a defensive prop, and in some cases even that was not sufficient protection against suicidal tendencies; it had failed to save Jacques Vaché from suicide.

Freed from his military obligations and possessed with an urgent desire to cut himself off from all bonds, Breton was still tied to his medical studies, although his attendance gradually fell off; his total dropping out brought his angry parents to his modest hotel room. Upon hearing that her son had quit his medical studies, Mme Breton said, according to her grandchild Aube, "I would have preferred to hear that he had died on the battlefield." The father was more sympathetic although skeptical of his son's future in the Parisian literary milieu. For many years he was to hover quietly but faithfully in the background of his son's activities, giving him a modest financial transfusion now and then out of his own meager income, saving him in moments of extreme economic crisis; but the fact remains that when Breton permanently interrupted his medical studies—he had been only a medical apprentice during the war—he was totally on his own, and his Brownian movements in the quest of chance and adventure were to be interrupted sporadically in order for him to meet the need for food and shelter, even as the freedom of the fly is curtailed and his course modified by the necessity to seek nourishment. Breton was eating less and less; and as he confesses candidly, the days of total fasting weakened his physical stability and produced a psychic state more conducive to automatic writing and spontaneous dreaming.

Fortunately he had rich companions who could come to his aid; fortunately also, through his connections with Paul Valéry and Apollinaire, he made contacts with the publishing world and got occasional editing jobs. But his mind was not on copy reading and he made a poor editor as Proust in a letter to Soupault pointed out ever so delicately and discreetly: "I see that my next book, though copy-read by M. Breton, contained so many mistakes that if I did not list an erratum I would be dishonored." It had taken the disgruntled Proust eight days to find two hundred mistakes in twenty-three galley pages, which comprised half the book. He reached the height of politeness not unmarked by benign innuendoes when he added: "But by no means let M. Breton take this for a reproach." [2] Let it be added that the same sinned-against Proust was generous enough, and saw enough talent in the early poetry of Breton, to propose him for the Blumenthal prize which could have brought the needy young poet twelve thousand francs—a veritable fortune which would have kept him free from economic pressure for a long time, when we consider that he mentions elsewhere in his correspondence that one could keep body and soul together for six hundred francs a month. The committee postponed his candidacy for two years despite Proust's warm support of the young man. Proust added sadly that in two years the prize would do no good.

With the death of Vaché in January and that of Apollinaire the previous November, Breton had attached himself to the friends he had made through common admiration of Apollinaire or common studies at the Sorbonne. The two common grounds converged in the case of his two closest friends, Philippe Soupault, whom he had met through Apollinaire, and Louis Aragon, whom he had encountered at the bookstore of Adrienne Monnier, La Maison des amis des Livres, rue de l'Odéon. Together Breton and Aragon had gone to Val de Grace to take auxiliary training as army medics. He had also entered into collaboration with two avant-garde magazines: *Nord-Sud*, under the direction of Pierre Reverdy, the leading poet under the aegis of the cubist coterie, whom he had also met through Apollinaire at the Café de Flore; and *Littérature*, which he himself took part in founding with Philippe Soupault after his apprenticeship on the staff of *Nord-Sud*. Of course the little magazines were totally nonpaying enterprises, and it was a labor of love to keep them going.

Breton had been drawn to Pierre Reverdy, in whom he recognized not the sidekick of the cubist painters but a master of the poetic image, along with another poet who kept himself aloof from literary schools, Saint-Pol-Roux. The latter was a recluse; the former was more available and had notions of poetic composition that were distinct from those of the cubist group with which he associated. They were to serve as a springboard for Breton's own poetic theories, but soon he became disillusioned with the man Reverdy while he remained sensitive to his breakthrough in aesthetic theory.

> I liked and I still like—yes, I love—that poetry practiced in broad strokes which circles daily life with a halo of apprehensions and indices, floats around our impressions and actions. He chiseled it as if by chance: the rhythm which he had created was apparently his only

tool, but this tool never betrayed him, he was marvelous. Reverdy was much more of a theorist than Apollinaire: he would even have been for us an ideal master if he had been less passionate in discussions, more truly concerned with the arguments with which we opposed him, but it is true that this passion was part of his charm. No one meditated better than he nor made others meditate on the profound methods of poetry. . . . We found him in spite of everything a little too withdrawn into his own world.[3]

We might say * that Breton's relationship with Reverdy was the reverse of his friendship with Apollinaire. He never lost his love for Apollinaire the man when he became disenchanted with his poetic talent; whereas he became disillusioned with the character of the man Reverdy, in whom he saw streaks of jealousy, and whose anger he aroused by his own unwillingness to become the exclusive disciple of any one being: "I never see Reverdy anymore, jealous (can you imagine) of my affection for you, of the place you hold in the thoughts of Soupault and in mine," he writes to Tristan Tzara.[4]

Between the years 1918 and 1924, Breton was disillusioned with society, with education, with the venal motivations of literary men: the questions he asked them in his fervent letters did not bring the answers he hoped for. He was sometimes overcome with a sense of futility, moments of total isolation and boredom, which he would spend sitting alone on a park bench at the Place du Châtelet;[5] he would identify with the melancholy of a street by Chirico or retreat to his lonely room at the Hôtel des Grands Hommes. He had inherited friends from the entourage of Apollinaire, and through Jean Paulhan of the publishing house of Gallimard, which was the center of the writers who had started La Nouvelle Revue Française twenty years earlier on the same basis that Littérature had been launched by the younger writers with whom Breton had come into contact. And now La Nouvelle Revue Française and its founders were the Establishment. Through Jean Paulhan he met Paul Eluard; their relationship was to be of long duration.

Breton tries to make life in Paris an extension of the time in Nantes. Vaché's companionship is replaced by that of Aragon, Soupault, and Eluard. But none of these men rejects both art and society in the way that Vaché did. Eluard is delicate, refined, literary in his attitudes. Soupault

---

* Breton's correspondence collected by Michel Sanouillet in his monumental *Dada à Paris* is of invaluable help in tracing the effusions and dejections of the young poet in Paris, his enthusiasms and his disappointments, his instinctive quest for a replacement of the Vaché image in his need for friendship, which led him ultimately to the discovery of Tristan Tzara and the Dada movement.

has a finesse and a sophistication in literary circles that stems from a more affluent, cultivated family ambiance; he has an extraordinary facility to write verse any time anywhere and an eye very responsive to feminine beauty. As for Aragon, he has a tremendous zest for life; he is highly articulate; his verbal eloquence shines in the company of his friends and at Adrienne Monnier's; he has read everything, has a prodigious memory. He is like a Don Quixote, and Paris is the scene of his adventures, about which he will write flamboyantly in *Anicet* and in *Le Paysan de Paris*. Everywhere he finds mystery and charm as he romanticizes the streets of Paris. Many years later Breton says of Aragon in *Entretiens*:

> I see the extraordinary companion he was in our walks. Even the most neutral places through which we passed in Paris were for him jacked up by several notches because of his fabulous power of romantic magic which never failed him and was sparked by each turn in the street or by each window display. . . . No one has shown more ability to detect the *insolite* in all its forms, no one could have got so carried away by intoxicating dreams about the existence of the secret life of the city.[6]

But Breton's description of his friend Louis Aragon in the dimming light of memory is as nothing to the vibrant on-the-spot portrait that Aragon made of Breton under the faintly disguised name of Baptiste Ajamais in *Anicet*, that cloak-and-dagger account of the Brownian moment in their lives. The authoritative character of Breton is immediately sensed by Aragon, as it was felt by so many of the young men who came in contact with him even before he became the leader of the surrealist movement. Aragon's description suggests Breton's power over him, a position that Aragon does not seem to have resisted but on the contrary encouraged. He shows the two of them in search for the "new beauty," *l'esprit nouveau* (Mirabelle); but whereas Aragon is prepared to be seduced by Mirabelle's obvious sensuality, Baptiste Ajamais (Breton) can look coolly through her sensual nudity and avoid the easy temptation for something beyond and apparently quite impossible to attain. Aragon attributes to his character Baptiste Ajamais the biographical circumstances of his friend André Breton. (Notice that the initials are reversed.) He uses the fact that Breton is still obsessed with the loss of his friend Jacques Vaché to make Baptiste look like someone lost in space, searching for something undefinable, certain of what he must reject but not sure at all of what he must find. In imitation of Vaché's dispassionate manner; Baptiste Ajamais remains impervious to easy conquests. He attracts women, looks at them with X-ray eyes; through them and beyond them he sees something else with his steel-like expression and haughty lip. He is searching for the sense of vertigo that no man has yet experienced. The words Aragon puts in his mouth are like direct quotations; they give an intimate insight into Breton's character:

> What happened is that nothing has happened since the world is world. The atrocious ills that men have imagined to forget the immense anguish which gnaws at them are a child's games. It is easier to bear humiliation, poverty, hunger, cold, all physical sufferings, than the least of those "whys" that the mind incessantly raises. Although it appears general, Newton's law does not suffice to explain a simple flicker of my eyelid.[7]

Aragon feels his friend's frustrations, constrictions. When they are inevitable, as during the years of military service, Breton tolerates his condition with sarcasm; but when normal life turns out to be simply an extension of military life, what is one to do? Insanity is no solution; nor is suicide. No, says Breton-Baptiste Ajamais: "The game consists of attaining one's limit in all directions before dying." [8]

We are indeed prisoners of life unless we decide for ourselves the exact importance we shall attribute to things. In the quest for a new hierarchy of significances, Breton-Ajamais chides his friend for his normal reactions: "You let yourself live; your docility is frightening." [9] Unlike in many ways yet alike in all that distinguishes them from the previous generation, the friends venture upon a modern quest of the Holy Grail within the confines of Paris:

> Their elders lived in cafés and asked for various *filtres* to embellish their days. *They* found their enjoyment in the street and if, by chance they stopped at a café terrace they drank only grenadine for the beauty of the color of that beverage. As they lived in the fresh air of the boulevards of Paris, they felt no need to go to the country.[10]

Later when Breton looked back on those years, it seemed to him that the war experience had been less traumatic for Aragon; he had borne with a certain ebullience the inconveniences of military life, enjoyed his *croix de guerre*, and suffered no profound crisis; he had made a stable adjustment to civilian life. Breton sums up his impressions in *Entretiens* with the opinion that "in him at that time little rebellion" was discernible.[11]

As for himself, Breton says that he experienced an ever-mounting sense of moral concern—"the moral question preoccupied me"—and an intensification rather than a relaxation of anger: "No compromise possible in a world to which an atrocious misadventure had taught nothing." [12]

The only hope, then, is in poetry, which Breton places a few rungs above philosophy as he confronts the complex and deep-seated problems of life.

In another part of Europe in 1916, at the time when Breton was making his first literary contacts, experiencing the mental and physical devastations of war on his hospital rounds, reading Rimbaud, and establishing companionships with others, like him uprooted from their studies to defend their country, a group of young men were convening in a café in Zurich, the Café Voltaire, much like those of the Café de Flore, and they were all young, but not quite so young as Breton and Soupault. Tristan Tzara was twenty-seven in 1919 as he writes to Breton, which makes him twenty-four at the birth of Dada: "since it interests you I am twenty-seven years old, and I see pretty clearly, question of habit and trade,—the disgust I spoke of somewhere is real, and I have recovered after a greater one: a few years lost in philosophy." [13] This means that he was four years older than Breton. Four years is a great distance in the development of a young man's life. In 1918, outside of a few Mallarméan poems, Breton's work is in gestation. Tzara had written a considerable amount of verse, some in his native Rumanian, others in fractured French. More important, he had written manifestoes during his stay in Zurich and was a leading figure in an international group, which included the German Hugo Ball (a poet friend of Kandinsky), Richard Huelsenbeck (a German physician-psychiatrist with a marginal interest in African dance), and the Alsatian, Hans Arp (to be known as Jean Arp after the Armistice which gave Alsace back to France). They had sympathizers abroad: Marcel Duchamp in America, Max Ernst in Cologne, Francis Picabia in Switzerland and later in Paris. The group in Zurich had been draft dodgers, had fled to neutral Switzerland from their native countries in order to make their rejection of war a living reality rather than a verbal expression. They were pursuing their quasi-artistic activities in a non-national context; their behavior was distinctly subversive both socially and politically. They practiced total unemployment for a while. Destruction and revolution were in the air; at a nearby café Lenin could be seen playing chess. The psychiatrist Jung was also in Zurich.

Which one of them invented the word Dada? They were to argue over it much later, but at the time nobody cared because, as they said, "everyone is President of Dada." Everyone practiced leadership, and no one followed, and no one cared who wrote what because, like all else, writing was considered a vanity, and it did not matter if you signed your name: it was not a thing of value; there were no values anymore. The aim of the young rebels was to destroy all values because they found those of their fathers in a state of default. As Tzara put it: "Dada never rested on any theory and has never been anything but a protest."

Huelsenbeck claims that he found the word while he and his friend Hugo Ball were looking through a dictionary for a name to give to the cabaret singer they had hired. On the other hand, Hans Arp states:

> I hereby declare that Tristan Tzara found the word Dada on February 8, 1916, at six o'clock in the afternoon. This occurred at the Café de la Terrasse in Zurich and I was wearing a brioche in my left nostril. I am convinced that this work is of no importance and that only imbeciles and Spanish professors can take interest in dates. What interests us is the Dada spirit and we were all Dada before Dada came into existence.[14]

It meant nothing and everything because everything was to be reduced to nothing. In the Manifesto of 1918, Tzara was to proclaim: "What is divine in us is the awakening of antihuman action. Let each man cry out: there is a big job, destructive and negative to be accomplished: sweep, sweep clean." [15] Appropriating the *table rase* formula of Descartes, they cried, "I do not want to know if there have been men before me." [16] (Yet had there not been men before them, against whom would they have directed their protest?)

They chose as their archetype the idiot, and what they wrote, enacted, or painted had as its aim the dramatization of the idiocy of mankind evidenced in the fracture of language, in the disconnected construction, with its built-in destruction called collage, in its exhibitionistic derision of social mores and social garb—of stiff collars, high hats, horn-rimmed glasses. Pamphlet No. 2 of Dada screamed: "We are a furious wind, ripping the wet wash of clouds and prayers, preparing the great spectacle of disaster, ire and decomposition." [17]

There was a concerted attack on and ridicule of all highly acclaimed writers and artists because as they thought success had made them stupid and sedate. In their place, a new recipe to make a new kind of poetry:

> To make a dadaist poem
> Take a newspaper
> Take a pair of scissors

Choose an article as long as you are planning to make your poem
Cut out the article
Then cut out each of the words that make up this article
                                   and put them in a bag
Shake it gently
Then take out the scraps one after the other in the order
         in which they left the bag.
Copy conscientiously
The poem will be like you.
And here you are a writer, infinitely original and endowed
                         with a sensibility that
is charming though beyond the understanding of the vulgar.[18]

In a more serious mood Hugo Ball explained the purposes of Dada:

> the dadaist fights against the death-throes and death-drunkenness of his
> time. Averse to every clever reticence, he cultivates the curiosity of one
> who experiences delight even in the most questionable forms of insub-
> ordination. He knows that the world of systems has gone to pieces,
> and that the age which demanded cash has organized a bargain sale of
> godless philosophies. Where bad conscience begins for the market-
> booth owners, mild laughter and mild kindliness begins for the Dada-
> ist . . .
>
> The bankruptcy of ideas having destroyed the concept of humanity
> at its very innermost strata, the instincts and hereditary backgrounds
> are now emerging pathologically.[19]

The Dadaists had a passion for liberty, but in their derisive representation of man in modern society they admitted that there was no liberty:
"We know that we are not free and we scream liberty," [20] said Tzara. The
manifestoes were noisy; their protest was explicit in collective demonstration, and not an individual attitude as in the case of Breton's friend
Jacques Vaché.

After the war the German Dadaists went to Berlin, where their protest
took two different directions: on the one hand, it was amalgamated with
other underground literary movements; and on the other, it found its
identification in the communist movement, which was eventually swallowed up by fascism. Dada is mentioned in *Mein Kampf* as a virulent
disease which must be checked before it becomes an epidemic.* Hugo
Ball remained in Switzerland in the Canton of Ticino until his death in

* The story of Dada in Germany still awaits the type of close study that has been
given Dada in Paris by Michel Sanouillet.

1927; there he produced a body of work, poetic, philosophical, and critical, having no further relation to Dada. Arp went to Cologne where he was joined by Max Ernst, and they developed together new forms of art and eventually joined the group in Paris when surrealism was born.

Switzerland had provided rather sterile soil for a protest such as Dada. Perhaps it was politically too sinless, and in the absence of a target it is hard to insist. Switzerland had neither fatuous writers to defame nor a guilty government to attack. France had the right climate for Dada: it had the belligerence, the guilt of success, the complacency of wealth. It also had another great attribute: a tradition of tolerance to subversive movements. Dada would not be its first youth riot; it had had the romanticists and the *Jeune France,* and it had enough sense of national security not to muzzle rebels or imprison them. Memories of the Bastille were carved in its stones, and barricades were frequently part of Parisian scenery. Paris would be an excellent culture for the germ of protest lodged in Dada. It would bring to a head the indignant restlessness of young intellectuals returning from war: their experience would substantiate the theoretical nihilism of the Dadaists. The flag of rebellion was raised in Zurich; the army was waiting in Paris.

In 1919, André Breton, having lost the companionship of both Vaché and Apollinaire, is looking for new friendships; Aragon and Soupault are not garrulous enough or sufficiently subversive for him. He thinks that he can find a substitute for Vaché in Tzara and one for Apollinaire in Tzara's friend Picabia. The character of Breton shines through his correspondence with the two men: his quick and openhearted offer of friendship, the almost naive revelation of his weaknesses, and his aspirations as a poet. He is quick to understand in himself and explain to Tzara why he seeks him out: Tzara's resemblance to the lost Vaché who was what he loved most in this world, and from whose death he has not recovered. Vaché has left him in a vacuum which Paris friends have not quite filled, perhaps because none of them quite felt the revolt that Vaché had communicated to Breton. In his very first letter to Tzara he brings out the connection between Tzara and Vaché: "He [Vaché] would have recognized your mind as a brother of his and together we would have done great things. He was twenty-three and the war was about to give him back to us." He goes on to say: "It is toward you that I turn today all my attention. You do not know exactly who I am. I am twenty-two years old. I believe in the genius of Rimbaud, of Lautréamont, of Jarry. I have infinitely loved Guillaume Apollinaire, I have a profound tenderness for Reverdy." [21]

In the next letters, addressed to Tzara from the Hôtel des Grands Hommes, Place du Panthéon, Breton's admiration reaches hero worship as he asks for a photo of Tzara and declares: "Of all living poets you are the one who moves me most." [22] He asks for advice from one whose disgust with the world seems to him to be more evolved than his own. He thinks that Tzara can deliver him from what prejudices remain in him. He considers his heart the knob of his door; in regard to Tzara the knob is turned, the door wide open, and Breton impatiently awaits Tzara's arrival at Picabia's home in Paris. So much was expected of the well-heralded arrival of the chief of all Dadas! In all Breton's letters to Tzara that Michel Sanouillet collected in his appendix to *Dada à Paris*, there is no other tone than reverence, respect, the hope of being liked by Tzara, of being able to serve him when he takes over the avant-garde movement in Paris. All Breton's hopes of doing something are centered on Tzara: "I think of you as I have never thought of anyone except Vaché." [23] In the meantime he hints to Tzara that he is working on something "earth-shaking," which he hopes Tzara will like. The summer before Tzara's arrival Philippe Soupault and Breton had produced what they will deem thereafter the first surrealist writing: *Les Champs magnétiques.*

Tzara's arrival was several times delayed, and Breton with childish solicitude runs five times to the station in the hope of meeting him. Characteristic of the absurd aspect of life to which he had raised a monument in his brief stay in Zurich, Tzara's arrival (in January 1920) at Picabia's home occurs just as the artist's mistress is giving birth to a son. In the unusual circumstances his first meeting with Breton is a rapid one. The great man was actually small, he wore glasses, his voice lacked resonance, his French was miserably weak. But at the outset there is no apparent abatement of Breton's enthusiasm. He rallies his friends around Tzara. He swings into the spirit of Dada demonstrations involving all his friends, those whom he had known at Apollinaire's, those at Reverdy's *Nord-Sud*, and those who had participated in *Littérature*. He dons round glasses, parades as a sandwich man. He finds for Dada particular targets to attack among literary men, rather than literature in the abstract. Maurice Barrès is singled out for a particularly severe mock trial for having changed from the free-spirited man of his early years as a writer to a nationalistic, regionalistic spokesman for the war and for patriotism. But even the trial, systematically arranged by Breton as a play with a cast of players, is turned into jest by Tzara, and is thus aborted. The fact was that at that period in his life Tzara meant it when he said that nothing could be taken seriously. Even protest was absurd in its futility. Breton learned a lot from Tzara in those early days of their meeting: to be more of an extrovert, to be more audacious, to learn to laugh at himself. Tzara in turn learned from Breton; and if in his Dada days his words and gestures lacked specific features even as in his words Dada lacked a countenance, later when he entered the surrealist group, he was to offer serious, deliberate treatises on style and the relationship of politics to art, and poems written in much-improved French.

The agitations continued from January to August 1920. But the fruitlessness of the activities was soon apparent to Breton and began to tell on his nerves. "There were at least two or three of us who wondered if this Battle of Hernani, which was resumed each month with complacency, and whose tactics had so quickly become stereotyped, was sufficient unto itself. The red gilet, perfect, but on condition that behind it beats the heart of Aloysius Bertrand, of Gerard de Nerval, and behind them those of Novalis and others." [24] The pamphlets were many, the words abounded, the harvest was meager. In his two articles on Dada, which have been collected in *Les Pas perdus*, we see, on the one hand, Breton's adoption of the Dada tone of tragicomic skepticism and, on the other, his disappointment: the red gilet in the case of the Dadas hid no profound thoughts, and everyone was beginning to realize it. Dada's very character of rebellion had a tyrannical hold—what he calls "the dictatorship of the mind." [25]

Basically the difference was one not only of character but of training. Tzara was for the abolition of all literary schools and traditions. But Breton from the very first, in the most intense moments of his revolt, felt that he belonged to an intellectual lineage: that of the great rebels of the past, the religious heretics, the hermeticists, certain literary moralists. Early in his correspondence with Tzara he had made this qualifying statement in relation to rebellion: "As much as you I have a passion to destroy, but must not one be wary of it? Sooner or later you risk becoming disqualified." [26] In characterizing himself as having *l'esprit frondeur*, he was identifying with the seventeenth-century princes who fought the monarchy to defend their autonomy. He was a rebel within a certain framework. Tzara was for the demolition of all frames and for total alienation from literature. He had had no intention of creating his own literary school, and he protested against the journalists who turned Dada, a free spirit, into a formalized Dadaism. He squelched any move on the part of Breton to give a serious character to any of the demonstrations that were organized. Dada had been welcomed as an open door by the French rebels, but the protest for lack of specific purpose was losing its effect. It was becoming redundant. "One discovers that the wide open doors of 1918 lead to a corridor that goes nowhere." [27]

The sequence of Dada activities has been given elsewhere, particularly in detail in *Dada à Paris*. Gradually, dissatisfied with the sterility of the demonstrations, Breton with the aid of Aragon tried to take the leadership. He had an idea for transfusing new vigor into the failing Dada: it must cease, he thought, to operate in a closed vessel and must situate itself in the wider channels of the avant-garde. He proposed to organize a massive Congrès de Paris to set in motion a vast dialogue among men of the arts, gathered from all over the world, to discuss and defend the modern mind. His proposed organization was as bureaucratic as the Third Republic with departmentalized divisions and subdivisions.

The Congrès de Paris was the first of many opportunities Breton was to create in the course of his life to ask questions of colleagues, to classify the answers, to organize exhibits. It was also his first serious attempt at leadership, and although it was abortive, it gave him insight into the type of role he might play under more propitious circumstances. Basically his inquiry was to delve into the nature of modernism. He had *a priori* notions about its origins and direction, and his questions were somewhat weighted by them. Tzara could not see what such a dialogue had to do with Dada which harbored no theories, and whose free spirit was unclassifiable.

Anger was sparked in Breton—the first of a series of angers that in the course of his life were to alienate many of his friends. The group divided into factions, and what was at first a case of derision responding to Breton's enthusiasm and dedicated action turned into anger responding to anger, as Breton in a temper called Tzara a foreign opportunist and lost some more of his friends. He had a little job at the time with the art gallery of a philanthropist, Jacques Doucet, who had promised certain funds for the running of the congress.[28] But the whole thing was a fiasco and led to the final and total disintegration of Dada's group activity in Paris.

If we linger a while on some of the questions that went unanswered, we can see that Breton's protest, indentified for a moment with Dada, aimed at a reconstruction of the tenets of modern art beyond the immediate destruction of the status quo: "Can there be knowledge outside of the confines of reason?" "What is the true sense of religion?" "Has the modern spirit always existed?" "What is the first condition of splendor?" "Can there be judgment without reservation?"

In the meantime Breton had met Benjamin Péret, who at first was not as close to Breton as were Aragon and Eluard but who was to become eventually his most loyal friend and, next to Breton, the most consistently surrealist writer. Péret sensed the coming break with Dada which he characterized as follows: "I take off the Dada eyeglasses and am ready to go. I look to see the direction of the wind without worrying what kind of a wind it will be and where it will lead." [29]

Breton was ready to wash his hands of the Dada adventure. It is in these circumstances that he wrote the little poem "Lâchez tout" which is often quoted as an example of his Dadaism. Actually it was his adieu to Dada, which he was ready to toss off along with all other involvements. His most extreme Dada protest was protest against Dada itself. He was also able to determine even then the place that Dada would take in the course of his life: "Dadaism cannot be said to have served any other purpose than to keep us in the perfect state of availability in which we are at present, and from which we shall now in all lucidity depart toward whatever calls us." [30]

He had wondered as he went along with Tzara's manifestations and public provocations in the early months of Dada in Paris: if the world was to be destroyed, would it end in a beautiful book or in a poster advertising hell? Slowly, quietly, for five years he had been preparing a platform in his mind. He was seeking roots, roots in the discontent of previous uprooters. He wanted a rebellion that would identify on the one hand with Rimbaud and Lautréamont, and even push back to the Marquis de Sade, and on the other hand with Hegel, Marx, and the illuminists. He wanted to proceed with the scientific methods that had been ingrained in him; and in breaking the old barriers between idealism and materialism, he would be careful to keep his orientation in the direction of the new scientific principles.

Although Breton, like Tzara, disdained men and their institutions, he still had a faith in the high potential of man. He had in mind a program "to remake human understanding." If nationalism deserved to be destroyed, it was to be followed not by the reign of the idiot but by the restoration of the primordial powers of human imagination, which had so long been held at bay.

This period not only marks for Breton the break with Dada; it is the beginning of a new chapter in his life. In 1921 he married Simone Kahn whom he had met by that mysterious chance that had begun to fascinate him, and that he was always to associate with love. She was the cousin of the fiancée of his schoolmate, Théodore Fraenkel—chic, well informed, inquisitive, extremely attractive with her luminous brown eyes. Her family was from Alsace, and her father was a modest manufacturer. He gave his daughter a small dowry, which the intelligent Simone was willing to invest in a painting or two, which in turn André and Simone were able to sell for profit soon thereafter. Almost in spite of themselves the Bretons had become part of free enterprise: André had found a form of livelihood that did not interfere with his Brownian movements. And he had acquired a wife with a rational head on her shoulders who could with sane calculation counteract his exaltations and distractions, who kept his things in order and mitigated his economic crises.*

Before his marriage, André Breton had moved restlessly from hotel to hotel, from the Left Bank of the poets to the Right Bank of the artists. (Most of the Symbolist poets had stayed on the Left Bank.) Apollinaire had vacillated in much the same way and finally had chosen the Boulevard St. Germain, perhaps signifying unconsciously his adherence to the coterie of poets. It is portentous and significant that Breton finally chose Montmartre, and at the end of 1921, up on the hill, just below Place Blanche, he took an apartment at 42 rue Fontaine, which was to be his permanent address for the rest of his life.

* Later she married a mathematics professor, and her beautiful apartment serves splendidly to set off a collection that would be the envy of any museum of modern art. Many of the paintings are acquisitions she and André had made together, cherished and sometimes sold. The collection was divided at the time of their divorce. She was able to buy back a number of the ones they sold in some of their urgent circumstances.

V

AUTOMATIC WRITING:
LES CHAMPS MAGNÉTIQUES
AND
POISSON SOLUBLE

"We listened to ourselves think."
—"Lune de Miel," *Les champs magnétiques*

It was in the summer of 1919, six months before Tristan Tzara arrived in Paris, that André Breton and Philippe Soupault wrote what Breton later was to call the first surrealist text. If *Les Champs magnétiques* is the first example of sustained automatic writing as conceived in the context of the psychiatric studies of Dr. Janet, which had so greatly impressed Breton in medical school, of greater significance is the fact that it is the first of a series of writings that create a new structure for communication, based on a new orientation of the creative mind. Molière's jocular distinction between verse and prose had suggested the simplistic equation—with considerable satire on his own part—that what is not prose is verse and what is not verse is prose. In the nineteenth century new forms had been created to bridge the gap: on the one hand, free verse—that is, poetry freed of metric restrictions—and on the other, the prose poem described by Baudelaire as a miraculous form of poetry, the language of dreams, more supple than verse. The symbolists experimented extensively with both the new forms and tended to create verbal music through instrumentalization of words and the attraction of sound to sound in a new priority of sound over sense. By the time of Rimbaud the distinctions in form were inconsequential; and as Breton was to observe in *Flagrant Délit*, Rimbaud's prose poems are really a more advanced form of poetry than his free verse.

The great contribution of the surrealists, and particularly of Breton in this area, beginning with *Les Champs magnétiques*, was the position that it is not through *form* that prose is distinguishable from verse but through the *process of thought* permeating the writing. Logical sequence of thought produces prose, as in the case of many inferior poets, even when patterned in impeccable versification, as in the case of Alexander Pope and Voltaire. On the other hand, true poetry is based not on logical but on analogical sequences of thought; it is poetry, no matter what exterior form it takes, because its poetic state is determined by its inner structure.

As we examine the writings of Breton, we shall discern three distinct structures: free verse, which he used continuously—no one has avoided rhyme as consistently as he; there is probably not a single forced rhyme in all his poetry; logical prose, which is the structure under which can be classified all his critical writings, philosophical essays, and manifestoes and addresses; and finally—perhaps his most original form—analogical prose, which unlike the prose poem takes on vast proportions, often the dimensions of a short novel. The main difference, however, is that his analogical prose proceeds not on the basis of narrative sequence or systematic description, but it is free of both time and place and moves in accordance with word and image associations, not as elliptically as free verse but analogically even in the discussion of objects, events, and states of being; it is so totally and exclusively dependent on the unfurling of spontaneous association that, as the critic Carrouges has characterized automatic writing, it is "an entirely different 'gearing' of the verbal mechanism." [1]

Six of Breton's works can be classified in this category: *Les Champs magnétiques, Poisson soluble, Nadja, Les Vases communicants, L'Amour fou,* and *Arcane 17.* The first, *Les Champs magnétiques,* was experimental and was inspired, as I have noted, by Pierre Janet and by the graphic representations of a physical magnetic field in an exposition in the Bois de Boulogne that Breton and Soupault had noticed in their aleatory movements.

It has been pointed out that the Dadaists had also practiced automatic writing; in fact, as Freud said in an interview with Breton, automatic writing had aroused as much "common" attention as had oneiric writing. But for Breton automatic writing assumed a triple convergence: the psychological concept of the liberation of psychic inhibitions, the mathematical one of the coincidences of chance verbal encounters, and the hermetic one of the oracular function of the medium-poet. The absence of critical intervention in writing, which is Breton's definition of automatism, precludes mechanical coupling of words by the deterministic function of the mind; automation as we know it today is a controlled movement of calculation, the very opposite of automatism as conceived by Breton; he thinks of it as "magic dictation" in the general category of dreams, as a verbal continuation of these, the overflowing of the fountain whose source is the collective self, the universal conscience. Breton felt that automatic writing had the power of hallucination over its practitioner, as evidenced by the state of euphoria in which he and Soupault found themselves at the end of each day of writing *Les Champs magnétiques*. It was in this context that he understood Rimbaud's "alchemy of the Word" and the notion of the reasoned derangement of the senses, which he considered— as he clarified some years later in "Le Message automatique"—the re-education of the senses: "The education (practically the diseducation) of all the senses remains to be accomplished." [2] Where psychiatrists had been using the device of automatic writing to uncover psychic blocks and aberrations in the so-called abnormal patient, Breton explains in this essay that the experimentation can illuminate in fact the very nature of preception and representation and revise our concept of their relationship to each other. In line with his general philosophy of *l'un dans l'autre*, the evidence of automatic writing tended to prove to him that man had artificially divided what was originally a single faculty, and the distinction, which is an artificial one, is due to the equally false separation that the adult and civilized mind—in contrast to the minds of the child and of primitive man—make between the inner image, creation of the imagination, eidetic, and the outer object which in truth has no independent value outside of human receptivity, which alone gives it meaning. In automatic writing Breton thought that he had found the first of a series of devices whereby a whole series of antinomies might be eradicated, thereby contributing not to the transcendence but to a clearer comprehension of the flexibility and scope of the human condition.[3]

In a broader context, man's very notion of liberty is involved if through a tighter interrelationship of the product of imagination and the object, exterior reality, we can make of the world what we wish. The pioneers in forging this channel between inner and outer reality are the saints such as Theresa d'Avila, and the mediums; the poet, in this sense of the word is a combination of saint and medium, in combining active faith and the willingness to serve and observe his own mechanism at work. "*Je est un autre*," as Rimbaud had said.

Automatic movement and automatic writing are actually two manifestations of the same phenomenon that Breton discerned. In the material world this movement can be observed in the polarization and repulsion of molecules coming to a center and moving away from a focus; in man, blessed with language, the mind gravitates toward a central image and digresses from it. Much of Breton's writing was to be so structured. It is significant that these secret movements of the consciousness had for him an element of magic, and that the verbalizations emanating from them seemed to him to emit the Word as from a kind of *bouche d'ombre*.[4] There is an element of the sacred in writing thus extracted from the bowels of the universe and its mysterious network, which is far removed from both the psychological and the Dadaist attitudes. Moreover, contrary to Dadaist automatic writing and to the clinical observations of automatism, Breton and Soupault's syntax is perfect; whatever ambiguity there is in meaning is caused not by a grammatical lapse but by the dislocation of objects, events, and sensations.

Another aspect of automatic writing connected with both physical laws and hermetic practices is the presence of two agents that alternately attract and reject, causing perpetual movement. According to Eliphas Lévi, the state of sympathy that is propitious to verbal revelation consists of the collaboration of two beings, one expansive by nature, the other attractive. This was indeed the distinction between Breton and Soupault that made the combination ideal. They worked two weeks according to Soupault, two months according to Breton, seeing each other daily and working from eight to ten hours; the divisions in the work corresponded to the end of the day, with a minimum of outside interference; "we listened to ourselves [or each other] think." [5] When the work was finished, neither poet made any attempt to identify publicly which part belonged to him, and the impression of continuity is expertly maintained. However, in discovering on a marked up copy who wrote what in the collaboration, I was able to observe the dialogue character of much of it, which makes the automatism appear like a game of ping-pong.

> —Est-ce que vous avez oublié que la police est neutre et qu'elle n'a jamais pu arrêter le soleil?

> —Non merci, j'ai l'heure. Est-ce qu'il y a longtemps que vous êtes enfermé dans cette cage? L'adresse de votre tailleur est-ce qu'il me faut.

In general, various movements can be detected—the melancholy and ennui of the first part: "Tonight we are two before the river which overflows from our despair." [6] There are the childhood memories of Breton, the voyage theme more inherent in Soupault's writing, the caricature of Paris life, containing in its phantasmagorias a mockery of life itself, the alchemic relation of man to earth (particularly in the parts attributable to Breton), the contagious character of the meteors and eclipses of Soupault.

Among the images with alchemic tints are "the flask of self," the rivers of milk, a trail bordered with stars, androgynous plants, asbestos which resists fire, the marvelous chain of keys (which will recur in a hermetic poem of Breton "Au Regard des Divinités"), the interplay of sun and snow, the iridescence of the earth and the "crispation" of stones; particularly striking is the intimate network that connects the human with the earth in an image such as this: "Do not disturb the genius planter of white roots my nerve endings underground." [7]

What ties the imagery together is the sense of imprisonment evoked by the two friends, and the outward movement toward expanding frontiers through the mystery of words, pictured as coming out of their mouths but actually born from the movement of their hands on a piece of paper.

After the experimental collaboration with Soupault, which was followed by two collaborations in an effort to write for the theater (dramatic fragments which today are of no more than documentary interest), Breton passed through a period of dejection, partly caused by disappointment with the Dada phenomenon for which he was not too well qualified by nature, and perhaps because *Les Champs magnétiques,* written in a state of elation and published in installments in *Littérature,* did not quite come up to his expectations.

Breton's depression had reached such a depth that finally his parents invited him to Lorient in the latter part of 1921. This proved a good excuse for him to abandon the job at *La Nouvelle Revue Française* which he disliked intensely. More than four years elapsed between the writing of *Les Champs magnétiques* and *Poisson soluble.* These were more noteworthy for personal contacts, such as his meeting with Picasso and Giacometti, than for his literary accomplishments. Any attempts he made to write as a Dadaist were total failures.

But when in that brilliant year of 1924 the First Manifesto as well as *Poisson soluble* appeared, he stated that five years of preparation lay behind him. The two distinct characters of Breton's prose are dramatically evident in these two manuscripts.* Whereas the many corrections and modifications in the First Manifesto show the struggle of the word to convey an idea and the efforts of ideas to seek organization, evidenced by many corrections and modifications, the manuscript of *Poisson soluble* is virtually free of any change, the hand having covered the page as if propelled by some magic and infallible force. The contrast is dazzling. The

* Mme Collinet, who preserved these manuscripts most carefully, kindly allowed me to examine them. Their authenticity is sustained by her testimony. She observed him as he wrote: one had demanded great effort and confronted him with a series of obstacles and frustrations; whereas he had written the other in a feverish frenzy as if possessed. The appearance of the documents confirms her recollections.

impeccable handwriting of Breton in total composure and without a sign of struggle seems to have flowed from a pure and inexhaustible source. *Poisson soluble* is indeed a rare case in the history of literature. It is the most authentically automatic writing, apparently free of any contrivance or artifice. There seems no labor involved, as though the author in fact acted as a sort of medium between his subconscious memories and their transformation into spontaneous images whose only organization is the tripartite structure in which they seem to be automatically cast: the inner life; the outer environment, principally the parts of Paris and its outskirts through which he wandered in his youth; and a mechanism of analogy largely based on cabalistic, hieroglyphic emblems. In fact Breton establishes out of his youthful poetic verve a whole structure of metaphors which will be the trellis of his future poetry. Like that of the hermetic mystics, his symbolism is obscure but not private; the door to his meaning is left half open even as the oracular word of the old sages. If the First Manifesto can be compared with Rimbaud's famous letter defining the new poet's mission in the world, the *Poisson soluble* is Breton's *Illuminations:* that is, the illustration of the principle and the expression of the marvelous vision.

Breton has often explained that he took great care in his search for titles. In *Poisson soluble, poisson* derives from the fact that he was born in late February under the sign of Pisces; *soluble* because indeed as he thought all men are solvent in the vast pool of their thought. *Poisson soluble* as automatic writing is more successful than *Les Champs magnétiques* in the range of its images, in the general impression it leaves of being cast in an alien sequence of thought; it contains the first poetic harvest of André Breton. Like his later analogical writings, the basic subject of *Poisson soluble* is self-identification. The core memories are no longer of childhood but of youth: love, liberty, adventure through the streets of Paris. The recital in the first person, the abrupt ending of each of the thirty-two parts, and the disconnected character of the parts from each other create the general effect of dream transcriptions. The last image is that of a man with eyes bound who carries the key to the mysteries: the blindfolded prophet is Breton himself. The persona of the last image is significant in clarifying, if not the meaning, at least the intention of this work and of almost all the poet's other creative works. In fact the last title of his collected philosophical and critical essays is *La Clé des champs;* and throughout the writing encompassed between these two limits, the emblems of the key and the field are preponderant. They have a distinctly alchemic sense. There were supposed to have been twelve keys to the mystery of life and its revelation. The *clé des champs* in the totality of the emblem is the key to the liberty of man. Breton's search for revelation is the pursuit of liberty as a modern Lucifer, through layers of darkness, treading on uncertain ground, a "terrain vague," the field, which has its own analogical meanings: field of consciousness, field of the magnetic movements of physical necessity; he is blindfolded as evidence of the obscurity of the ground to be covered in the spirit of high adventure and almost of piracy, like a brigand on forbidden property.

The images in *Poisson soluble* waver between the marvelous and the absurd; and as in *Les Champs magnétiques*, the grammatical structure is correct even though there is not enough continuity to produce a logical pattern. The most consistent single frame of reference one can detect is hermeticism: references to the magic fountain, the eagle and the Chameleon, Prometheus and other rebus analogies, the struggle between the eagle with its volatile celestial nature and the lion, the earth force, fixed and solid. As in the case with many of these symbols, the meanings are multiple; and this multiplicity of meaning occurs in all of Breton's poetry thereafter because he adopts the rebus as his basic structure. For instance, for the hermeticist, Camée Léon is also the green lion, *le lion vert*, or, anagrammatically, vitriol, which in another form becomes mercury or *le vitriol vert—l'or y vit* (gold is therein contained), a magical substance, the object of the philosophical search. And the multimeaningful lion is indeed Chameleon or in still other appellation, Proteus, the everchanging.

One image sets off a whole kaleidoscope which Breton evokes in saying that the Chameleon spoke to him. With the concept of "one in the other," an obscure allusion opens up like the petals of a rose. The green lion is the vitriol, which is the mercury, which is the magic salt, which is not soluble in water, but which contains an internal fire, which is the secret of life, the transforming agent, the Philosopher's Stone. And assuming this principle of creation, Breton views all nature as a continuity, in a state of dynamic metamorphosis. Much of his vision in *Poisson soluble* is based on this fundamental concept. Life, then, is a continuous quest for the Great Work, which can be revealed through the network of nature. But the Great Work has various phases. Breton's references to the White Gate (Porte Albinos) is an allusion to the "work in white" associated with the moon in its early phases—that is, to youth and purity, which corresponds to the youth of the poet and to the candor of his quest.[8]

In a general sense then *Poisson soluble* is the account of a series of apocalyptic dreams, interspersed with the scenes of Paris most familiar to the young poet and part of his daily pattern of life: the mountain of Ste Geneviève, the Porte Saint-Denis, the rue Etienne Marcel, and the rue Lafayette—which are to be referred to many times more in *Nadja* and in *L'Amour fou*; the Boulevard de Dieppe, the Boulevard des Capucines, the rue Cujas. All these streets teem with marvels, which establish for surrealism a whole series of street images: the street lights, a sensitive and mobile image, permanently entrenched in Breton's poetic idiom; the electroscopes in the shopwindows; the worker coming home; the women going nowhere; Breton creates new legends around a miraculous turkey who sits at the dike of the sea and scares the schoolchildren who pass by; the mysterious hunter with the magical finger glistening with brilliant stones. Stone, star, diamond, glass, crystal, mirror are the steps of one scale of the harmony that the universe offers the poet; another scale consists of water, source, fountain, rain. Crystal is the purifying agent; water the conductor, the agent of communication between things and beings.

> The source is all that passes from me in the whirling of the leaves watching overhead, above my moving ideas which the least draft displaces, it is the tree that the ax attacks unceasingly, it bleeds in the sun and it is the mirror of my words.[9]

The star is white as the Porte Albinos and directs him into a transparent network of algae against a telegraph pole. Rain is a column of crystal; it contains the transparency of the eggs of bird-flies and the sound of voices in their uncountable echoes. It is sacred and is conjured by the poet. The rocks contain water, and their imposing summits reach the eagle whose feathers fall on them; and in the falling there is revealed in the forest, the burning wood.

His identifications with nature are in cadenced steps with his pursuits of love: a series of mysterious women mark his poetic vision; and in a passage called "a kiss is so quickly forgotten," he takes us into the burning forest where his eyes become flowers of the hazelnut tree, the trails beckon to him, his hair is transformed into mushrooms and pine needles; he creates an atmosphere of chase, but with delicacy and fluidity as if the fruit, the forest, the seashore contain the kiss, and the kiss and the girl float in the purity of the elements. The haunting words *noisette* and *écureuil* are later to become key emblems in *L'Amour fou*, the parts of a rebus by which he will identify his newborn daughter. The early evocation of these words seems to contain the oracular image of the love to come and its cherished fruit.

Poisson soluble is in fact totally oracular in that it foresees all the fundamental images of Breton's poetry: the fountain, the castle, the fish, the rose window, fire in all its manifestations, birds, the weighing of stones, wood, burning wood, the ship, the lamp, the rain, the white bear, crystalline substances of many objects (aigrette, diamond, brilliant stone). The awakening of the universe, Breton's awareness of the mobility of natural forces are expressed by conversations with its many forms. The animism of nature extends to inanimate objects as well, such as the street lamp, radiators, etc. They carry on dialogues with him which have overtones of Biblical language.

The mutation of nature's physical properties, which was to become a characteristic of all surrealist poetry, has its nucleus here as we view a great blue sun and hear its echo, and listen to the song of the dust. The miraculous character of his visions, with their roots in Paris, in his room, in his earthly loves, in his daily newspaper, is described as he regards himself with a "five-leaf clover" over his left shoulder,[10] made possible by the magical power of the dream that has spilled over into the waking state. Awakening gives substance to the dream, like a bas-relief (he uses the word *anaglyphe*). The mingling of the two states gives an intimation of the pure state, of the golden age, the lost paradise, which is also what he calls the "Absolute Spring." "Later, when the bottle of dew explodes, and you enter silently into the leaves, and when the Absolute Spring which is preparing itself opens its dike, you will remember the lover of Porte Albinos who will be reposing on a bed of pleasure, asking to take back from God what God took away from him." [11]

It was to become André Breton's extraordinary purpose in life to give back to man what man in his clumsiness, as he thinks, gave up to God. Rallying the forces of dream, of language, and of the subconscious is analogous to the medieval search for the Philosopher's Stone or the Holy Grail, or to the ancient search for the Golden Fleece; poetry is for him nothing if it falls short of the desire to recuperate lost human powers, and this desire permeates the automatic writing of *Poisson soluble*, perhaps with more verve, more innocence, a more brilliant flurry of analogies of the earth with its inner bonds than in any other work. There is in *Poisson soluble* a mingling of sun and rain, flashes of fire, animism of man-made objects and cosmic manifestations. The poet seems a winged, mercureal messenger, hopping through the Paris landscape, his ubiquitous eye linking the unlinkable, creating humble legends in an atmosphere electrified with high voltage. He alone this time is the center of a magnetic field whose poles constantly shift, leaving the reader with an impression of perpetual motion. *Poisson soluble* is authentically without subject, without sequence, from the point of view of our normal concept of subject and sequence; but it is truer to say that it is a work where no subject is foreign to the search for self-identity, and its sequence is that of the psychic rhythm of the poet's flow of language, out of which explode like a cluster of fireworks all the future ingredients of André Breton's poetry.

VI

THE SURREALIST
REBELLION

"You are the man one must meet two or three
times in the course of one's life in order to have
the courage to live."   —Picabia

There is a point in human life when a man's relationship to others
changes direction. If in youth he gravitates toward his elders and relates
his thought and action in terms of their values—whether in seeking direction or producing a reaction—he measures himself on the scale of those
older than he. In general it is only around his fortieth year that man's
eyes begin to turn the other way and giving replaces receiving; and man
begins to watch the reactions that he himself produces on those who have
come after him. He watches himself be watched. In the case of the artist, if at this crucial time in his life he has gained and continues to
gain only the adherence of his elders, he is an overripe child, and even his
excellence or his perfection in terms of his art is a rear-guard action; he
bathes in neolights. This was somewhat the case of Valéry in relation to
the symbolist movement; Gide saw the danger and looked for younger
readers.

What is unusual about André Breton is that those older than himself to
whom he might have turned as guides suddenly disappeared when he, still
in his twenties, felt a keen need for encouragement. He lost some, like
Proust and Apollinaire, through death, Valéry and Reverdy through dis-
enchantment, Gide because he turned from the orbit of gratuitous characters like Lafcadio, which was what attracted Breton to him in the first
place. Picabia and Tzara, though closer to him in age, were also to fail
him. At twenty-eight—at the time of his First Manifesto (1924) and the
creation of the surrealist movement—Breton is pushed, almost against his
will, into leadership. He finds himself in a reversed perspective where

others look to him for direction, and the other side of the spectrum is suddenly empty. He can no longer expect anything from anyone older than himself. In the Symbolist *cénacle* Mallarmé had become the mentor to a group who were some twenty years younger than he; André Breton as the leader of the surrealists was to be mentor among his peers by the strength of his convictions, by the power of his verbalizations, by the magnetism of a personality warm and rigorous at the same time, which drew those of his own age to follow every one of his brainstorms. Among the many friends whom he was thereafter to win and lose, Marcel Duchamp remained a constant. In answer to the question why he never became the target of Breton's numerous angers, Duchamp knowingly answered: "Because I was older." In fact he was one of the few older people —another was Trotsky—from whom, after the death of Apollinaire, Breton was ever again to seek wisdom. Any subsequent influences on him were through books and events, not through persons. The break with the older generation was total. If there is a certain codification in his thoughts thereafter, it is apparently because he was put so early in a giving position.

From Jacques Vaché the lesson that André Breton had learned was that literature was not as important as life, that any vocation was a limitation of the free direction that ideally opened before man. From Tristan Tzara and the Dada experience he learned that protest for its own sake was a dead end as far as the need for liberty that motivated the protest, a mouth swallowing its own tail, energy beating on a nonresistant vacuum; worse, it was an activity that bred tedium. In his short article "Après Dada" [1] he situates the funeral of Dada in May 1921 and calls it a noiseless end to a noisy phenomenon. For Breton, Dada's quest for liberty had turned into a total tyranny; it had become a yoke that he felt compelled to shake off. In *Entretiens* many years later he gives an account of a more prolonged demise: "In the spring of 1923 Dada, very sick for the past two years, enters into its agony." [2] Its last sign of life was, he says, the performance of Tzara's little play *Le Coeur à gaz* in 1923.

At the time of the unsuccessful Congrès de Paris, Picabia had said to Breton: "There are a few of us whose eyes are turned to you." [3] Besides Picabia, Breton's closest friends of the moment were Aragon, Roger Vitrac, Benjamin Péret, Robert Desnos, and Jacques Baron, barely seventeen, the son of a rich man. Eluard had stayed faithful to Tzara and was not to play an important part in the early experimental work of surrealism; at the height of its gestation he took a trip around the world. Picabia's complimentary remarks were to carry no great weight in the organization of "something new." Nor did his other artist friends give much support to Breton's new activities. Marcel Duchamp was kindly but detached, as he was always to remain in the margin of movements *au dessus de la mêlée*. Picasso in 1923 had made such discouraging remarks that Breton had been plunged in what was perhaps the deepest dejection of his life; the thought of suicide had crossed his mind, but as he put it, he was not cut out for it.

Breton analyzed in a number of his writings the state of mind of impending creation, the floating in a sea of inaction that characterized the period between *Les Champs magnétiques* in 1919 and the fecund year 1923–4 that was to give in quick succession *Clair de terre*, the volume of his earliest poetry: *Poisson soluble*, the more perfected form of automatic writing; *Le Manifeste du Surréalisme; Introduction au discours sur le peu de réalité;* and *Les Pas perdus*. For Breton the story of his life was ever the story of his mind and heart. He gives his own self-portrait in "Une Confession dédaigneuse," in *Les Pas perdus;* describing the scandals of a mind that refuses all conformism, he examines the character of his own rebellion.

Breton rejects all the pragmatism that men of letters use to accommodate themselves to the human condition: hope in the future, the skeptical affirmation of the vanity of all things, the concession to earthly happiness, the solace of religion, and most of all "the abominable terrestrial comfort." He views himself as a subversive on all counts. The *esprit frondeur* character of his rebellion in the midst of moral, social, and cultural patterns that give a semblance of harmony and unity to European civilization is doomed to failure, even as that of the princes of the seventeenth century had failed. But failure is—and will always be—for Breton an element of exaltation. Failure simply means that the goal is unrealizable.

But if the goal were attainable, it would not be acceptable: he would be working within the limited context of those whose myopic pattern of life he was rejecting. The acceptance of failure is an innate feature of Breton's mechanism of protest. The validity of the protest lies in the acceptance of its very futility in terms of immediate effectiveness. The greatness of man, a greatness that modern man has forfeited, lies in envisaging the unfeasible; and in assuming this attitude, he found support in the men of science who alone in modern society aim at the impossible. "All that can be *realized* in the intellectual domain appears to me always to attest to the worst servility or bad faith." [4] Therefore, protest that has a specific target, immediately realizable, is protest on too pragmatic a basis. The other side of the coin is that success in its worldly sense is an anathema to Breton; it simply means attainment of limited goals, lack of that element of risk that is the moral as well as the physical badge of courage;

success more than anything else brings with it complacency. Not only successful persons, but successful nations, including his own, are the object of his scorn.

Examining further the concept of creativity, he rejects the evaluation of creative power on the basis of its products—that is, a poem, or a painting, or an object—but considers that its exterior manifestations reflect the total power of the human organism to extend its field of perception and its understanding of its relationships with the organisms of the universe.

Starting with "Une Confession dédaigneuse," the journey of André Breton through life is to recast the Theseus journey through the labyrinth, to which he refers so often as he moves along holding staunchly to the thread. The labyrinth is the cosmography of analogies that seem confused only to the mind that is out of focus. The contradictions that confront man are in Breton's view simply evidences of the improper use of the mind, and the world is a labyrinth because of improper focus. The myth of Theseus converges with the hermetic quest for gold. However, the search for the Philosopher's Stone that turns metal into gold is an end in itself: the purification of the agent is a higher attainment than the purpose for which it was purified. The extension of the double-decked symbolism to the poet of latter-day civilization is obvious. The creative product, the poem, is the offshoot of the creative process and a barometer of the intensity of life. If the poem is the futile gold, the poetic activity is the Philosopher's Stone, of greater worth in the existence of the man than the work itself. In Mallarmé's view, a work of art had the quasi-sacred quality of the Great Work and gave the poet a vicarious sense of immortality, as he projected his work into a future he would not experience. Breton was at the age of twenty-seven (when he wrote his "confession") little concerned with the posterity of the work; this attitude prevailed all his life, so that little of what he wrote was ever reprinted beyond a first small edition until almost the end of his life. From the beginning it is to him the poetic act, rather than its product, that is sacred, if indeed it succeeds even in a limited way in finding new doors to perception. And if immortality is the elimination of time and space limitations from the human condition, then this state of immortality can presumably occur in a number of human activities whose fields of operation can be developed and enlarged beyond the accepted criteria of the arts. These channels to immediate immortality were for Breton the study of the dream state, the revelations of automatic writing, and the exploration of hypnosis.

After the initial impetus given to automatic writing in the company of Philippe Soupault, Breton found later exercises with others less rewarding. He found the problem of "inspiration" closely linked with automatic writing; an exercise of will set off the involuntary activity of mind in controlling conditions that would provoke the uncontrolled organization of the mind. This was a particularly difficult task, a veritable paradox. Another difficulty arose from the fact that the established aesthetics for any form of writing assumed later correction and selection of texts: thus the critical faculty kept in abeyance during the writing appeared in the editing that followed. The fact is that what had documentary value for Breton was mistaken by many of his colleagues for a literary work.[5]

One might well ask how long man can tolerate his naked self, even though committed to nudism, if he is compelled to view the image of his nudity in a mirror constantly held before his eyes? Are not mores and taboos in reality a collective acquiescence to censure the naked reality of the human condition? The fact was that, as Breton admitted years later in *Entretiens,* few of his comrades were free enough of vanity to let the testimony of automatic writing stand under the glaring light of public exposure. The partial failure of automatic writing did not cause Breton to modify his view that it was the most direct key to the Great Arcanum, not only because it liberated the mind to varying degrees from social and sexual taboos and from the mechanism of self-censure, but also because it liberated the language from habitual word associations which in turn bridled mental activity by canalizing thought within these linguistic patterns. He believed that, even when only partially successful, automatic writing could take giant steps to alleviate the sclerosis of modes and verbal expressions, and to restore language to its original innocence and purity.[6]

In the case of the dream, the obstacle lay in the failure of memory in the waking state to recuperate the experiences of sleep. It was these two types of failure in experimentation which had depressed Breton so profoundly in 1923, as well as Picasso's cavalier attitude toward such latter-day mystics as Breton and his friends appeared to have become.

If Philippe Soupault had been the collaborator par excellence in automatic writing, it was Robert Desnos who was adept in the description of dreams. He was introduced to hypnotic sleep by René Crevel, a doctoral student specializing in the rational materialism of Diderot at the Sorbonne; he had brought a medianic agent, a woman identified as D., into the circle of the young poets. D. had instructed them in spiritualism, finding in Crevel qualities (no doubt of mental imbalance) that made hypnotic or self-induced sleep readily possible. Again, as in the case of hermetic magic, Breton makes it clear that his interest was in method rather than in the objective of mystical quest. Through the hypnotic climate of turning tables they sought communication not with the dead but with their own psychic selves—what Rimbaud had called *la vraie vie* ("the real

life"). It turned out that not Crevel, who introduced the method, but
Desnos was the best equipped to fall into hypnotic states, as he had been
the most apt to translate his dreams. In fact subsequently, histories of
surrealism tell us, his spontaneous trances became so frequent that the
fear of the medical man Breton overcame the curiosity of the poet Breton,
and he forestalled the extension of these experiments. He himself was too
self-controlled to be a medium; in fact at the end of the article in which
he describes these séances, "Entrée des mediums," he confesses that he,
Eluard, and Ernst were incapable of falling asleep. It is obvious that the
role Breton himself played was that of magnetizer, as Crevel and Desnos
became the mediums.

In the struggle between his very human misgivings and his scientific and
poetic curiosity, Breton turned 42 rue Fontaine into a virtual laboratory
between 1922 and 1924 with his collaborators who were all under thirty.
They called him, first in fun, then in anger, the "Pope of Surrealism." The
analogy was false in many ways. Breton was not venerable, and he did not
claim to be the spokesman for a higher authority. His position was closer
to that of a research director, a presenter of hypotheses that needed imple-
mentation and verification; he was not the interpreter of accepted dogmas.
An eyewitness, Victor Crastre, describes Breton's relationship to his companions at the outset of surrealism:

> Certain of his friends—some day to become his enemies—called him
> the pope of surrealism; it is true that there was a great deal of majesty
> in the attitudes of Breton and a certain solemnity in his immobile
> features. In 1924, the entire surrealist group recognized him as its
> leader, without there having been any question of investiture; authority,
> a spiritual one of course, emanated from his entire countenance: with-
> out effort he carried his head high and his eye was as fixed as Aragon's
> was roving; his eyes of a light blue in hours of calm, eyes of a thinker
> and poet, were lost in an interior drama; but as soon as a discussion
> would arise, the blue of his pupils would darken like that of a lake
> in tempest. Calm in his bearing, slow in his gestures, he had sometimes
> —the pope of surrealism—the attitudes of a pontiff, attitudes which in
> him were exempt from all posing; they were natural and not studied.
> His voice, of a soft texture, agreed with his gestures; it is remarkable,
> by the way, that this instigator spoke relatively little; one felt that he
> spoke only when necessary and nothing was more foreign to him than
> the voluble eloquence of Aragon for whom, by all evidence, speaking
> was a great pleasure.[7]

Clara Malraux, the first wife of André Malraux, tells an amusing story of
having persuaded her husband that his notions of life were not too far

removed from those of the surrealists; they were to meet at Breton's on a certain evening. But when they rang the bell at the rue Fontaine, there was no answer. Yet they had the distinct impression that the apartment was not empty. The morning brought its apology. An experiment had been in process that could not have been interrupted for the sake of letting Malraux enter. One can only speculate on the mutual effects of the collaboration of those two strong personalities had the door opened at the right moment.[8]

An important text of 1924 that summarizes the development of Breton's thought prior to the publication of the Manifesto is "Discours sur le peu de réalité," of which he was to say in the Manifesto, that he wanted all copies of it destroyed at his death. It is indeed a more personal expression of Breton's position in relation to the universe than the more generalized First Manifesto.

The basic image it reveals of Breton is that of a latter-day alchemist with "the conscience of a man of the fourteenth century." [9] The symbol-identification of the search for the impossible is there in all its failure-bound exaltation: "There is nothing in my opinion that is inadmissible." On the image of Theseus walking through the labyrinth, thread in hand, he superimposes the modern victory over the necessity of the thread. He shows his appreciation of the invention of the radio in a typically Breton-esque manner: not the object but the method, communication unencumbered by any visible thread. Another improvement over the classical Theseus is the composition of the labyrinth itself: "Theseus enclosed forever in his labyrinth of crystal" presumes the luminous material of glass even if the lens is still not clearly adjusted.

For the figure of the alchemist in search of gold he substitutes *l'or du temps*—that is, the precious ingredient of time, which might extend life itself, an aspiration to the immortal within the meaning of time itself: "to attempt the great adventure, to resemble a little the goldseeker. I am looking for the gold within time." It was to be the sentence he asked to be engraved on his tombstone.

Here again he defines the pitch of his total rebellion against the mediocrity of the world; his desire, destined to remain unrequited, to uncover a new paradise on earth; his willingness to assume the difficult role of poet in a world where poets have three times less chance of being read than philosophers who have two hundred times fewer readers than novelists. Breton defines what the future surrealist magazine was to assume as its motto: the declaration of a new set of human rights. For Breton it is "the right not to act and think like the horde," to refuse the eight-hour working day, to cast off the heavy burden of a system of education that binds us to a rational form of reality. In this proclamation of a creed Breton rejects any infringement on human rights, which he extends to language itself: "language can and must be delivered of its servitude."

The "Discours" had also a political extension. It nurtured the seed of the political protest that in the following six years was to become the most popularized form of the rebellion as it manifested itself in verbal demonstrations in the press and in the personal commitments of surrealists. It is inherent in its most categorical form in Breton's rejection not only of the Establishment but of certain facets of Western culture. "Latin civilization has had its hour, and as far as I am concerned it is time for a complete refusal to save it." Turning eastward he concludes: "Orient, triumphant Orient, you who have only a symbol-value, take me—grant me the means of recognizing your ways in the coming revolutions."

A climate of exaltation and high tension can thus be seen to prevail [10] on the eve of the two important events that launch surrealism: Breton's Manifesto which codified the findings and the ideas he had been nurturing for five years; and the launching of the review, *La Révolution surrealiste,* which was to be the journal of surrealist activities, the record of its experiments in the expansion of human consciousness.

The scope of surrealist activity was to be immense in the six years between Breton's two manifestoes, and it was to confirm the early position of Breton that life is more important than art: the experimental work that had preceded the First Manifesto on a limited basis did not cease but instead was intensified and proliferated. Never had a group of writers and artists worked in such close proximity to let down the barriers of the arts and push back the frontiers of its concerns: linguistics, philosophy, psychology, mathematics, physical laws, political action, religion, sexuality, and sociology were subject to an alternating current of reception of data, experimentation, and reorganization of received facts, and their transformation or rejection. The journals of the surrealists between the two world wars—principally *La Révolution surréaliste* and *Le Surréalisme au service de la révolution*—attest to the high pitch and continuity of surrealist activities, which were the antithesis of the nineteenth-century Symbolist concept of the alienation of the artist from society.

The success of surrealism, which a half-century later belied the philosophy of failure in which Breton conceived it, is evident in the number of works in art and literature that have proved viable and in the many talents that arose out of the coterie, or *Bund* as Jules Monnerot has called it.[11] In retrospect we can also discern the individuality that this close interrelationship bred despite accusations that were so often levied against Breton for his allegedly papal tyranny over his colleagues. Breton could not tolerate the defection of those who had accepted the surrealist credo, because he considered it more than a literary coterie; for him it represented a total transformation of the role and function of a man who chose to become "poet" in the modern notion of one possessed of an extended sense of earthly reality; in this context he could not conceive of anyone betraying the commitment in relation to which any subsequent commitments were concessions to the individual's integral liberty. In this light the "excommunications" of the Second Manifesto can be seen as somewhat more than personal quarrels.*

In the surrealist periodicals the areas of greatest interest in relation to the work of André Breton are politics, the development of techniques applicable to poetry and art, and the evolution of a new concept of sexuality. The latter two had a significant impact on his writings; the political orientations were to have a profound bearing on the course of his life. "Fun and games," as the peripheral associates of the surrealists judged some of these activities, had electrifying effects upon those closely involved. The problem of inspiration, which had earlier interested Breton personally, took on a broader significance; and as though by magnetic attraction, contact between artists was established, and each one's capacity for work was intensified. There proved to be a veritable contagion of talent, the creation of a culture (in the biological sense) propitious to the breeding of genius.

In this close, though sometimes turbulent companionship Breton's former situation as an only child had been richly compensated by the numerous friendships that he seemed to attract without effort. The number of his associates grew very fast. How did one gain acceptance? There was a rigid entrance examination. One had to be introduced to Breton by someone close to him and endure scrutiny in a face-to-face confrontation in the lion's lair. Dali tells us that after Miró introduced him, he immediately began to refer to Breton as "my new father, André Breton." [13]

Maxime Alexandre, in his *Mémoires d'un surréaliste*, describes in particularly vivid fashion the ins and outs of the brotherhood in the years between 1924 and 1939. There were degrees of intimacy in the friendships: the broad exchange at the Café Cyrano at apéritif time, then the invitation to an impromptu dinner at the rue Fontaine, which Breton would

---

* The multitude of surrealist activities revealed in the prolific production of pamphlets and articles in surrealist reviews have been dealt with in histories of the surrealist movement [12] and will in future years be considered in greater detail, as the surrealist magazines and all the sundry writings appearing in limited edition again become available.

extend to those closest to him at the moment; others would be happy enough to be asked to join the inner circle after dinner. For the rest, the evening would end in a vacuum to be filled by attendance at the movies or in a card game.

According to Victor Crastre, the spirit at the rue Fontaine was one of disinterested give-and-take: "no one at rue Fontaine presumed to incarnate 'French intelligence,' no one thought in terms of history, no one dreamed of glory: each one obeyed in his creations or in his refusal to create, an obscure but all powerful inner necessity." [14] How many were there at a time? Ten, twelve, says Crastre. All were young. They filled the atelier with their laughter, and sometimes with the silence of their intensity. Breton had said early in his association with Aragon that he believed more in the future of Aragon than in his own. He adopted this attitude toward many of his associates. The discovery of the distinct qualities of a Dali, a Miró, a Péret was as exciting to him as the discovery of a scientific truth. What these and others like Yves Tanguy, Max Ernst, René Char, and younger artists and writers who came in contact with Breton owe him is not a nucleus of abstract notions, but his communication of an outlook on life that brought their individual psychic fibrillations to artistic fruition. If Breton gradually assumed the appearance of a pope, it may have been that those around him looked to him to set the pitch of the motivation and the standard for their nonstandardization.

A word here about the miracle of the printed word! The artist in a society where printing fees are prohibitive and where most editors are committed to accepted patterns of publishing, may look with envy at the permissive printing activities of the surrealist writers. Many of them were virtually penniless in the days of their highest creativity, and they had the stern eye of Breton on them if ever they fell prey to economic temptation. Financial collaboration went in step with intellectual collaboration, and group collections of funds made often possible the publication of works that would otherwise have remained in manuscript. Publication generates publication as reaction sparks inspiration. The generosity of the artists in the coterie was even more striking, as evidenced by the number of gifts of paintings to the writers in their coterie; these portraits and illustrations for the books made a lasting bond between the writer and the painter.

The political question had been of course with the surrealists from the beginning. On no point did they agree with Dadaists more than on political rebellion extreme enough to verge on anarchy. Yet while the Dada political nihilism had been a vague but absolute opposition to all institutions, Breton had, from the arrival of Tzara in Paris, wanted to give the political protest specific targets. As a foreigner this was rather awkward for Tzara. For total Frenchmen like Breton and his colleagues, Eluard, Aragon, and Soupault—as well as Baron, Crevel, and a number of others—the tone of protest was close to that of the heroes of the French Revolution, Saint-Just and Robespierre.

The first major stand was against war and colonialism—the war in Morocco. The Surrealists' demonstrations, their open letters were a series of stabs at the heart of the government. Under Breton's watchful eye every incident that smacked of aggression or of a pragmatic political compromise brought indignant reaction from the surrealist press.

While Pierre Naville and Benjamin Péret, the most militant, had taken on in 1924 the direction of *La Révolution surréaliste*, the first authentically surrealist journal, Antonin Artaud—the black prince of surrealism, the one who, as Breton says, was "most in conflict with life"—started the Bureau for Surrealist Research in the rue Grenelle.*

As the nature of the surrealist protests became too verbose and too sensational, and the targets became more numerous, Breton sensed that some of the principles he held most dear, those that "kept [him] on this earth," were being crushed. He stepped in when the climate became too nihilistic and brought surrealism back to its fundamental issues, to what he calls *positions préalables*. It was to put the break on such excesses that Breton took over, as he says, the editorship of *La Révolution surréaliste*; but although the diatribes were toned down, the strong political line had been an integral part of surrealism and could not be softened. The fourth issue of the magazine was based on a revolutionary theme: "In the current situation of Europe, we remain committed to the principle of all revolutionary action, even if it should take as its point of departure the class struggle and provided only that it pushes far enough." [15]

A disturbance occurred at a banquet in honor of the venerable poet, Saint-Pol-Roux, who, as it happened, was admired and respected both by the surrealists and by members of the literary establishment. Among those in attendance were Lugné-Poe and Mme Rachilde; loudly the surrealists accused the former of having been a war spy and the latter of being a Germanophobe. The disruption of the banquet, the affront to two well-known personalities in the arts, created such a scandal that some of the surrealist activists were threatened with expulsion from France. Moreover,

---

* It was supposed to implement the theory that surrealism resembled scientific investigation and promoted experimentation in the field of psychology and linguistics. Unfortunately, although people from various parts of Europe sought out the research center, it also attracted crackpots and became the locus of many belligerent confrontations. The project was shortlived, but a similarly conceived institute in Amsterdam still exists bearing the same name, and flourishes as a center for writers and artists.

their demonstration alienated the Paris press, which had previously found their sensational activities newsworthy. They were strangers in their own country, a foreign and hostile element in the national culture. There was no regret on the part of any of them; no one was seeking a literary prize or a seat in the French Academy. But the canalization of the surrealist rebellion toward political action had begun.

A number of factors were to bring the surrealists into the arms of the Communists in the period between Breton's first and second manifestoes. It was not an isolated phenomenon. The middle twenties saw the inspirational phase of Russian communism, which, after beginning as a ministerial crisis, had eventually involved a radical transformation of life. Many writers in no way connected with surrealism joined the Communist Party, among them Malraux and Gide. Had not the surrealist motto of "a new declaration of the rights of man" and the aspiration "to change life" been answered by the Moscow government? The surrealists had friends in the socialist press of France, principally in L'Humanité; and one of their number, Pierre Naville, was backing a journal called Clarté.* The pressure was on Breton to join the ranks, and he did in 1927 with some misgivings. His stay as a party member was of very short duration for a number of reasons, which are more illuminating as they throw light on his character than as they reflect on the Communist structure.

Breton's best analysis of the relationship of communism to surrealism is in his essay, Légitime Défense (1926). Before the Communist Revolution the word "revolution" had had a parochial context for Breton and a monolithic scope: the French Revolution, the Commune of 1871. What sparked his imagination was the international character of communism, with its foundation in the dialectical materialism of Hegel, in the pragmatic applications of Marx, in the humanistic thought implementations of Lenin and Trotsky. When in 1925, eight years after the Soviet Revolution, Trotsky's work on Lenin reached Paris, Breton had had it published in La Révolution surréaliste. The aspect of communism that captivated Breton was rather abstract; in his incorrigible search for unity and correlation he was attracted to the philosophical heritage of a political movement. He was touched by the human traits of Lenin as represented by

---

* Crastre's book tells the story of the relations of the surrealists with the Clarté group and their initiation to communism. In The Left Wing Intellectuals Between the Wars 1919–1939, Robert S. Short gives a detailed account of the political involvements of surrealism and Breton's role in this context. In reference to surrealist protests, he concludes: "It seems that they [the surrealists] committed themselves to little tasks in order to avoid commitment to bigger ones." "Little" and "bigger" are relative and depend a great deal on one's vantage point. Some men seek power over other men's actions; others over their minds.

Trotsky and by the superhuman task he had set for himself—perhaps the same type of aspiration doomed to failure which characterized his own impractical dreams. His knowledge of the writings of Marx, Engels, and Lenin was very limited; he entered the cell with little indoctrination. The more shocking as a result was his confrontation with the Communist reality in the Paris of the 1920's.

Breton had already stated in *Légitime Défense* that he could accept communism only on condition that the amelioration of the human condition have primacy over that of the social condition. As the son of a modest bourgeois—like most of the other surrealists—he was willing, even eager to see political power pass from the hands of what he considered a discredited bourgeoisie to the proletariat, but on condition that the transformation of the physical life of the poor be in step with the enrichment of the "interior life." For if it is true that man cannot live by ideas alone, he would gain nothing if he were simply fed better under a new system and allowed to retain as limited a mind as he had previously had. Breton was particularly wary of any infractions that might be made by a political power, demagogic or communistic, on the autonomy of man's movements in the expansion of his inner life. Breton's whole concept of surrealism had originally been based on the refusal to relegate to abstract idealism the crucial problems of mankind, but he was not ready to admit to the primacy of matter over spirit, just as he had refused to subordinate material reality to ambiguous idealisms. Insofar as the elimination of economic indigence might lift the curtain that separates the individual from his real, human problems, Breton welcomed communism; but if it confined man to economic questions and controlled his human desires and nonmaterialistic aspirations, if the search should turn to real gold alone and lose sight of the gold of man's time on earth, then Breton could not go along with communism.

A number of incidents occurred within a short time to confirm his fear that this was indeed the case. The story of his defection is in the Second Manifesto. Assigned to a "gas cell" (consisting of a group of utilities employees), he was principally asked why he had to continue to be a surrealist now that he had earned the privilege of being a communist. He was given the task of writing a paper on the conditions of workers in Italy. His immediate rejection of the assignment was not due to any dislike of Italian workers but because it jarred with the basic principles of autonomy he maintained in politics as in his private life. Breton had not taken orders from anybody since the day he left his father's house. He had started life as a leader. He had his own formula for the transformation of man on this earth, and each man for him had an individual face; the experiments in automatic writing had been undertaken not to establish norms but to discover for each his own inner flame. This little bourgeois had for ten years made every valiant effort to shed the prejudices of his heritage, such as nationalism, such as rationalism, such as adherence to Christian rites that in his opinion had outgrown the meaning of their symbols; but what he had perhaps not realized was that traits of independent thought, of free will, that passionate love of liberty and individualism were also part of the heritage he was combatting, and had remained intact despite bad governments. If he deplored elements in his own education, such as sophistry, he still had a deeply inculcated power of critical judgment that made it impossible for him to accept bad writing as good writing simply because it carried a worthy thought.

He was to be faced with that dilemma a number of times in the case of the poor quality of the articles in *L'Humanité* and more dramatically in the matter of "Front rouge." Aragon, on his return from Russia, had written this poem, frenetically praising communism and insolently scorning his own country. The *Affair Aragon* quickly became a *cause célèbre* as he was threatened with censorship and imprisonment. Breton, who was ever on the front line of defense of anybody's civil liberties, made it clear nonetheless in his article-pamphlet, *Misère de la poésie* (1932),[16] that he was defending the right of his friend to write, and not the poem that had resulted. He believed that the attitude of mind that produced an inferior poem as a "service" to a great cause was as deplorable as the reaction it precipitated. The fact that in a state of exaltation Aragon could do no better than to write such a circumstantial piece was as depressing to Breton as the attacks of bourgeois society on the poem, which gave it an importance it did not deserve in his artistic judgment. In "Front rouge" he saw poetry used as a form of political propaganda. Its message was circumscribed by specific events, to circumstances of public life, reminding Breton that it was written during Aragon's stay in the U.S.S.R. He judged it a poem "without tomorrow because poetically regressive," in other words a poem of circumstances.

Breton did not include a poem such as "Front rouge" in the destiny of the poetic art. In reading this essay one can see how hard it must have been for him to write it; the stand he took in the scandal surrounding the poem was equivocal as it involved a twofold integrity: purity as a poet, purity as a revolutionary. Breton wanted to make it clear that in opposing committed literature he was at the same time equally adverse to the art for art's sake philosophy. He repudiated an attitude of withdrawal on the part of the artist from the scene of political action, but the role of the artist within the political arena should not be, in his opinion, the same as that of the political man. To relax critical judgment in such a situation would be "to misconceive the profound significance of the poetic act." It was a sacrifice he was not prepared to make, even though as strongly as any other libertarian he deplored the prosecution of the author of "Front rouge." Strangely enough, the very manner in which he defended his friend displeased Aragon and triggered the break in their collaboration, as Breton tells us in *Entretiens:* "Paradoxically it [the break] was consummated the instant the brochure [*Misère de la poésie*] saw the light of day although its purpose had been to defend him." [17]

A number of events totally alienated Breton not from communism but from Stalinism: the first was the banishment of Trotsky; the second, his own exclusion from the International Congress for the Defense of Culture, sponsored by the Communists in Paris in 1935. Breton could not forgive what he thought to be Moscow's imitation of the type of hypocrisy and connivance that he had associated with capitalistic regimes.

The severity with which Breton regarded any moral default was in direct proportion to the degree of trust he had harbored in a human being, an idea, or an institution. Each of his disappointments with communism was marked with a feeling of regret at the shattering of a hope; but where some of his friends vacillated for many years, once he had rejected communism as identified with Stalinism, he never went back. The position, as in the case of all his positions, was irrevocable.

On several other counts he began early in the surrealist movement to have differences with his friends. One of these was drug addiction, which Breton, as a medical man and a stable personality, barred under any pretext from the experimentation into psychic exploration. His adamant position produced a break with Antonin Artaud particularly; Breton always commiserated with the tortured life of this ailing, unbalanced friend, but he early eliminated him as a serious contributor to experimental discoveries in the field of the human psyche. It was the most dramatic illustration of the fact that Breton's interest was not in clinical or abnormal psychology but in the power for translucidity in the lucid mind; Artaud's mental imbalance and strong drug addiction made him an object of compassion but not of exploration.

Breton also condemned sexual abnormalities. Although discussion of sexual activities was very much part of the surrealist program, it was eroticism in relations between man and woman that was the subject of questionnaires, as it was the core subject of surrealist poetry. It was a much-neglected subject in the symbolist coterie of poets whose concerns appeared rather asexual. The surrealists gave an almost sacred character to the erotic embrace, to copulation, to sexual beauty and mystery in woman, to the liberating powers of orgasm, and discussed these questions freely and openly. If some of these preoccupations verged on the pornographic, an almost laboratory purity was involved; the end result lost some of its scandalous character as the focus was on the means rather than on the purpose of the erotic communication. Such is the case of the collaboration between Breton and Eluard, called *L'Immaculée Conception*. With this restoration of the feminine element at the heart of literature, Breton frowned severely on aberrations in the direction of homosexuality. As he had on so many other counts, he stood against popular fads in this instance, opting for natural love in the face of a massive trend in literature, headed by Proust and Gide, toward the exploration of homosexuality. It was deplorable enough that in the literature of the Establishment, homosexuality should have primacy over heterosexuality, but its practice within the fold was intolerable. In the surrealist *cénacle*, there was a feminine presence: the wives and mistresses who participated in answering questionnaires on love and in all the other exercises of art or experience that took place: the list of surrealists has included a number of women artists and writers; it was perhaps the first *cénacle* ever to admit them to equal rank. One of the reasons that Breton disliked Cocteau intensely and kept him outside of the surrealist group despite his surrealist propensities, was the fact that Cocteau was an admitted homosexual.

Finally, the greatest number of rifts in the surrealist ranks were due to Breton's suspicions that surrealism was being exploited for personal gain, that it was being prostituted and involved in the manipulations and trade customs of a capitalist society. It is on this level that Breton was to brand Salvador Dali as Avida Dollars, an appellation on which Dali with good humor capitalized to great advantage.

Finally, if the portrait of Breton in the years of his active leadership of the *cénacle* looms somewhat stern and puritanical, it is because there are so few examples in literary annals of such intransigent control on the part of one man over the destinies of so many of his peers, all talented writers and artists.

But there was another aspect of his personality that friends and enemies remember of the young Breton in the heyday of surrealism: his enormous sense of humor, which was not a gift for clever punning or witticisms, but brittle, sarcastic, with a tinge of the malicious, the sardonic, the devastating irony against which he was to measure the authors he included years later in his *Anthologie de l'humour noir*. In the wake of his death friends remembered the effervescent and the humorous character of the scandals he perpetrated. He would turn the tables on the meek and the sedate, shock them by remarks unexpected and touching them exactly at a vulnerable spot. Sometimes the prank was a means of retaliation and a source of almost cinematic hilarity. One such anecdote concerned a bartender who after months of extending credit to insolvent surrealists finally refused them a drink. Quietly Breton walked out. Sometime later a group of movers and demolition workers arrived and began to dismantle the bar under the horrified eyes of the proprietor. What was the reason for the action? They had orders to redo the bar and had several pianos to install! The incident had the dimensions of a Mack Sennett comedy. Another time, says Breton's son-in-law, Breton and his friends had gone to see *Nosferatu*, a phantom-movie, but to their disappointment the program had been changed. Sardonically Breton found a form of vengeance. When the lights went on and the program discussion began, as was the custom in that particular cinema, the surrealist group began to discuss, at a signal from Breton, not what they had seen but what they had come expecting to see, to the astonishment of the rest of the audience who could scarcely believe their ears or trust the eyes with which they had just viewed the film.

It is true that Breton did not have a constant smile on his expressive face; but according to his friends, when he laughed he roared like the lion to whom he has often been compared, or, as Soupault recalled, like a child or a cock. He laughed with the force of thunder, and his whole being participated in the joy of the *détente*. The laughter was as brisk as the rancor was sharp. Both were marks of fervor, of a tenacity, of an earnestness in respect to the high adventure to which he thought man was committed here on earth.

VII

THE SURREALIST
MANIFESTOES

"Let us remember that the idea of surrealism
aims simply at the total recuperation of our
psychic force by means of what is nothing else
but the vertiginous descent within ourselves—a
perpetual walk in the forbidden zone."

—Second Manifesto

André Breton's two manifestoes (1924, 1930) [1] are much quoted documents as the most characteristic expression of his definition of surrealism and delimitation of its scope. Indeed, so comprehensive are they of his philosophy that were all his other prose writings destroyed, the reader would still know from these the quality of the man, the range of his associations, the influences on his mind, his critical opinions on literature of the past and of the present, his political attitudes, his proposed innovations in the field of language and poetic imagery—all expressed through the formidable structure of his prose.

The manifestoes contain a series of ideological capsules which Breton utilizes more extensively in the rest of his essay. Because of the disjunct and discursive character of the manifestoes, allusions to them are generally made through isolated quotations. Viewed in the light of the fervent activities that implemented the concepts of the First Manifesto in the six years that elapsed between the two documents, one becomes aware not so much of diffusion as of continuity and development or enlargement of surrealism when one juxtaposes them. There may be further elaboration, but there is never contradiction in Breton's work after the publication of the Second Manifesto.

What is a manifesto? It is a proclamation made generally in a didactic, categorical vein; it stems from a need to inform and convince; it is a resolution, a call to action. It often spells out in trite form a series of dictums or attempts to popularize an elusive concept. If Breton got the notion of manifesto from Karl Marx or Tristan Tzara, in content his two proclamations of faith were a far cry from the genre *manifesto*. Except for the two brief definitions of surrealism in the First Manifesto, there is no formal presentation of dogma. In fact, Breton maintained all his life that there was no function more distasteful to him than that of pedant. Nor is there any desire to popularize, for he is distrustful of the general public, and journalism—what he calls *l'immode reportage*—is an anathema to him. If they are not true manifestoes, neither are they essays in the strict sense of the word because they have neither a uniform theme nor a contrived logical development of ideas. They constitute philosophical meanderings—a genre particularly characteristic of the French tradition: much of the meditative character in the writings of Montaigne, Pascal, Rousseau, and Chateaubriand manifests itself in communications of philosophical attitudes without categorizing them into a system.

The manifestoes are a two-tone soliloquy, closely related to Breton's activities in the five years preceding the first and the six-year interval between the two. The abstractions are the echoes and repercussions of actions; the manifestoes are like the log book of the navigator, the "work in progress" of the scientist. They are not written as an escape or cure from life but as a corroboration, a documentation of life in high gear. On the one hand, they reveal a temporal man in a specific society, moved to rebellion against conventions and mores, against institutions, and mostly against the habits of thought developed by Western civilization, and at the same time harassed by discords in his personal relations. As personal confrontation between Breton and associates, the manifestoes are an apology, a one-way conversation which consists of answers to public denunciations on the part of erstwhile associates who were breaking away for one reason or another; or they constitute Breton's reactions to current political events. On the other hand, they present in its most naked form an ideological challenge which he believed to be universally viable regardless of time and place. As a man of creed, a fanatic—"I insist on passing for a fanatic" —he scorns our concerns with circumstantial problems and, unrelentingly probing the human essence, reaches a grandiose summation at the end of the First Manifesto: "It is living and ceasing to live which are imaginary solutions. Existence is elsewhere."

Although there is a certain degree of repetition in the manifestoes, the first one might be said to propose, and the second to dispose. Many of the propositions of the first are elaborated in the second document; many of the implications find specific applications. As Breton indicated in his letters to Tzara and Picabia, it had taken him five years to crystallize his concepts and arrive at his definitions.

Like Descartes, after due confrontation of the human condition, Breton focused on a specific vision of man and on a personal course of comportment which define his principles of morality, attained after a process of *table rase*. But the visionary and the personal stance is marked by an intense desire to share his personal code of ethics: the "I" turns often to "we" and to "man" in a general sense, although he is loath to acquiesce in the compromises and tolerances that leadership entails.

At the beginning of the First Manifesto we are in the presence of a man of twenty-eight who has stripped himself of the conventional crutches that are necessary to attain spiritual serenity in the modern age, but who nonetheless refuses the cynicism of his time. He detests the social mores not because he finds them unsuccessful, but on the contrary, too smugly adjusted to the complacent and superficial grasp of the human potential; he has rejected all religious faith—that is, belief without proof of a hereafter; yet he seeks intimations of the marvelous and the unwonted (*insolite*) within the reasonable limits of human destiny. In fact he wants to substitute the marvelous—which is revelation—for the mysterious, which is symptomatic of blindness and ignorance, as he sees it. "The marvelous is always beautiful, any form of the marvelous is beautiful, only the marvelous is beautiful." He seeks human affiliations in the midst of the apathies of the rabble. If the romantic spirit, identified with Rousseau, Chateaubriand, and Lamartine, pictures the sensitive individualist as a man alone in the desert of the crowds, Breton dreams of the solidarity and reciprocity of a self-chosen group which is willing to pursue the free spirit regardless of cost. He revolts against everything in life as society has determined life, and searches for life in its primitive, bare, paradisaic form, which we sensed as children, and over which our memory and our training in rational thought drew a final veil by the time we were twenty. Had the training of the imagination rather than the development of logical thinking been the objective of our education, memory would have been sharper and allowed us to retain the innocent sense of life and its aura of magic throughout our adult existence.

Assessing what is still recuperable in the condition of man, Breton alights not on the legislated rights of man, but on his inherent, physiological traits that have survived the pressures of all yokes. On the first page he mentions one of these in his very definition of man: "Man that incorrigible dreamer, each day more discontented with his fate." The other is the notion of liberty that still exalts him in the midst of all inhibitions. As with the notion of life, the notion of liberty is detached from its impact on social manifestations. Like Descartes he came early in his career to the conclusion that to be master of one's own mind was the greatest freedom of all. "Among so many disgraces that we have inherited, one must surely admit that the most total liberty of mind has been left to us. It is up to us not to misuse it gravely."

Basically what distinguishes the manifestoes is that in the first he is primarily involved in finding inner targets for the practice of liberty, whereas liberty in terms of exterior action was to be more prevalent in the Second Manifesto.

"Man proposes and disposes," says Breton in the declaration of this inherent liberty's power to shape human destiny; and the liberty is manifest only if it is preceded by knowledge of the self. In seeking this knowledge, Breton, as we have seen, alighted on two channels of psychic revelation: the dream, and automatic writing, which was, as he thought, expression in its unmitigated form; both avenues lead to the recuperation of imagination, the vital and highest faculty of the mind. If imagination is generally known as a falsifier of reality, Breton redefines it as an illuminator of reality, as the unveiler of forbidden zones:

> Imagination alone makes me realize what *can be*, and that is sufficient to lift the terrible ban a little, sufficient also to let me surrender to it without being afraid to make a mistake (as if it were possible to make a bigger mistake). At what point do things begin to get bad and the mind feel no longer safe? Is it not true that the possibility for the mind to err is all to the good?

As a medical student he had discovered in the science of psychiatry two devices for strengthening the imaginative power: the exploration of the dream through the methods of Freud; the practice of automatic writing through the revelations of Janet. His definitions of surrealism incorporate his commitment to these two areas as the means by which, through sensory rather than supersensory processes, man may seize and identify the metaphysical with life *here and now* and resituate the imaginary not as the antinomy of the real but as its nucleus. Reality, then, in its dynamic sense proceeding from an interior state, nurtured by what we call imagination, and brought to an exterior existence through the capture of dreams or subconscious verbalization, is what Breton calls the "surreal," in a sense that has no connection with the *unreal* or the intervention of the fantastic, which is understood to be exterior to human perception. He felt that although he had borrowed the word from Apollinaire, the meaning he attributed to it brought him closer to Nerval, who in his personal derangement had managed more totally than Apollinaire to erase the boundaries between the wakeful state and the dream, between the irrational and the rational.[2]

The First Manifesto was written under the aegis of Freud, who more than anyone else in his time had shown, in tangible manner and not as the basis of faith, the interrelationship of dream and reality and had revealed, without having been specifically aware of it himself, the possibility of expanding reality by the utilization of the dream. The encyclopedic meaning, then, of surrealism is based on this confidence in the superior reality that man can attain through the powers of the dream and of the free play of the mind. The more limited meaning Breton gives to surrealism is closely linked with expression, and judging from the contents of the manifesto, literary expression as it reveals, through the exercise of psychic automatism, the "real functioning of the mind"—the possibility through art expression to view the mind freed of social, moral, and even aesthetic sanctions. In this sense the arts would be not an end in themselves, destined for pleasure, but a means to knowledge of man, a means to effect a convergence of the aesthetic, sociological, and philosophical aspirations of man.

In his insistence on expression as a source of understanding of man, Breton sought antecedents among the most controversial literary figures, those whose metaphysical cries had most prevailed in their writings, and who in various but never total ways had groped toward the comprehension of the surreal. His own literary patron saints, Rimbaud, Lautréamont, Apollinaire, were of course his principal supports.

As an introduction to a new literary movement within the tradition of the untraditionals of the past, from the English writers of Gothic novels to Jarry, Reverdy, and Roussel, the First Manifesto became at the same time an extensive criticism of existing forms, which in retrospect was to make of Breton a demolisher of established literary hierarchies.

With the passage of time and the sifting of the perishable from the imperishable in literature, we begin to wonder if the epoch between the two world wars, which has been presumed to be the age of the novel, was not more truly an age of poetry. The presence of Valéry, St. John Perse, Claudel, Supervielle, Reverdy, and the many in and out of the ranks of the surrealists whose works seem to have survived their time, persists. There is a cumulative evidence that, as Breton thought, the art form that communicates the mysteries of the human spirit is more resilient in the face of changing literary tastes than are those that relate to social and psychological behavior of man in a given and passing epoch.

Sharing his contemporaries' opinion that the dominant literary form of the time was the novel—unfortunately, as he thought—Breton attacked it as the major literary evidence of society's dependence on the rational and the unimaginative, and he sought to dethrone it single-handed. There is no evidence of any other such total attack on the novel by any of his colleagues. He derided the narrative form, the descriptive postcard style, the novelist's *petite observation*. Ever since the Symbolists of the late 1800's, poets had discovered that the best way to reaffirm the primacy of poetry as the major literary art was to discredit narrative and descriptive writing.

> And the descriptions! Nothing compares to their nonentity; they are simply superimposed pictures taken out of a catalogue, the author uses them more and more carelessly, he takes every opportunity to slip me these postcards, he tries to make me see eye to eye with him about the obvious.

He was unabashed in his choice of examples of novelistic weakness; far from confining his criticism to minor works of his contemporaries, he alluded to no less a master than the saint and model of the novelists of his time—Dostoevsky, with reference to *Crime and Punishment*. In contrast to his engrossment with psychiatry in its clinical physiological form, he berated "psychology" as it pertains to the analysis of personality by the layman; this only explains away human actions and leaves the observer— and in the novel, the reader—no nearer the discovery of the human essence particularized in each individual. The diversity, according to Breton, is so great that the "mania" of reducing the mystery of each into a general, known quantity is a futile game, of which some of the best novelists of the time have proved guilty. This time his references are to Maurice Barrès and Marcel Proust. "The result is a series of long developments whose persuasive power is due merely to their strangeness, and which are convincing to the reader merely by means of an abstract and rather ill-defined vocabulary." Psychoanalysis in the novel leads to generalizations and categorizations instead of revealing the actual functioning of the mind and its capacity for associations.

Each human action, according to Breton, carries its own inner justification, and analysis weakens the plot by limiting the relationships of the human psyche. Stendhal's characters are most interesting, according to Breton, when the author abstains from evaluating them or commenting on their behavior; it is when he forgets to point out the sources of their motivations that we really discover them. He wonders why the novelist has to identify characters by specific physical and moral traits and thus submit the novel to the tyranny of time and place. Rejection of the dimensions of time and place in narrative art is parallel with banishment of perspective and proportion from drawing: in both cases there occurs a mutation of reality. But Breton, as we have seen, is not so much destroying—as was the case with Dada—as forecasting a revision of the notion of reality. The transfiguration of the narrative form as an antidote to abstraction is the counterpart of the transfiguration of the plastic arts that stemmed from Picasso. The purpose of all art, according to the First Manifesto, is an interrogation of the universal and presumably "forbidden" mystery (*le grand interdit*) by the nondescript, undefined man—identified by an initial, if there is indeed any need for identification—detached from his temporal and special marks rather than a representation of the finite man in his social relationships.

We are in a position to see the effects of Breton's challenge to the novel form. He had intended to draw the creative artist away from that literary genre; what he actually did—and, ironically, without writing a single novel himself—was not to destroy but to reshape the destiny of the novel. He became a major frame of reference for the French novelists who after World War II were to create the new novel according to the general lines that became self-evident when the characteristics attacked by Breton were obliterated.

But for his own generation Breton's most important precepts in the First Manifesto were those that affected the nature of poetic composition and actually the notion of poetry itself. Breton's statement, "Language has been given to man that he may make surrealist use of it," has, on the surface, a pedantic tone that is immediately dispatched when we translate "surreal" in terms not of a specific style of writing but of verbal expression as the exteriorization of the psychic resources of man. Language in this sense is a vehicle by means of which intrinsic truths surge from the psychic depths of conscience, precluding the possibility of the existence of abstract thought separate from its symbolization. Breton's most important statement in this respect had its germs in Hegel and Von Kleist and has since become a basic premise of structural linguistics: "The speed of thought is not superior to that of speech." In short, words are the symbolization of thought, its coefficient; they shape thought so totally that we cannot say which comes first. If symbolization was one side of the coin, deciphering was the other. In other words, the "fortuitous encounter" of words is the basis of the poetic image and induces the spontaneous revelation of associations, creating successive images which combine to form the poetic metaphor. "Words, images only offer themselves as springboards to the mind that listens." The important part of the sentence is "listens": attentiveness to words, to their emblematic character, to their oracular content, to their magnetizing effect on other words. If autom-atism implies the need for spontaneity and the nonfocusing of the mind, the second operation is one of mental labor and deciphering without which automatism is no more than the *grand jeu* it was for the Dadaists. That is why there is no contradiction [3] between the nonwilled, self-propelling dictation of the mind proposed in the statement "the speed of thought is not superior to that of speech" and the deliberation implied in the state-ment: "I had begun to fondle words immoderately, to discover how much space was allowed around them, their tangential relationships with in-numerable other words that were left unpronounced."

The concept of "words without wrinkles" incorporated in *Les Pas perdus* develops this thought more dramatically and identifies it as the basis of Rimbaud's alchemy of the Word: that is, the metamorphosis of words by their friction with each other, by their copulation—*"les mots font l'amour."* They are resplendent in their alliances, not by the mystery they produce, but by the illumination they provide the attentive mind and eye. It was Breton's conviction that the two processes used together could make poetry an ecstatic state and a universal communication on the level of alchemic hieroglyphics. What Breton was trying to make clear in the First Manifesto was that surrealism was not a reform in prosody but a *reforma-*tion of the mental process of the writer—and by extension of the reader—who would call himself "poet."

In identifying the new metaphor, Breton agrees with Pierre Reverdy's statement that "The image is a pure creation of the mind. It cannot be born of a comparison but of a *rapprochement* of two realities more or less distant." He pointed out, however, that the association was not a creation of the writer but a discovery. The more obvious the association and the less deciphering necessary, as in the case of correspondences and similes, the less luminous is the truth or beauty it uncovers; deriving from Eliphas Lévi rather than from Swedenborg, Breton understood analogy to be based on the unreasonable, unexpected *rapprochement*, on the attrac-tion of contradictory qualities in the conciliation of antinomies, just as the spark produced by the connection of electric conductors of varying voltages creates a light whose intensity depends on the degree of difference in voltage.

These notions—frequently repeated and developed not only by Breton, but by his colleagues Aragon, Eluard, and Tzara in other writings, prin-cipally in the pages of surrealist reviews—are spelled out in the First Mani-festo not as an *a priori* poetic principle but as the outcome of work in progress. When Breton suggests specific ways in which far-fetched realities have been made to gravitate toward each other, he draws his examples from the poetry of his colleagues. He mostly omits illustrations from his own poetry, although a number of poems, which comprise the volume of *Clair de terre*, have already been written under the impetus of automatic writing and free image associations. He prefers to publish as his basic illustration the prose format of *Poisson soluble*. All through his life there is a certain reticence on Breton's part where his verse is concerned; yet it is in the network of his broad free verse that the surrealist image is most actively used.

Breton found approval and consent among other young writers who shared his stand against the world they had inherited. This prompted him to name them as cofounders of the surrealist movement. In situating the personal commitment in the framework of a collective search, he named most of his companions in the First Manifesto.

But if the First Manifesto creates a sense of solidarity, the Second Manifesto opens on a note of disruption. We witness a certain disintegration as Breton reveals himself unable to accept what he considers the waywardness of his erstwhile associates in the personal and political confrontations that followed the First Manifesto. In the manner in which the ancient alchemists treated their followers, the enunciations of the First are followed by the abjurations of the Second Manifesto. Breton gave a bitter roll call of those who had proved unable to resist the demands of bourgeois life and were therefore unable to maintain their artistic integrity. High on the list of alleged corruptions was the need to earn a living, to which so many had succumbed: it led some, like Robert Desnos, to journalism and others, like André Masson and Francis Picabia, to popularize their art forms. Breton accused Roger Vitrac and others of his former friends of stooping to inferior forms of writing or of oversimplifying the tenets of surrealism for ulterior motives, of exploiting art—as he had accused Antonin Artaud and Philippe Soupault. He was also angered that some comrades had confused the principles of surrealism with the political tenets of the current communism in which he, Breton, could find only a feeble and limited application of the concepts of Hegel, Marx, and Engels.

Economic compromise, political compromise, artistic default for the sake of material gain: these were intolerable sins for Breton, the moralist, the man of conviction and of unmitigated principle, who found himself constantly in discord with an age in which it was the fashion to indulge in "anxieties"—that is, to be troubled by grave questions but never to be sure, or at most, like André Gide, to express the sincerities of the moment rather than to shape a philosophical directive of a lifetime.

There was a passion for integrity in the vindictive vituperations with which Breton, as a fanatic, seemed to want to destroy those he had so dearly loved. His verbal blasts equal Voltaire's; they were acid erosions on human personality: one man has the *"graces de tétard,"* another is a *"serpent boa de mauvaise mine,"* a *"petit volatile,"* *"révolutionaires malintentionés."*

The attacks cannot be seen in their true light unless considered as answers to journalists' provocations which questioned his most precious asset, his integrity. But as in the case of his earlier quarrel with Tzara, the anger had undertones of disappointment, a sense of loss; and in later years the ferocity of the condemnation was softened in a number of instances.

The most serious indication of weakness in the surrealist *cénacle* was its alienation of a younger generation of adherents. Those who had gathered around a new magazine, entitled *Le Grand Jeu,* were not in disagreement with the major surrealist tenets, but in effect they accused Breton of not having made enough progress in the directions in which his first proclamation had pointed: social rebellion and psychic occultism. It was particularly painful for Breton to lose these, including René Daumal, Roger Vailland, and the literary critic, Rolland de Renéville, the last of whom has done much interesting research into the occultism of Rimbaud. In 1928 the first issue of the magazine had appeared; it greatly resembled Breton's revues in format, in orientation, in tone, in its association with painters. But without attacking Breton's integrity, these young writers were voicing their disappointment in the slow pace with which surrealism was advancing in the field of reality; however, their own efforts had neither produced earth-shaking results nor induced Breton to change from theorist to activist. In fact, as the Second Manifesto demonstrates, he was plunging deeper and deeper into the philosophy of surrealism, perhaps because the area of greatest possible pragmatism—that is, association with communism—had so rapidly collapsed.

The effect of these disputes upon the Second Manifesto is to dilute with circumstantial detail the basically philosophical tenor of the work; yet it is a much more important and far-reaching document than the First Manifesto, and the very rancors that interfere with the continuity of the concepts intensify the drama inherent in the treatise.

As we have already noted, one of the major events in the life of André Breton between the two manifestoes was his brief involvement in the Communist Party. In this connection he had also done considerable reading in the sources of dialectical materialism. The activities of the surrealist *cénacle* had been oriented more and more toward social preoccupations and action. In this interim political and diplomatic miscarriages had so accumulated that the Second Manifesto opens on a note of social and general crisis whereas the First was impelled by a personal spiritual crisis.

It was written under the heavy sky of "the malaise of the times": "It is indeed around 1930 that perceptive minds are warned of the imminent, unavoidable return of the world catastrophe."

In the Second Manifesto, which is much longer than the First, he elaborates on the encyclopedic meaning of surrealism—that is, on its resolution of the problems of life, rather than on its direct application to writing. Not only are many previous associates repudiated but most of the antecedents as well. "It seems less and less necessary to look for antecedents and, as far as I am concerned, I am not opposed to having chroniclers, those who pass judgment, or any other kind, consider it [surrealism] specifically modern." As a result, Rimbaud, Poe, Baudelaire, and many others receive a less complimentary treatment than they had in the First Manifesto. In a spirit of nonaccommodation, Breton considers mercilessly the compromises not only of his friends but of Rimbaud. Only Lautréamont survives the purge of the past, a past that is suddenly inadequate to solve the problems of the future.

The point of view is different; while in the First Manifesto, Breton attacked the older generations and spoke to his peers, in the Second he is thirty-four years old and turns toward youth, to youth who, despite all the leveling attempted by schools and by military barracks, has refused to be brainwashed. He has here a supreme faith in youth, which he was to sustain to the time twelve years later when he spoke at Yale University in the midst of the Second World War. "It is only to them that I address myself. It is for them only that I undertake the justification of surrealism against the accusations that it is after all nothing more than an intellectual pastime like any other," he asserts in the Second Manifesto.

There is a shift in Breton's attitude toward literature. Its significance for surrealism lies not on an aesthetic basis but in its subversive quality: "It is true that the poetic question has ceased in these last years to be considered in an essentially formal angle, and to tell the truth it interests us more to judge the subversive value of a work." "Subversive" indicates a shift in Breton's notion of liberty. Whereas earlier he seemed to be satisfied with Descartes' position that liberty of mind was the lion's share of liberty, in the Second Manifesto he associates liberty much more closely with the will to action. It is in this context that one must read that most quoted and sometimes loosely understood sentence of the Second Manifesto: "The simplest surrealist act consists of going down into the street, revolver in hand, and shooting at random." He immediately points out that the most important word of the sentence is "simplest" and explains what it means: that the only remedy to the increasing and overwhelming power of "vilification and cretinization"—what we call today "brainwashing"—which is rampant, is to possess the sense of rebellion so totally as to be willing to be shooting-mad. He is calling for a more fervent indignation than most intellectuals had yet shown; and the reason for his urgency is that he observes an accelerated pace in the deterioration of society in the Western world of the thirties, and an imminent disaster.

"In the matter of revolt," says Breton, "none of us should need ancestors." The problems that trigger revolt differ from age to age. The symbol of the revolver is to dramatize, he says, the pitch of despair amidst the complacency of the Establishment. In the face of the necessity for absolute revolt and insubordination, problems of aesthetics seem to pale. He does not want surrealism to stay on an ideological plane: a will that acts only for its own account is not valid. When questions of top priority invade the mind so completely, the distinctions and nuances that are indicative of philosophic serenity fade. It is in this light that one must read the famous sentence in which Breton declares the insignificance of the old antinomies; he believes they were created to give man the feeling that he was surrounded by unconquerable barriers, to clip his wings by convincing him that flights into the domain of the *insolite* would be not only risky but futile because of man's basic insufficiencies. He hurls his challenge against those he calls "the library sitters" (armchair critics).

Whereas the First Manifesto had been written under the banner of Freud, the Second is in the orbit of Hegel, in whose dialectical materialism Breton found support for his desire to overcome the contradictions and grasp the long view. While with Freud he explored inner consciousness, in a movement of subjectivism and interiorization, with Hegel he is oriented toward the possibilities of projecting ideas and images into the concrete, exterior world. It is not insignificant to note that the "point" of elevation from which he erases the antinomies is not abstract but is in the poet's eyes identified with a peak of the Alps from which he could verify *concretely* the disappearance of the contrasts of topography. With this concrete image in mind it is in the realm of reality that the dream of unity and harmony is envisioned. "Everything leads us to believe that there is a point in the mind from which life and death, the real and the imaginary, the past and the future, the communicable and the incommunicable, the high and the low, cease to be perceived contradictorily." In the determination of this point, Hegel was of more help to Breton than French philosophers, as he highlighted the need to know the material world exterior to man as well as the inner, psychic phenomena.

In repudiating all previous antecedents and relating to Hegel's *Phenomenology of the Mind*, Breton locates surrealism under the banner of dialectical materialism, but not as an agent of the Communist Revolution.

Rather he sees two independent streams rising out of a common fountain-head, and he holds more hope for the surrealist revolution than for the Communist regime of his time. As we have seen the latter was proving in his experience pathetically abortive. If the social application of Hegel's dialectics is a necessity, there are other necessities without which the system cannot work, and the abolition of the class system is unsatisfactory and incomplete without the eradication of the notion of caste within us: agents much more powerful than economic revolution must be put to work. He gives as an example of the limited vision of communism his own experience in the Party where his nonconformism made him readily "one of the most undesirable of intellectuals." To demonstrate the corruptibility of Communist structures, he accused Pierre Naville of having bought his position in the Communist Party with the money of his father, a banker, and he concluded that the Communist structure was as corruptible as the capitalistic.

Breton's position in regard to dialectical materialism and communism is the distinction which we have come to recognize as the New Left. While relating surrealism to dialectical materialism, Breton dissociates it from deterministic materialism as practiced in university circles and crystallized, as he thought, in the writings of Georges Bataille. His attacks against Bataille must be viewed in a different light from those against his other colleagues. The discord goes beyond personality and personal comportment; it is a serious ideological one, aggravated by Bataille's apparent power to popularize his philosophy and exploit his relations with surrealism.

If Hegel replaces Freud as the guiding spirit in this phase of Breton's thinking, his inspiration from occult philosophies is also heightened as we go from the First to the Second Manifesto. The call to action, which is an exteriorization of surrealism, is coupled with an equal desire for "occultation," which is taking a new look at subjectivity. Breton points to the apparent failure of psychic automatism and exploration of the dream; they failed because those who practiced them were dazzled by the picturesque results and did not apply their attention to what was happening to themselves in the process of psychic automatism. Although it created striking imagery, it did not have the liberating effect on the mind that Breton had hoped. It got no deeper into "the bottomless box" of human conscience. It threw no light on the character of inspiration. The alchemy of the Word was taken as a quest for literary style, rather than as evidence of the mental structure. Before the modern linguists' emphasis on the distinction between style and structure, Breton saw the one as exterior to the soul of man ("soul" used by Breton in a nonreligious sense as the better, if not unperishable part of the human psyche) and the other as the essential expression of the soul. True automatism should produce spasmodic releases of the human essence, like meteors illuminating truths that otherwise can be unraveled only through long machinations of the ordinary processes of the mind. Automatism had erroneously been used as a means of cultivating language for language's sake, instead of taking verbal expression beyond language, to break the shackles of style; for the liberation of language was a prerequisite to the liberation of thought, just as the social revolution could only succeed as a condition of the moral revolution. The alchemy of the Word, toward which Rimbaud had aspired but which he had not clearly defined, takes on a literal meaning in the Second Manifesto. As Breton explains:

> Let it be observed that surrealist research has a common goal with alchemist research: the philosopher's stone had no other pretext than to let human imagination have a glorious revenge on all things. After the mind had been domesticated for centuries and been taught a foolish resignation, here we are trying once and for all to liberate the imagination.

The alchemists sought not the garments but the "furor" of language; it is also what Breton aspires to find, as in the cabalistic sense of the word "alchemy" he makes specific references to the third and fourth book of *Magic*.

In regard to hermetic philosophy Breton reveals himself as much of a purist as in the case of dialectical materialism. His search for purity, which made him evoke "the miter of the ancient conjurers" and declare a situation of "moral default," called forth the derision of many of his former colleagues, who accused him of acting like an old druid or a religious ecstatic.

Indeed there is in the Second Manifesto a strange co-existence of the revolver and "the key of love," the blood of vengeance and the milk of human kindness, the penetration into the problems of darkness and the aspiration toward light—the alchemist's astral light, *l'oeuvre en blanc*, "the light that will cease to be faulting." Breton plays the role of Lucifer, not as the fallen angel of Christian dogma, but as the dark prince of light, rebellious in the search of knowledge. The "marvelous" is no longer "beautiful": it moves from the orbit of aesthetics into that of science, of the search for truth, of light.

Again, Breton pursues his philosophy of failure. The last pages of the Second Manifesto are full of the word "vaincu," only because he thinks the possibility of failure is contingent on the will to risk all, which in the case of a man of letters meant to jeopardize literary reputation, to lose personal friendships and a niche in the world. In full realization of this he says that anyone who cares for his place in the world has no place in surrealism: that is why he would like to place the destiny of surrealism in the hands of those who possess both anger and innocence, who are unspoiled by the temptations of society, who would be willing to recognize in surrealism's failures only wordly failure: "vanquished—but vanquished *only if the world is world.*" If by 1930 the surrealist group had lost all semblance of cohesion, Breton was willing to take upon himself the fault, but considered the fault a virtue—that is, his own obstinate refusal to deviate from fundamental issues: "putting back into question its original premises, that is to say, a return to the initial principle of its activity."

While the First Manifesto was a call to recuperate the powers of imagination and to recharge the weakened batteries of reality, in the Second, Breton ponders on the futility and the irrelevancy of a freed mind and sharpened imagination if they do not enter into the field of action: if the power to see finds no effective target outside itself, and if the power to change life in terms of the individual does not extend to a broader metamorphosis—the transformation of the world. That is why the Second Manifesto opens the doors of the surrealist *cénacle* to a new and younger generation.

As younger writers and artists enter the field, the relationship of Breton to his associates changes; he assumes more and more initiative and direction, he has the power to create a reputation. As others look to him for judgment, he finds himself in the center of a vicious cycle: he can bring an unknown name to public attention, but when the recipient of the sudden fame shows signs of enjoying the recognition and of reaping some material advantages from it, he becomes the object of Breton's denunciation. What is clear is the increasing base of the proliferation of surrealism, as foreign artists and writers join the French nucleus of the early years. It is at this point that in Breton's eyes the artists seemed more adept as surrealists than the writers. It is around this period that Salvador Dali and Yves Tanguy enter the ranks, compensating for the loss of a host of literary men. It is also a time of increased concern with social problems, for in spite of Breton's unfortunate experience as a member of the Communist Party, he showed an intensified concern and gave increased expression to the mounting political dilemmas of his country. As from all over Europe young artists come to join the group, the effect is not an internationalization; surrealism produces, as it had been in the case of the Symbolist movement, a *de*nationalization of the artist who comes within its magnetic field. It causes an obliteration of ethnic differences: while Breton's associates varied in the years of the twenties and continued to drift in and out of the ranks in the thirties, one constant remained: no nationalist ever came into the circle, and no work that emanated from it had any trace of regionalist habits of expression or parochial dimensions; the surrealist's concern and subject was the condition of man, his reception of the data of his senses, in the face of the colossal enigma of his ageless, non-historical destiny. Even as Breton tightened the precepts of surrealism, he widened its perspective and aspired toward a broader catholicity. By defining the surrealist writer and artist as dreamer, lover, philosopher, he gave the role a character it had never assumed before in the history of the arts: that of a militant, his militancy directed toward such seemingly unattainable targets that measurement of success was unthinkable. "To cast a bridge over the abyss," to attempt to link the perceivable with what is yet entrenched in the pith of mystery was a task to which he set no time limit, projecting the failure of the moment into the possibility of future success. Thus he thought it impossible to set a historical limit to the surrealist movement.

VIII

TOWARD
A NEW
STRUCTURE OF WRITING:
ANALOGICAL PROSE:
NADJA
LES VASES COMMUNICANTS
L'AMOUR FOU

"Is it true that all the beyond is in this life?"
—*Nadja*

"We are on the track, or rather lying in wait for this 'objective chance' according to the term used by Hegel, and I shall not cease to spy upon its manifestations, not only in *Nadja*, but later in *Les Vases communicants* and *L'Amour fou*." —*Entretiens*

The groundwork for the type of writing that *Naja, Les Vases communicants,* and *L'Amour fou* comprise had been prepared in *Les Champs magnétiques* and *Poisson soluble* and was to culminate in Breton's last major work, *Arcane 17.* These three works are related in subject and structure and contain an originality matched only by Breton's poems in free verse; in fact they create a genre in spite of his determination to destroy all genres. We have seen that in the manifestoes he attacked both the novel and the verse of the past: the one because in representing life it had robbed life of all its spontaneity; the other because it had preserved the shell of poetry and filled it with materials unworthy of poetry, drawing its anemic blood from worn-out symbols and tired word associations. As for the theater—for which he had avowed a distaste a number of times, as the most prostituted of the arts—he had admitted that dialogue was the form of verbalization most suited to surrealism. But his own attempts at dramatic writing had been at most fragmentary, and those of his colleagues had not fared much better.

Actually Breton aspired to the breakdown of all genres as determined by literary form, and beyond the breakdown, he hoped for an amalgamation of the notions inherent in the genres into a unity called poetry which would include the best attribute of prose, that is, its flexibility. The distinction between the two was for him not of form but of structure, the structure of the writing directly a reflection of the process of thought. The process consisted of giving the lead to the imagination over the logical controls of organization and sequence indicative of nonpoetic writing, but adhering to prose *form* as the more supple. For him any form of writing could be classified as poetry if it utilized as its mental movement the powers of analogy and proceeded on the basis of the unpremeditated relationship of images and of the mind's reaction to the phenomena of the exterior world. The affective intensity of these phenomena was dependent not on a preliminary mental adjustment to them but on an *a posteriori* psychic acceptance of the mind's surprised reaction to events. The first process is effective for the interpretation of man and his world; the second is, as he thought, conducive to its transformation and extension. Although he favors the latter, it does not mean that he does not utilize the logical prose form in others of his works. The manifestoes, his literary and art criticism, his philosophical and social essays all follow the most intricately analytical structure, making of him a significant essayist in a class with Valéry, Gide, Ortega y Gasset, and Unamuno.

But the antithesis of this analytical prose is not the free verse he wrote concurrently between 1920 and 1947. We expect, of course, the power of the analogy in verse; but when it appears in prose as it does in *Nadja, Les Vases communicants,* and *L'Amour fou,* it does not mean that Breton is indulging in a prose poem. For him the old antinomy built into the designation "prose poem" no longer exists. Poetry in its extended sense, as understood by the surrealists, has to do with the channeling of the mind, freed of the exigencies of logical direction; it is not the injection of assonance, rhythm, alliteration, and other outer devices that makes prose more poetic. The two earlier works, *Les Champs magnétiques* and *Poisson soluble,* depended largely on verbal automatism rising out of spontaneous memory to communicate the mind's analogical powers. The three later works are based on the automatic coincidences of experiences whose relationships with the logical sequence of events are arbitrary and can be deciphered only *after the fact*. In the earlier works the spontaneous play of images is transcribed without rational commentaries.

These works are also linked by their subject matter or orientation: they are the autobiography of a sensibility, which begins with an initial interrogation in *Nadja*—"Who am I?"—and searches for an identity through a labyrinth of objects and events containing indices that eventually lead to the crystallization of desire. The quest for identity (tell me whom you haunt and I'll tell you who you are) coincides with the quest for love, culminating in *L'Amour fou* in a letter to Breton's newborn daughter in which he passes to her the only heritage he considers worth having: to be in her turn capable of being furiously loved.

Whereas *Les Champs magnétiques* and *Poisson soluble* are illustrations of the first definition of surrealism, which specifies psychic transcription as the basis of surrealist writing, the three later works written between 1928 and 1937, the decade of the highest surrealist productivity,[1] fit into the more philosophical definition: the belief in the superior reality of the dream and the free play of the mind "in the resolution of the principal problems of life."

As Breton tells the story of his affective life in the decade between 1926 and 1936—that is, between the ages of thirty and forty—he turns for guidance not to the French literary heritage but to German philosophers—Hegel, Engels, and Feuerbach—and to the findings of Freud who, he believes, did not understand the philosophical import of his own inquiries. He engages in a pinzer attack on both deterministic materialism and philosophic idealism. On the one hand, the systematic analysis of chronological events in a man's life, some of which he can shape, others of which he cannot avoid, are of no great help in defining his course or in understanding his most deep-seated motivations; on the other hand, he is no further advanced in the knowledge of self and of the universe if he seeks refuge in an ideal but nonexistent abstraction, whether through religious speculation, whose target is beyond reach, or through philosophical idealization, which intensifies the dichotomy between reality and the dream. His quarrel with Freud is that the psychiatrist came to an ambiguous conclusion incompatible with his avowed monistic philosophy. Freud was in fact accepting the duality of the universe when he suggested that we must not confuse psychic reality with material reality.[2] In effect, the basic aim of the three works is to show the contrary: that indeed psychic reality is a part, and the better part, of material reality, that it is the inherent reservoir of magic. A rich involvement in this world can resituate the notion of the "sacred" within the scope of human experience. In the enormous task of giving back to man what man has for so long attributed to God, Breton seeks to channel the sacred that exists in the human adventure, taking himself as a case history as it were, one that he knows better than any other, but not well enough.

The greatest intimation of the sacred character of physical life is for him the erotic experience. Love is the spiritualization of the physical and the objectification of the subjective. Love equated with pleasure lies outside his quest, since the sexual act as a form of casual pleasure precludes the spiritualization of the object of that act; and on the other hand, the idealized mental image of a loved one is equally irrelevant, since it tends to become a substitute for the realization of the love. Breton in his quest for love will never proceed from a mental image-ideal to a reality, but rather from nonobjective desire to a concretion or a crystallization of it, and from the particular he derives the feminine essence. He calls it "this major operation of the mind which consists of going from the being to the essence." [3] Love is the product of the inductive process, rather than a deduction from a preconceived image. Because to him love is the most complete manifestation of the integral relationship and unity of the subjective world with the objective, and the irreducible identification of the physical with the spiritual, into a single state, the search for love in these works is like the search for the Holy Grail, the Philosopher's Stone, or the Golden Fleece. It is the fundamental thread that runs through the trilogy, "a capillary fabric" he calls it, which keeps the link between the exterior and interior world.

Each of these works explores primarily one of the various phenomena that convince Breton of the continuity and unity of what a dualistic civilization has impelled its language to split into "real" and "unreal," "physical" and "spiritual," "causal" and "marvelous." The phenomena that belie, according to him, these dichotomies are mental derangement, dreams, and the aleatory character of events. Each book explores one of these areas in terms of André Breton's life adventure. In *Nadja* he wanders into the penumbral experience of a young woman who has let down the barriers between the rational and the irrational, thus showing to Breton how flexible they can be and how ambiguous is the frontier between sanity and insanity. In *Les Vases communicants* he places the dream in the world of material phenomena of our waking life and its powerhouse of accumulated desires and frustrations; if the dream is symptomatic of wish and constraint, so is our gravitation toward objects and our symbolization of them in life and literature. Finally, in *L'Amour fou* he seeks out the miracles of objective chance, the moments of coincidence between our voluntary movements impelled consciously or unconsciously by human desire or necessity, and their coincidences with natural necessity in the great scheme of mathematical probabilities. As the love wish, which in *Nadja* is undirected and nonobjective, reaches in *L'Amour fou* its ultimate and concrete realization, life assumes for André Breton a sublime character and confirms his hypotheses.

The fact that his criticism of the novel form was not a theoretical postulation is evident in the way in which these three works are structured. He avoids both narration and description as they are known to exist in the novel or in an ordinary biography.

The vital statistics constituting the basic structure of the trilogy are his separation from his first wife, Simone; a free liaison with one whom out of discretion he calls "X"; his eventual marriage with the "scandalously beautiful" Jacqueline; and the consummation of that love in the birth of his only child, Aube, with which *L'Amour fou* ends. He was to idolize Aube for the rest of his life.

Earlier, in "Une Confession dédaigneuse," Breton described how he guarded against having his life fall into a rut: "Each night I would leave wide open the door of the room I occupied at a hotel in the hope of waking up at last next to a companion I had not chosen." [4] Nadja is an unknown quantity intervening in a fairly regulated marital life. She slips as it were through a half-open door with her promises to one who had subconsciously made himself available again for the love adventure. *Nadja* ends in liberation from bonds that apparently had lost their significance; Breton was always wary of the symbol that outgrows its significance. But *Nadja* serves as a hyphen from one bondage to another.

Les Vases communicants opens with a new bondage, as Breton appears in the role of spurned lover. X has disappeared from his life, but he cannot free himself from the persistence of memory. He reveals the efforts at substitution, which prove unsuccessful, but through which he learns much about the character of desire and the human power of sublimation. The book ends in the poet's liberation from memory.

In *L'Amour fou* the search finally comes to an end: the consummation of the "only love" toward which the substitution had unwittingly led. In retrospect the peregrinations, which had seemed haphazard and undirected, reveal the pattern of their continuity; all the fragments in the form of events, dreams, places, and objects had contributed clues to the solution of the search. As Breton passes ten years of his life in the course of these three works, he is seen to be walking—most of the time he is actually walking—not through a forest of symbols but through a forest of indices. If symbols are conducive to interpretation of something whose sense is hidden, they limit the field of figuration according to Breton. What is free of symbolic meaning is, on the contrary, an open door: "the least object to which a particular symbolic role is not assigned is susceptible of becoming a figuration of anything." [5] Indices are like pebbles for a man lost in a labyrinth: they beckon toward a revelation. In the case of Breton the revelation is twofold: whatever throws light on his own problems and desires helps him to a better understanding of the world without; these are in fact the two objectives of surrealism. [6] He is not an empirical sensualist since he proceeds from definite hypotheses; and since perception and representation are interchangeable in his scheme of things, the intercourse between the senses and the intellectual evaluation of their data is almost spontaneous, so that it is hard to say where the man of heart stops and the man of intellect takes over: the power of love, in its overwhelming sexual sense, is so intricately involved in the aesthetic sense, in the metaphysical transformation of the data of the visual sense, that as painting or writing is a projection of the subjective image into the exterior world, the image of woman that produces the notion of love is an interiorization of the object, a penetration of the outer image within the psychic apparatus. At the end of *Nadja*, Breton says "the heart is a seismograph"; and indeed, as he proves in the course of his three volumes, it is a reactor to psychically charged atmospheric conditions that constantly and in varying degrees forewarn of the convulsions of the being. "Beauty will be convulsive or it is not beauty" is the conclusion of the first stage of the journey.

None of these three works can be defined as a novel in any sense of the word, unless considered a forerunner of the "new novel." He eliminates from "plot" all the things that people do when they are not directly concerned with the fate of their souls, with the meaning of their lives. Incidents are not indices—that is, they do not throw light on the fundamental concern; they are sifted out just as things and places that do nothing to illuminate the character of the writer are left undescribed: "to extract from the milieu to the exclusion of all the rest, what had to be of use in the reconstitution of this self." [7] In fact whenever the environment takes on the character of décor, it simply means that life has fallen into still waters, waste and putrefaction—a warning to the poet that he has floundered.

Breton insists on giving a documentary character to the diarylike notations of these events: their seemingly disconnected character, as revealed in their outwardly arbitrary juxtaposition, is pertinent to the sacralization of the human adventure. In his introduction to the 1962 edition of *Nadja*, Breton emphasizes the fact that it is a "document extracted directly from life." And in *L'Amour fou:* "The use of the immediate, confounding irrationality of certain events as evidence necessitates the strict authenticity of the human document that registers them." [8] The striking effects of this psychic selectivity of milieu are apparent in each of these works.

The eclectic character of time and events has the condensed form of dream narration. The principal occupations of social man are bypassed completely, and the acts to which our attention is drawn are measured by the power of psychic duration rather than by chronological time. According to Breton's long-standing contention, among the barriers to the psychic adventure is routine work as a device for the securing of a livelihood. Never in the network of the events related to work is man likely to find the event "out of which everyone has the right to expect the revelation of the meaning of his life." [9] Among the selected activities in these three works which so intimately concerned his personal life there is no mention of work. This does not mean, of course, that he did nothing to earn money in those ten years, but the lack of mention of these activities conveys the conviction that they in no way contributed to the essential flow of his life, to his knowledge of self, or to the accomplishment of his desire. This may be hard to understand in a society where most people center their existence around their work pattern: friendship, aspirations, even recreation. This denial of any significance to events related to work is the keynote of Breton's insubordination, what he calls in the final testament he leaves to his infant daughter "my nonslavery to life."

Most of the action of *Nadja* takes place between October 4 and 13, 1926, although the book was not published until 1928. Of *Les Vases communicants*, he says: "All that has occurred for me between that 5th and 24th of April [1931] is contained in the small number of facts that I have reported, and which if put end to end, without counting naturally the waiting periods in between, would not occupy more than a few hours." [10] Publication followed the actual occurrences by one year. As for *L'Amour fou*, the most crucial adventure occurs during a spring night, May 29, 1934; but other events complementing the critical moment occurred between April 1934 and the spring of 1936, with vaster lacunae between them than in the other two books.

The central milieu in the three books is Paris, the dearly loved caldron out of which so many works of art have emerged, Paris which knows when to efface itself to give its characters the element of universality, when to provide French authors with the most fascinating brand of regionalism in literature.

Breton's Paris is like no other writer's, not even Apollinaire's or Aragon's. As Breton himself indicates, the affective character of Paris was part of the education of the surrealists from their earliest affiliations in the

1920's; and Aragon's *Le Paysan de Paris,* although published in 1926, is chronologically a companion piece to *Nadja,* as is René Crevel's *Êtes-vous fous?* to *L'Amour fou.* Aleatory ambulation was a surrealist activity parallel with automatic writing. The self-revelation inherent in the chance meeting of words corresponded with the chance encounters of persons and objects in aleatory, nondirected walks through the streets of Paris; they would throw light on the nature of objective chance and create the daily miracles that contribute to the understanding of the latent magic of life. What other city, except perhaps New York, could have offered the diversity of phenomena, the enchantment, the impression of unreality within the very real, unshakably real manifestation of life in its total spectrum, a phantasmagoria of the most obvious devices of modern industry, creating *terrain vague* by the ambiguous intentions of spectacle and event—Paris with its streets that flowed into each other in irrational, illogical patterns, delivering its multitude into each other's arms; Paris the ideal locale for Brownian movements, where even the most intentionally directed movements appear in their collective impression chaotic, and at the mercy of arbitrary chance. Another author, a poet in his own fashion, Jules Romains, was trying in his monumental novel, *Les Hommes de bonne volonté,* to show the patterns of group dynamics, the elements of unanimity in the multitudes of Paris; and he centered his kaleidoscope on the unifying pattern of the work routine: Paris descends to work, Paris returns from work. The surrealists were to give to Paris the exactly opposite treatment: the dreamer in Paris, the wanderer, the free spirit who does not forge his way through the city but lets himself be propelled by the powers and baits that Paris contains in her movements, in the cafés, the *places,* the signs of Paris, in the storehouses of memories where each stone and statue is as a bark of a tree layered with events one on top of the other. Aragon, Crevel, Péret, and Desnos (who sees what others do not see) discovered and conveyed this miraculous phantasmagoria of Paris, with its fauna and flora, with all it held of the mysterious and unexpected, all that made it a source for meditation, a fire for the imagination.

For Breton, Paris was all this and something more. It was the *champs,* the *pré* in the hermetic sense, a magnetic field in the physical and the occult senses, with various poles toward which he was drawn and which had oracular meanings for him; it was the nest of indices, his fountainhead as it was eventually his tomb. Through Paris he felt a continuity, a unity with the ages, because Paris was the receptacle of events and the intimate link of his being with the objective world. Paris had been the recipient of so many subjectivities that had left their imprints there. He was drawn

to the statues in particular, to that of Etienne Marcel as to an oracle, to
La Porte St. Denis—beautiful and useless, as he thought—to La Tour Saint
Jacques—a monument to the heretics of the fourteenth century.

His walks through Paris can be traced in the three books, somewhat
different in each but having common traits, and common rallying points:
the Place Blanche, where he lived; the Sacré Coeur, that church of the secular, casting its benediction on the wanderers and dreamers of Paris; down
to the rue Lafayette where Breton meets Nadja for the first time; the Fau-
bourg Poissonnière, the Boulevard Bonne Nouvelle, the Place Dauphine,
Les Halles, and the flower market. Paris is the great catalyst of encounters;
in its charged atmosphere the poet feels constantly renewed and revital-
ized, in an intensification of the sense of life. This is in sharp contrast with
the role that Paris originally played in his early youth when in fact the
streets had for him the melancholy emptiness of the canvases of Chirico.
Like the painter, he had been inspired with their sense of mystery, a mystery that at first he equated with rarefaction and found void as they
appear in the imagery of symbolist poetry. But for André Breton, mystery
moved from abstraction and unreality to transfiguration and revelation.
The empty streets in Chirico's paintings became teeming with images and
promises, of which *Nadja, Les Vases communicants,* and *L'Amour fou*
were the fruition.

In each of these works there is a flight from Paris as well: in *Nadja* the
mind of the deranged heroine finds a more poignant sounding board in
the ancient palace of St. Gemain en Laye. In *Les Vases communicants,*
Breton, prey to solitude, obsessed with a lost love, seeks solace in the mountains of the Maritime Alps. In *L'Amour fou* love is crystallized in the
grottoes of Vaucluse and in the exotic vegetation of the Canary Islands,
the Pic du Teide à Tenerife; its moment of uncertainty occurs against the
background of a desolate mansion of Lorient, which had been, as he found
out later, the scene of a recent act of bloody violence.

But in each case when Breton resorts to description, what he gives is the
account of the convulsive effect; and for the curiosity of those who need
the static reality of the place or object, he provides an accompanying
photograph. All three books are thus richly illustrated with photographs,
which are both a concession to the reader and an integral part of the
physical format of the work itself. The concession, however, is superficial:
the photographs dramatize the disparity between static reality and the
"convulsive" beauty with which it is endowed through the poetic vision.[11]

The *"Je est un autre"* of Rimbaud's famous letter explaining the function and the materials of the poet is substantiated here as the alchemy
of the Word was in *Poisson soluble.* There are two "I" 's in the works:

the "I" who is the object of the adventures and the "I" who explains the relative significances of the experience to which he has been subjected. Breton is indeed, as he says in *Nadja*, living in a glass house. It is an auto-psychoanalysis in which the poet, impulsive, younger than his years, starry-eyed, highly impressionable, vibrant in every fiber of his body, rising to the challenge of every dream, object, or phenomenon that looms before him, is confronted with the rational analyst, who finds the meaning, who appraises its direct relation to the psyche, and who keeps track of the various erotic states that reach their peak in what Breton calls—adopting religious terminology—"a state of grace."

In the beginning of *Nadja* the subject is in a state of passive freedom: that is, despite the fact that he has marital bonds, not to say moral ones, he feels in a state of availability. In his discussion of love and in his metaphors about love, Breton will always claim that the sense of sin must be dispelled from sexuality. Libertinism is something else; the casual possession and pursuit of more than one woman at one time is unsavory to him. For Breton the pursuit of love is total and overpowering, untainted by ulterior motives, disinterested in terms of social conventions; "the mysterious, the improbable, the unique, the perplexing, and the *certain* love" is a form of miracle. By conveying a sense of innocence, an openness, a freedom from subterfuge, he is able to maintain the aura of sublimation in all his relations with woman. It must be remembered that the notion of the purity of woman, accepted and extolled by the surrealists in the years of the 1920's and 1930's, was in sharp contrast with the role assigned to woman in most of the literature of the time. Elsewhere, woman was a cause of stress, distress, and misfortune to man, and she was portrayed as either passive, wanton, or cruel by the many homosexuals and misogynists who were predominant among the novelists. The surrealists, under the direction of Breton, restored the love theme to French poetry and gave woman the sublimated role she had not played since the salutary heroines of the Middle Ages. "A certain conception of love, unique, reciprocal, realizable toward and against all, which I had conceived in my youth and which those who have seen me closely can say that I have defended." [12]

It is in this frame of mind that, going nowhere, Breton meets Nadja, who was going nowhere. He tells us that she has called herself "Nadja," taking the beginning of the Russian word that means "hope": "she tells me her name, the one she chose for herself." [13] The interesting word in the sentence is "chose," which immediately suggests that the name is fictitious. One wonders how far the things that Breton makes Nadja say subsequently are as authentic, as "documentary" as his own reactions. In the case histories of women hysterics described by Dr. Janet in almost romantic terms, Nadia harbored the memory of her mother, dead for many years, as if she were alive; this same lack of a sense of time is prevalent in Breton's Nadja and her general, anemic, wide-eyed appearance is reminiscent of the young patient described by Janet. May not the actual encounter have triggered a memory of clinical days, and may he not have been the one to "name" her thus? And if the first step in the modification of reality may tip the balance a little toward fiction, is it not also possible that the poetization of the irrational world of Nadja is Breton's rather than that of the little, uneducated waif he met by chance? "The blue and the wind" (the blue wind she sees passing in the trees) has the quality of a surrealist sentence rather than of a wandering mind. As they look deep into the Seine in the glistening sun, is it Breton or Nadja who sees a hand in the water? The words, put together like a rebus analogy of one in the other, are attributed to Nadja: "That hand, that hand in the Seine, why that hand aflame in the water? It is true that fire and water are the same thing?" Yet the words seem to echo the hermeticists who had inspired Breton. It is curious to note that of the three heroines, Nadja, X, and Jacqueline, only the first is allowed to speak or to lead a life of her own, to be, so to speak, animated by the author; the other two are known only through the effect of their beauty and their love which has power over the poet's soul—as is also the case with the series of other women who produce a series of substitutions for each other in Breton's quest for the ideal.

But what expresses Nadja's position in life better than the words Breton may have put in her mouth is his observation that she "cares little but marvelously for life": "little" in the sense of life's social meaning and duration, "marvelously" in the intensified sense of the immediacy of the life experience without concern for past or future. It was this same immediacy that surrealist poetry was trying to capture. Nadja's situation outside the context of the human routine provokes Breton to attack the work pattern which absorbs in most people the individual pattern with which nature has endowed them.*

In their various haphazard meetings so different from conventional love trysts—an unplanned dinner in a café, a walk along the Quai Malaquais, along the capriciously winding rue de Seine, a train excursion—he highlights the incongruity between the traditional pattern of the awakening of love and the nonlove that goes its course, where the mounting attachment of Nadja for the stranger whom she seems to have known since the beginning of time and Breton's reciprocity which is sympathy, compassion, com-

* "The kind of *brave gens* who put their shoulder to the wheel are like those who get themselves killed in a war," says Breton in *Nadja* (pp. 88–89).

panionship, but not love, allows him to channel the *insolite* and gives her, pathetically, a power to ward off the ills of the world, a power which is mercurial, elusive, at the end completely futile. She makes Breton live for a few brief hours on a different wave length, creates a metaphysical sphere as in reality they sit in crowded cafés, and order very ordinary meals. The fact is that within the confines of an oppressive reality, amidst problems of money, of health, of human relations, the curve of Nadja's derangement reaches its apex, no doubt under the effect of sexual excitement. She is less and less able to distinguish between the real and the illusion; and the presence of the nonexistent feather of her hat is so tangible that it convinces Breton, at least momentarily of its reality: "With what grace she hid her face behind the heavy, nonexistent feather of her hat." Being near her is not the supreme experience that signals the awakening of love, but her presence makes him gain proximity to the things to which she is contingent and most of all to the beyond: "Is it true that all the beyond is here?" A veritable contagion of insanity now triggers for the poet numerous symbols of the fantastic which had been quietly stored in his psychic reservoir, and which he now projects upon the sights of Paris and upon the behavior of the deranged girl. We are reminded of the night chase of Gérard de Nerval after Aurélia, but there the poet, not the woman, is prey to the type of transfiguration caused by Nerval's insanity. As Nadja crosses the barrier that separates insanity from sanity, the poet cannot follow her even though for a brief moment he had reached the threshold of non-distinction between the rational and the irrational. The fact that he cannot follow her all the way, symbolizing his inability to love her truly, shows the restricted character of this particular channel of psychic force for a normal though wary man. Only for a moment can he partake of life that literally puts one out of breath: "*la vie à perdre haleine.*" The star "in the heart of the infinite" is as elusive as Nadja, for the social mores of our time are quick to segregate those who deviate even in the smallest degree from the pattern of the rational.

Breton's vindictive attack on psychiatry and asylums is to be understood in the larger context; it is an attack against the forces in general that bind the human imagination. He also realizes how precious human liberty is, and how much it must be cherished: "liberty acquired here on earth at the cost of a thousand—and most difficult—renunciations, must be enjoyed unrestrictedly, while we have it." The incarceration of Nadja at the end of the book is symptomatic of the abject situation of man in general, which Breton's political involvement of the moment related to the need for revolution: "Human emancipation conceived definitively in its most revolutionary form . . . remains the only cause worth serving."

The plight of Nadja comes to symbolize the plight of humanity as a whole as she vanishes behind prison bars. This is the first of Breton's elaborations of an individual problem with the universal problems pertaining to the human condition.

In terms of the personal, if Nadja did not satisfy the quest for love, if she did not prove to be the object of the search, she nonetheless served as medium. She emancipated the poet from his bonds at the very moment when he might be settling down to a conventional domesticity. She freed his imagination for the free union; and—in the first of the substitutions that Breton made in his search for the unique love—he comes to believe at the end of *Nadja* that he has found it in X. If the book ended with the heroine vanishing behind bars, it would have terminated on a tragic tone, and it would have been *her* case history. Indeed, as a "literary work" the book should probably end with Nadja's commitment to the mental hospital. But *Nadja* as the record of a moment in Breton's own psychic history begins before he meets the heroine and ends after her disappearance. Through Nadja he understood himself better. Whether Nadja really found the words herself, or whether Breton put in her mouth words that coming from him would have appeared too egocentric, it is *through* her that he defines his destination: "It was truly a star, you were going toward a star. You could not fail to reach that star. To hear you speak I felt that nothing would stop you, nothing, not even I. . . . You could never see that star as I saw it. You don't understand; it is like the heart of a heartless flower."

Nadja proved to be only an intervention. The orientation was strictly surrealist, since the enigma that had haunted Breton through the pages of his book remained undecipherable in his pursuit of Nadja; but when he met X, the revelation of love destroyed the enigma: the love that replaced the presentiments of love he had previously had, of which Nadja was the most acute. "Without meaning to, you replaced the forms that were most familiar to me, as well as a number of the faces of my presentiment." The mystery was overcome by the marvelous, a sequence that Breton's adventures always followed.

But there is something more significant from the point of view of the development of Breton's own creativity; in proving his major hypothesis concerning the relativity of the notion of reality, he projects enough objective existence into Nadja to lend credence to her attitude toward the exterior world, to give her imagined objects and situations the reality of the deranged imagination. We believe as we read the book that she has established in her innocent way the continuum between the exterior world and the objectification of the subjective. She is in terms of Breton's life the blue wind that passed in the trees.

Like *Nadja, Les Vases communicants* starts with the end of a relationship: in this case with the woman who had become the substitute for Nadja, who in retrospect was herself to become an intermediary, an agent rather than the object of the unique love. But whereas *Nadja* opened on a note of high expectation and effervescence on the part of the author, *Les Vases communicants* announces that the year 1931, some five years after the events that led to the *union libre*, opens on a somber note: the definitive break with the loved X, at whose insistence Breton had divorced Simone, not without tears.* To add to the intensity of the disappointment, X had married subsequently a man whose economic status was somewhat more stable than Breton's, as Breton saw the situation. It reinforced his contention—the leitmotif of *Les Vases communicants*—that society must be transformed so that love could be liberated from economic factors, making the choice free and therefore pure.

The second stage of the quest of this latter-day *Roman de la rose* starts with the poet's struggle to free himself of an image; therefore the effort of passing from idea to object is the more urgent, as X has fallen into the domain of abstraction through her absence, and desire is again unleashed on the reactive field of daily experience.

Les Vases communicants begins as a study of dream, with Breton taking a position on the nature of dreams: they are part of life, the residue of past experience and the indication of the direction of desire.

The dream is to life what poetry is to literature; in their power of condensation, in their ability to synthesize experience, both illuminate the essentials among the miscellany of sensations and phenomena. Suddenly, *"je est un autre,"* and we are put before a dream transcription. In deciphering it, Breton is plunged in the "torrent of data that constitute a life," and building analogy upon analogy he interprets every detail of the incongruous image which, as in a surrealist poem, creates relationships unacceptable to the rational mind. They are unacceptable because of the tensions that outwardly contradictory metaphors created in respect to their credibility. In the analysis of this dream, Breton demonstrates perhaps better than anywhere else in his poetics what he means by the conciliation of contraries, which he had found in Hegel as early as 1912, and which became the

* In an interview in 1966, Simone Collinet relived those days and without rancor related to me the bittersweet ending of their marriage.

driving force of his philosophy. Where, as much as in the dream, is there a field for this conciliation? But if the dream is part of reality, which we make circumspect in its identification with our waking hours, then the same conciliation may be achieved in the wakeful state. Then the dream not only loses its character as escape, and expands reality, but has the power to transform that reality. Instead of being an index of latent human conflicts, as considered by medical technicians, it contains qualities that can be directed toward mental serenity. Since stress is a symptom of contradiction, the state of grace is the ability to erase contradictions. The dream is a force for good; and it is in this vein that in his wanderings in the year of 1931, Breton seeks to introduce the forces of the dream into the material world, as he had sought in the episode with Nadja to utilize the forces of insanity to reach a more exciting concept of reality. In each case the need for transcendence is overcome by a deeper probing of reality instead of becoming an escape from it.

Whereas in *Nadja* the scene opened in a field of receptivity in which Breton met in unexpected places those who were to become his best friends, such as Aragon, Eluard, Péret, *Les Vases communicants* opens on a note of solitude, a solitude precipitated by the facts that he has been deserted by X and that he has rejected a good number of his companions, as evidenced in the Second Manifesto. The immediate effect of the solitude is to turn his physical surrounding suddenly into a simple and inanimate décor: "Whether I turned this way or that, solitude was the same. The exterior world had resumed its appearance of pure décor." [14] It will remain inert, he knows, unless and until he can reactivate its power of magnetization by finding in the material world links with his subjective world, and can reinforce the threads that can effect the relationship between desire and objectification.

The analysis of the dream identifies the constraints he had endured, particularly the sexual frustration and the obstacles that were put in the way of free choice. Through the imagery of the dreams he summarizes the events of his immediate past not in the normal sequence but in the order of their importance to the present. This total disturbance of sequence, which today is expected and accepted in the novel form, was revolutionary in 1931.

Proceeding on the analogical basis to the reconstruction of his state as fallen from grace, which is the theme of *Les Vases communicants*, Breton goes from one dream to another, the sequence determined by their relative power for revelation. Using himself as a subject, he tried to go further than Freud in breaking down moral reticences. The entire first part of the book reads like a scientific study, with many references to dream studies besides

Jacques Vaché—self-portrait appearing in *Lettres de guerre*, 1919 (edited and with an introduction by André Breton). Courtesy Mme Simone Collinet.

The Soupault apartment on the Ile St. Louis, 1922. From left to right, Tristan Tzara, Simone Breton, André Breton. Courtesy Mme Simone Collinet.

The Surrealist Cénacle. From left to right (standing): Jacques Baron, Raymond Queneau, Pierre Naville, André Breton, Jacques Boiffard, Giorgio de Chirico, Roger Vitrac, Paul Eluard, Philippe Soupault, Robert Desnos, Louis Aragon; (seated) Simone Breton, Max Morise, Mme Soupault. Courtesy Mme Simone Collinet.

Jacqueline and André Breton,
Marseilles, winter 1940.
Courtesy Mme
Jacqueline Lamba.

Max Ernst frontispiece for
Les Vases communicants.
Courtesy Mme Elisa Breton.

Cover by Toyen to illustrate the essay, "La Lampe dans l'horloge." Courtesy Mme Elisa Breton.

Cover by Dominguez for *Anthologie de l'humour noir*. Courtesy Mme Elisa Breton.

Illustration for *Arcane 17*
by Matta. Courtesy Mme
Elisa Breton.

Elisa Breton, 1945. Courtesy
Mme Elisa Breton.

Cover by Miró for *La Clé des champs*. Courtesy Mme Elisa Breton.

At the top of Montségur, August 1956. Left to right, Yves Elléouët, Aube Elléouët, Annie Dax, André Breton. Courtesy Mme Aube Elléouët.

Breton's home in Saint-Cirq La Popie. Courtesy Dr. Michel Lanoote.

Freud's, including those of Haffner, Havelock Ellis, Haeckel, Bernheim Jouffroy, Spitta, Maury, and Hervey. It was this paradox in Breton that exasperated his friends: on the one hand the free, poetic spirit, passionate and spontaneous, and on the other, the erudite, exhaustingly well read, deeply analytical man, as dispassionate in his vivisection of himself and his friends as if in a clinical laboratory. In no other book do the two aspects of his character converge and confront each other as in *Les Vases communicants*, where the dreamer and the analyst of the dream connected as in communicating vessels.

As a poet he seeks the aid of the scientist in breaking down prejudices connected with the dream. First, he denies that it is an illusion, indicative of man's escape from reality, or an intimation of his future transcendence from material existence into something better; and second, that it is a mark of mental disturbance to identify with one's dreams. (Had not the dream been primarily studied in terms of the mentally ill?) Third, he rejects the idea that the dream should be defined in Kantian terms as an emblem of idealism, as an extension of the image of non-realizable desire—that is, what "might have been" if we had somehow acted differently or if we had been directed in other ways. As a figuration of the good things that did not occur, it is a source of pessimism; as a nightmare to which reality is blessedly impermeable, it is a source of security, giving us comfort in the realization of the impossible alternative. Seeing himself guillotined in his dream only increased Maury's prejudice against Robespierre. In both the French and the Kantian notions of dream, reflected in the art work of the symbolists, the cult of the dream reinforces the human withdrawal from active participation in the world. On the contrary, in Breton's thinking it should reinforce man's mental function, his effect on the world of phenomena. In art Breton discerns the first evidences of the introduction of the dream into reality in the phantom figures created by Dali, Ernst, Picasso, and Giacometti. In poetry he sees the transfer of the dream wish into verbal metaphors. But the greatest significance of the dream can be seen in the context of Breton's heightened political concern of the 1930's. The social revolution cannot, in his opinion, be effective unless the dream is spelled into action; and since the dream has by its nature an individual character, the whole problem of the individual's role in social transformation is put in question. In the maze of his poetic analogies Breton makes a greater challenge to collectivist politics than in any of his purely political writings. He fortifies his position by quotations from Engels to suggest that he who transcends reality by the objectification of his dream is more accurately expressing the nature of that reality. Political revolution, then, is viewed in the context of a new metaphysics; in extricating from the dream the prejudicial element of mystery and unavailability, Breton proposes it as an agent of revelation, utilizable in the field of action, a wasted element of society's material resources waiting to be put to work. In this way the cult of self takes on social proportions that it did not have in *Nadja*. Group dynamics can proceed only from individual dynamics; mediocre men, despite any general ideas of a more perfect society, can produce only a mediocre collectivity; the sum of the parts is not able to form a dimension different from those parts. From his forest of analogies Breton points an accusing finger at the Marxist ideology with which he had become involved but toward which he felt great misgivings. The bifurcation in his own life, which *Les Vases communicants* represents, is parallel with the conflict in his political thought. Ever adamant against the older order, he sees in the new one the reflection of the same mistakes. Most of all, he fears that in focusing the rebellion on the social condition, the individual may lose sight of the greater cause for rebellion, which resides in the precarious character of the human condition. As he had put surrealism at the "service of the revolution" in the second periodical, which succeeded *La Révolution surréaliste*, he places the dream as an unalienable right of man, "at the service of the Revolution," with revolution taken in the broadest sense. In a reversal of narcissism that reduces to individual dimensions the problems of man in general, Breton's movement is outward, proceeding from the individual problem to the collective one, the personal sensitivity translated in terms of its importance to the understanding of the collective conscience. Not that he has no sense of his own position as part of an "elite." He admits quite candidly the difficulty of adjusting to normal life when one has harbored for so long notions of one's higher wisdom. But he resolves the dilemma to a degree in his definition of the elite in terms not of higher intelligence or higher social rank, but simply of a higher degree of awareness of the problems of humanity: "the role is to preserve what might otherwise in some corner of a hothouse perish, so that it may find its place much later at the center of a new order of things."

As for his own personal problems, he seeks solution to them in nature's latent power to substitute for the things we have lost; he tries to capture all possible coincidences in the transient glances of the women of Paris, although to the end of the work the connection between himself and a new feminine face does not occur.

The last analogy, however, is one of hope in the life to be lived, in a turning away from the life that has been lived. One of Breton's most frequent expressions is "until further notice" or "a day will come," a projection of the dream into future events. The image is of Paris, which has shed the purely decorative character of the early part of the book and taken on its oracular role: here it is viewed in the context of dawn, the victory of awakening over night and sleep. His favorite hour is dawn, when human sensibility awakens, replenished by the forces of the subconscious, the magic warehouse of possibilities. Man's imagination, his sense of un-equivocal freedom, has its moment of gratuitous existence before it is engulfed in the routine tasks that society demands of the individual. Paris at dawn is like a woman rising out of a nocturnal embrace, her beauty the more devastating as well as the more innocent because it is uncommitted, because it harbors the image of potential, the power of direction when the object is yet undetermined: "without immediate destination, without her awareness of any destination, an unheard-of flower made of all its distinct parts in a bed that can aspire to the dimensions of the earth." The image of Paris as a woman available to all-encompassing love is extended in the analogy with the poet as a particular directing his embrace to the world as a whole. *Les Vases communicants* ends in a hymn to life's potentials as, extending the analogy, Breton views Paris, with its "monstrous reserves of beauty, youth and vigor," as "a woman who rises before dawn, and in whose tresses the last star has visibly descended, who comes out of a dark house and somnambulistically makes the fountains sing" in the morning sun.

In *Nadja* and *Les Vases communicants*, Breton demonstrated the pow-ers of the irrational and the dream as forces in the rearming of the indi-vidual, in transforming society, in renewing the arts, while he experimented with these same forces in the solution of his personal problems. In *L'Am-our fou* he resorts more fully to the intervention of chance in the shaping of human destiny. Here he takes a more sophisticated view of aleatory movement, although the same theme is very evident in the previous vol-umes. There it is held in abeyance in relation to the other two phenomena of dream and derangement; now in the third volume it is given full rein in the explorations of subjectivity.

Just as in *Les Vases communicants* Breton attacks idealism and its im-pact not only on human behavior but on the arts, in *L'Amour fou* he has the same open attitude toward objective chance and the same reversal in relation to Symbolist ideology as in his attitude toward dreams. Where Maeterlinck, Verlaine, Novalis, Hofmannsthal, and Villiers-de l'Isle Adam saw the dream as the refuge from reality, Breton sees it as a provocation of reality, a transformer, a metaphysical agent at the heart of physical reality. The end-of-the-century artists had taken a negative attitude toward aleatory phenomena. In Maeterlinck's plays this is particularly dramatic in the action of the elements upon human destiny: occult forces, albeit physical, which crush the human will, which put an infinite number of obstacles in the way of the realization of human desires. In *Un Coup de dés jamais n'abolira le hasard*, Mallarmé takes a defeatist attitude in the battle between man's feeble casting of the die—the human necessity—and the intransigent laws of chance. The image of shipwreck, characteristic of man's defeat, with only faint hope, is expressed in the "supreme conjunction with probability" as man casts the dice in terms of a thought flung upon the seas: taking the chance that the bottle will arrive at some shore is a gallant option on the benevolence of the laws of probability; but if Mallarmé's confidence in Providence was no greater than the surrealists', his atheism had a melancholy character, and so differs from Breton's, particularly as evidenced in *L'Amour fou*.

Whether the forces of physical necessity are benevolent or malevolent, is of no concern to Breton, for as in so many of the instances benevolence or malevolence depends on the uses to which man puts his opportunities for capturing the coincidences with human necessities or desires.

In keeping with Breton's inclination for laboratory investigation, with his supreme effort to force the doors of chance in the recapture of love, once won but lost, he had circulated questionnaires among the surrealist group asking "What was the major encounter of your life?" In his personal scale of values love is the most consequential of the products of the chance phenomenon. Love in Breton's concept is, as we have seen, love at first sight, not a growing sympathy—were it that, Nadja would have triumphed—but rather the *coup de foudre*, the sign, as blazing as a Magda lamp, sweeping, total, second only to the two other convulsive events over which one's personal human necessity has no power: birth and death. The coincidence is particularly hazardous and miraculous since in its essential character of reciprocity it is dependent on the junction of the objective power with the concordance, unpremeditated, of two human desires and the correspondence of their distinct aleatory movements. The law of probability has certainly been stretched beyond even the chance of the bottle of desire reaching a shore; it is rather the chance of two bottles, tossed by the same arbitrary movement of sea and wind, reaching each other.

The powerful imagination of Breton rereads the legend of Cinderella as an enigma revealing the miracle of the love chance: the slipper of desire, the foot receptive to desire, and the fairy godmother, objective chance, benevolent only in retrospect; for the whole thing might have ended in frustration, in which case the plight of the prince and the household drudge would have been worse than if they had never had the dream of the metamorphosis of their individual drab solitudes into a fusion of love.

Breton's years of movements through Paris had taught him that there is preparation, in terms of availability to love, which is an exercise of liberty; even as the right to dream, so there is a preparation for the capture of chance and its appropriation to our personal needs. The second part of *Les Vases communicants* is such a preparation if taken as an exercise in the new metaphysics, rather than as a series of open flirtations with street girls and passers-by. The training of the eye to capture the sources of erotic magnetism is followed up in *L'Amour fou* by the exploration of objects, no longer for what indices they might provide in the labyrinth of confusion; this time the responsibility has been shifted to the explorer: the unexpected, irrational uses he may make of the object, or the arbitrary functions he may attribute to it. One might argue that he has in fact made a *volte-face*; that whereas earlier he had rejected symbolization in favor of deciphering, he has reverted to attributing symbolic character to the inanimate. But with this difference: that the symbolization is subjective and open, the object is used not as a generalization but as a particularization, the mirror is held up to his own psyche.

In a curiosity shop Breton and his friend Giacometti find the emblem-objects necessary for their immediate desire, the substitute image for a previous default—in the case of Giacometti, the face of a statue he could not complete and the chance meeting with a mask which electrifies his creative powers to complete the work. The fortuitously discovered mask has no significance for good or evil in itself, acting as agent between the subjective image and its substantiation. In the case of Breton, he had for some time been haunted by an automatic phrase with which he had awakened one morning: "the ashtray of Cinderella" (more euphonic and therefore more hypnotic in French: *cendrier de Cendrillon*)—"bewitchingly evocative," as Baudelaire would have said. Among the many curiosities in the shop, Breton suddenly encounters a spoon, which his psyche transforms into an ash tray, which in turn opens up a larger symbolization: that of shoe, Cinderella's slipper. And in a flash, which is involuntary association pooled from the deepest wells of the subconscious, the object has retractive meaning even as do the images of a dream; the obsession created by the object engages his whole sexual apparatus. The fixation on the object transforms it into an erotic device: "slipper-spoon-penis-perfect mold for this penis." [15] The erotic desire in its condensation had made him utter *"le cendrier de Cendrillon,"* and had impelled him to crystallize desire into emblem: the spoon-shoe-slipper, that is, the search for the foot that fits, takes the proportions of a poetic analogy. And in a flash he has a deeper insight into the intensity of his desire and into the meaning that the legend held hidden from him, undeciphered but decipherable. The urgency of the love desire is reinforced by the testimony of a friend, Joe Bousquet, that the mask represents death; whereupon Breton concludes that there has occurred a polarization between the death-wish and the love-wish. Had he not himself predicted in *Les Vases communicants* the catalyzing role of objects? It is not surprising that soon thereafter there appears on his path a "scandalously beautiful" woman, whose smile reminds him "of a squirrel holding a green hazelnut." (In fact, Jacqueline Lamba's eyes are the color of hazel; she is small and delicate, agile and lithe as a squirrel.) The association is involuntary in its immediacy, in its spontaneity: *verre-vair-dos d'écureuil* (glass, fur, squirrel, fur of squirrel out of which the slipper is made); the slipper fits the foot. "To love, to recapture the lost state of grace of the first movement of love."

And the title becomes clear in the moment of exaltation. It is not in its pejorative, adolescent sense, but in the meaning given by Dr. Janet in his treatise *From Anguish to Ecstasy:* a physical transformation, totally overpowering, not unlike the religious postures of mystics. The mysticism of the flesh—Breton will not be abashed to mention it as the ultimate result of the sacralization of the universe: "I have never ceased to make one of the flesh of the woman I love and the snow on the summits in the rising sun." If poetry is all enigma, as Mallarmé thought, it becomes part of life, a vital part that can make life a little less futile, as Breton's journey in quest of love reveals. The enigma can open its doors and light the path of man. The capacity to love is part of the total irrational understanding of things and being, the openness to the convulsive power of beauty.

The light that illuminates the life of the poet in the last pages of the book is Aube, the daughter whose birth, exactly when desired, is the triumph of human desire over chance. Earlier in *Les Vases communicants,* Breton's steps unconsciously lead him to the door of a maternity clinic, and suddenly he realizes that the desire beyond desire is survival in a child. The quest for the unique love, if precarious even in its moment of triumph, had been announced to him in the psychic forces that had generated the automatic poem of *Clair de terre* in 1923: "Tournesol." In 1934 as Breton takes a nocturnal walk through the flower market in Les Halles, that former farm in the middle of Paris whose "windows opened on the Milky Way," he knows the realization of the enigma.

But if the matching of the foot to the slipper is the reality of myth in accordance with the mechanisms of objective chance, "they lived happily ever after" is the fiction perpetuated by the fantastic world of idealism, against which these three volumes are a prolonged protest. The only triumph over objective chance, and the only certitude of the link between desire and exterior phenomenon, is the birth of his daughter, whom he called Aube after a gouache of Victor Hugo that he had long admired. No poem Breton has ever written has the power and the passion, the intensity of love untainted by anything exterior to itself, as his letter to his daughter, written as he sat at the side of her cradle and watched her in wonder.

To Aube, Breton justifies his pursuits, which he knows will seem futile in the context of wordly occupations and concerns. The final and composite image that absorbs all the other images is one he had derived from Hegel in his earliest youth: the abolition of the antinomies. The dangers that life presented in the ten years between *Nadja* and *L'Amour fou* were indeed challenges to the concept of the moral victory that results from the attainment of the sense of unity of life and its conflicts. He tells Aube of the supreme peak to which he has aspired; and again, it is in terms of physical realities that he envisages it and not in abstract, idealist terms. He has measured the passage of the dream into reality, he has sought communication between the rational and the irrational, he has served as buffer to the conflict between a gratuitous world and the personal castles each man builds on the shifting sands of his personal desires. He has aspired to relay the knowledge he has grasped of his own psyche to a collective plane of action: what he terms the power of giving sight—*donner à voir.* Always remembering the limitations of the condition of man, he has battled against what he considers the mortal enemy of mental health and the obstacle to man's adjustment to his destiny: idealism, which at its best leads to inaction, at its worse to suicide.

The legacy he wishes to pass to his daughter spells his particular way of defining success and triumph in this world; idealists might call it "spiritual," but Breton, the furious realist, terms it his "nonslavery to life" and his commitment to love, both very earthly experiences. Liberty, love, and the means by which they can be conveyed—poetry—are the arms with which he will combat the waves of despair to which he, like all mortal men, is subject.

> Against everything I shall have maintained that *always* is the great key. What I have loved, whether I was able to preserve it or not, I shall love always. As you too will be called upon to suffer in time to come, I wanted to explain this to you in finishing my book. I spoke of a "sublime point" on the mountain. I never expected to make of it my abode. Besides it would have stopped being "sublime" and I would have ceased to be a man. Unreasonable as it was to expect to reach it, at least I never lost sight of it. I had chosen to be the guide, I had consequently willed never to become unworthy of the power which,

in the direction of eternal love, had made me *see* and granted me the privilege, even more rare, *of making others see*.

The truest identity of man is not with the things he leaves behind but with what he projects into a future reality. In terms of Breton's trilogy which started with an interrogation: "Who am I?", the answer lies in the crystallizations of love; he can find identity only in terms of those he loves. Thus the heritage he leaves for Aube is one that she will be in a position to receive when she is sixteen—that is, at an age when she too can look forward to love. For the father conveys to the daughter not the things he has left behind but the power of love, the desire that may become reality.

IX

BRETON
THE POET

"Les comètes s'appuieront tendrement aux forêts avant de les foudroyer"
—*Le Revolver à cheveux blancs*

Some of the most enthusiastic admirers of André Breton the man and André Breton the writer have remarked with unveiled regret that he was not a poet but rather an author who wrote poetically in prose; they have judged him on the basis of the old harmony and found him wanting, equating a refusal with a default. But in making these reservations about his poetry they have unwittingly demolished what is essential in Breton.[1] For his entire comportment in life, his notion of the uses and powers of language, his vision of the universe as it related to the world, and of the relation of the world to himself, the intensity with which he faced life and the lyricism with which he expressed his love experiences—all these reveal him as a poet; it is primarily as a poet that he will be eventually identified, even as Apollinaire addressed him in his very first letter.

Although from the beginning of the nineteenth century, French poets and critics had called for a radical renewal of the process of versification and for a new lyricism, it was Breton in the third and fourth decades of the twentieth century who transformed not only the concept of poet (this process had been started by others before him—Rimbaud, Lautréamont, Mallarmé) but also the structure of poetic language, which was then not quite grasped by the critics of his own country and has not been generally understood by foreign poets or by those who do not read French: just as the simple purity of Racine disappears in translation, so the severe baroque music of Breton is totally lost in the process of transmission into a foreign language. Even more extraordinary, his own compatriots seem scarcely aware that the change that they had been expecting for over a hundred years—heralded by Victor Hugo's *Les Djinns,* Paul Verlaine's *L'Art poétique,* and Rimbaud's famous letter—came finally with Breton.

The need for renewal of the patterns of poetry was felt by Baudelaire and Rimbaud, but they expressed it in *ars poetica,* not in actual practice. When a poet felt that verse had become too confined, as did Lautréamont, he simply expressed himself in prose and called the product a "prose poem." The Symbolists, instrumentalizing poetry, took a technical attitude toward poetic renewal and played with sounds and imitated musical patterns. Mallarmé, in a last moment, really broke with traditional verse, after having written a long number of sonnets; he created a graphic partita in "Un Coup de dés jamais n'abolira le hasard" as his manifestation of the new "orphic" poetry. Apollinaire wrote free verse, as did Reverdy, but for them, as for many of the surrealists, the absence of regularity and of rhyme are often compensated by assonance and other mnemonic devices that have evocative effects and bespeak a poetic ideal of image through sound. It is inconceivable that when music has changed its harmony so drastically, a composer of today should write like Mozart, but we accept Valéry's alexandrines in the 1920's and, more amazing, Aragon's in 1940. When certain modern poets shy away from rhyme, their refusal is of negative value, for in breaking down versification they have replaced it with no new pattern.

In Breton's verse, from the earliest *Clair de terre* to the *Ode à Charles Fourier,* there is a virtual absence of rhyme. If it were a conscious effort to evade, surely occasional rhymes would have slipped into the free verse, as they do in Apollinaire, in Reverdy, and in most of the other surrealists of Breton's generation. In Breton's verse even unconscious rhyme becomes rare; his ear does not hear it that way. In his article "Les Mots sans Rides" ("Words without Wrinkles"), he had discussed the importance of utilizing new words and new associations of words as well as old words in their etymological sense, much like the language of the hermetic cabala, which went to primitive Greek for its meanings, interchangeable, flexible, and sometimes reversible. In the First Manifesto, Breton lists the various types of imagery utilized by surrealist poets in the effort to grasp new relationships between disparate realities. But nowhere does he discuss poets and their uses of the poetic structure; when he talks of them, he discusses *content* and their philosophical orientation, even as in his art criticism it is metaphysical approach that interests him rather than specific techniques. It could, therefore, be inferred that the changes he produces in his own verse are not owing to *a priori* theories but are an integral part of his concept of art, reflected in his poems as in his "prose."

Breton's notion of language is closely akin to that of present-day structuralists. If, as he believes, "The speed of thought is not greater than that of speech," then language is the concrete realization of thought, the objectification of the subjective, which emanates as a block.[2] And if his rebellion has not turned into action, it arrives at its "reality" through the Word. Style is not a contrived process, an envelope attractively wrapped around an idea or an image. Each poetic image is born with its linguistic trapping, and the connection between one image and the next has the condensed quality that he found in his study of dreams. This eliminates immediately all the extra words that make for visual or auditory appeal. The fact that Breton's poetry does not flow gently does not mean that it is not good poetry, just as Richard Strauss's music, which has its own sonority and tonal pattern, does not depend for its value on comparison with harmonic standards of a past era. In fact, one needs a revision of critical lexicon to be able to speak of Breton's poetry.

First of all, Breton has thrown away the entire vocabulary of poetry and created a new one. His words are harsh, unpoetic, because many of them have never been pronounced orally; they are part of a silent, very precise, particularized vocabulary that is in the passive-recognition level of most French readers and not in normal literary usage. A scientific man, widely read in diverse materials, he uses as poetic language the terminology of the biologist, the geologist, the physicist, the botanist. His images are thus plunged deep into reality even as the magician's in contrast with the mystic's. In showing the distinction, Eliphas Lévi said that "the sphere of material experience is that of his knowledge." Breton replenished the exhausted metaphoric scale of the French poet. There are enough new poetic metaphors in Breton's poetry to last for the next two centuries. The poetic advantage of his erudite vocabulary [3] is that no traditional and worn-out images are associated with this fresh set of nouns. Whereas Mallarmé thought that the bouquet suggesting the absence of any particular flower was more widely evocative than a concrete description of an individual flower, Breton proceeds from the opposite position that the designating, nondescribed noun, pertaining to a rare generic category, not of species, but of subspecies, has a wider and freer range of association in its concreteness and freedom from previous poetic use.

It is a poetry that is hard on the eyes because of its harsh, most irregular disposition on the page. It is longwinded, crowded, with sudden breaks in the concussion of words one on the other, like a crack in a wall that lets the light suddenly flow in. It doesn't sing, but it echoes image upon image as the organ emits in its rich chords, sound upon sound. Each image contains not one possible connection of realities, but many on various levels. It is hermetic but strictly syntactical, leaving doors ajar for multiple interpretations. When you read Breton, you wander through a Gothic, primeval forest filled with trails, all leading to a certain burst of light. His imagery is constructed with the intricacy of a labyrinth, new chambers are revealed with every rereading, and new difficulties of meaning. As he calls life a cryptogram, so is his poetry. The images appear spontaneous, and yet it is clear that their relation to each other has been lengthily considered and highly contrived. As in the hermetic literature of the Middle Ages, which he emulated, Breton eliminates from his work the pleasurable, extraneously ornate element. His language is severe and mighty, full of archaic verb structures, particularly dramatized by his frequent use of imperfect and pluperfect subjunctives. What Fulcanelli, whom Breton admired, has said of hermetic literature can well characterize the poetry of Breton: "This literature has to a greater degree exercised the mind than served it." [4] In what way does it exercise the human mind? Breton identifies his fundamental poetic meaning with that of the hermetics of the fourteenth and fifteenth centuries. "What is the essence of this invisible and mysterious dynamism which animates substance?" [5] Each word has its secrets, self-contained, and each image its built-in philosophy. The purpose of art as conceived by the hermetics was not far from Breton's objective: "From obscure chaos, he makes light ooze after having reassembled it, and this light shines henceforth in the darkness as a star in the nocturnal sky." [6] The star is the North Star, which is Breton's guiding star in all the various darknesses of existence, the star he wanted to carry as his emblem on his tombstone instead of the traditional cross. There are constant references throughout his poetry to the northern lights. Another appellation of the star of bright light is "brilliant," which is a bridge between the emanation of light and its reception (crystallization of stone into diamond or other shining stone).

This is one of the many instances of the rebus, the cabalistic device much utilized in Breton's poetry; the multiple images are contained in the semantic variations of the word itself. This is not the kind of symbolism that calls for multiple subjective interpretations, as does Symbolist poetry, but it is symbolism of the Word itself, in the alchemic use of language. The words or the objects they designate have a multiplicity of meanings, each a chameleon, its range a spectrum of realities available if you look hard, if you have the mental orientation appropriate for cabalistic vision.

Cabala itself has many meanings, and as Fulcanelli points out hermetic cabala must be distinguished from Hebraic cabala. The latter is a device for the interpretation of the Bible. Hermetic cabala predates all organized religions in its interpretations of the universe. Its intricate hieroglyphics, based on the potential of sound similarities and visual approximations, are as close to a universal language as can be conceived short of the language of the birds or the sign language of the deaf. It came into French tradition through three sources: Mediterranean (the Hebraic influence), Hispanic (Arab), and Oriental (Byzantine). It has left its mark on the sculptures and engravings of many monuments of the latter part of the Middle Ages and is implicit in the *Roman de la rose*—the part attributed to Jean de Meung—in the code of chivalry, which is a variation of the cabala, and in the closed societies of the Templars and the Freemasons. If Eliphas Lévi, Fulcanelli, and others in their interpretation of these emblems and codes relate them directly to Christianity, they admit all the while that much of their foundation is pre-Christian, even pre-Judaic. Thus for Breton, as a heretic opposed to closed religions, it became possible to get involved in the entire gamut of hermeticism and to see in monuments that represent the Christian culture of France the hidden divinity of man in his nonpositivist attitude toward the movements of the universe. As in the case of hypnotism, spiritualism, psychiatry, and dialectical materialism—all channels for Breton's monologue with the world—it is not the end result or the objective of each of these activities that he seeks, but the *processus* of the mind involved in them. In the case of hermeticism he could read the books of the devout Fulcanelli and utilize the symbols that in their original sense supersede Christianity and fall into a common pool of myth identifiable with the natural mysteries of the world. If one removed the references to God and His Providence from the allegory, everything else was acceptable to Breton and provided him with a rich and formidable scale of poetic metaphors. As he says in *Les Champs magnétiques*, meanings beckon to him from every stone in Paris; in "Epervier incassable" he puts it in the form of an image of substitution: "There is a message instead of a lizard under each stone." [7]

Before delving into the specifically hermetic meanings of the poems from *Clair de terre* to *L'Air de l'eau*, which cover the period we have determined in relation to Breton's activities, it is well to specify the aspect of the cabala he embraces. There are the Open Book and the Closed Book. The Closed Book is supposed to contain those mysteries never to be revealed to man—that is, total mystification; whereas the Open Book is the realm of the marvelous or of revelation.

Hermeticism was not the private property of André Breton. The entire nineteenth century had been drawn to occultism. But most people were oriented toward the Closed Book. This is implicit in the closed imagery of Gerard de Nerval, whom Breton evokes frequently as a kindred soul, but whose efforts to bridge the gap were marked with reverence for the forbidden. It is equally closed and subjective in Mallarmé's cryptic verse.

The veil as in Novalis' image of Isis trembles but remains. When Rimbaud talked of the alchemy of the Word, he saw the power of words as effective agents of transmutation, but he relinquished poetry too soon to do more than point to the possible illumination. Baudelaire talked of the "evocative bewitchment" of words and wrote an equivocal poem "Correspondances," which starts as an interpretation of Swedenborg and proceeds to something closer to the sensual objective revelation of the universe inherent much later in Breton's poetry.

But too often and too carelessly the two outlooks are taken as a single manifestation of mysticism, and their reflection in poetry as a continuous chain in the history of poetics. They are, rather, opposite faces of the poetic coin. Correspondences imply a dualistic concept of the universe. During our sojourn here on earth certain emblems of nature give intimations of another plane of existence, and as we saunter along the pathways of our forest we recognize signs of a possible transcendence. In becoming more and more astute, the living creature comes closer and closer to this transcendence. Life, thus considered, consists of progressive steps rising ever higher toward a rarefied atmosphere. This transcendence was achieved through a moral purification by many of the romanticists, or by virtue of a sharpening of the senses and an ultimate synesthesia as with the Symbolists. Hence, among the symbols of ascendance used to convey a poetic vision based on a dualistic philosophy are the ladder, the wing, and the chain of Victor Hugo and the octave of Paul Claudel. What Rimbaud proposes, what Raymond Roussel does in a rather literally hermetic sense, and what Breton translates into a new set of poetic images, are based on a monistic view of the universe, in which essence and substance become one, the material entity provokes ecstasy not through a rising motion but through rotation and metamorphosis. The universe is not an octave but, as André Breton suggests, "a great circuit." The poet's mission is not to discover the signs that are the reflections of another world, not to interpret these subjectively, but to recognize the indices and lift the veils that obscure the way in the labyrinth or cryptogram of earthly existence. "We view the unbelievable and we believe in it in spite of ourselves . . ." (as he says in "Le Soleil en laisse," *Poèmes*). As Éliphas Lévi pointed out, and Breton paraphrased in many instances, mystery is not an *end* to be cultivated in itself but a *state of revelation*. Poetry must be apocalyptic, first as it reveals man to himself, and by repercussion as it becomes revealing to others, "In the obscure and terrestial signalization." [8] One of the primary reasons for confusion of two such divergent poetic outlooks is that the power of metamorphosis is as dependent as that of transcendence upon the keenness of the senses and, through the senses, on the power of imagery. The means are similar; the goals are quite different.

In the world of correspondences intuitive memory recalls previous existence to aid in the comprehension of the spiritual meaning of things. On the contrary, Breton considers memory an obstacle in the way of transformation. Memory can keep us in a static state, while forgetting facilitates the passage to new experience and even to new existence. Imagination reverts in his thinking to its original meaning—the act of creating images and making dreams become reality. "The imaginary is what tends to become real," as he says in "Il y aura une fois." It is the key with which man may attain whatever degree of liberty is possible here on earth. "The bars are inside the cage" as he says in "Les Attitudes Spectrales." [9] Where earlier poets sought liberty through disfiguration and abstraction, Breton uses transfiguration of life, expressed by hermetic symbols that contain the rebus nature of self-transformation. Absent from his poetry, on the other hand, are descriptive statement, symbolic interpretation, reminiscences, and confessionals.

Although his poetry is not objective but highly lyrical, the subjective experience from which it derives is constantly transferred to a universal level, the ego becomes the collective self, the personal vision provokes what he calls in *L'Amour fou* "the privilege of giving the power of sight."

Poet, magician, druid, as he has been called, it is "druid" that is particularly apt for it denotes both priest and oak tree, suggesting the mysticism of the earth. We have the movements of the imperceptible, as of plants and metals, the sounds of silences like: "This woman passes imperceptibly in the sound of the flowers" and "And the world dies a break happens in the rings of air." [10] The lights in the darknesses are suggested by *brèches* (cracks), stars in the dark sky, gleaming stones in the abyss. Light conceived as a sudden penetration in the darkness: "The seasons luminous like the interior of an apple from which a section has been cut out." [11]

Like that of the hermetic magicians Breton's universe is controlled by the four major elements: earth, air, fire, and water. The unions of these elements are indices of the unity and fusion which he is seeking with the universe, and of which love—physical fusion producing spiritual states—is the highest indication. As with the hermetics, the four elements are identified in his poetry with male and female, and these contacts of the elements correspond to male-female polarizations. *Clair de terre* suggests the metaphysics of space, the fantastic vision of seeing the earth as a moon from a point removed from the earth—quite acceptable in the era of astronauts and space travel, but visionary in 1923 (the imaginary indeed becomes real). There is a polarization of fire-male and earth-female, as in the later collection of love poems to Jacqueline, *L'Air de l'eau*, which represents the sexual polarization air-male, water-female, and the notion of *l'un*

dans l'autre which makes most of Breton's *de* prepositions signify *dans.*
The third title of these early collections of poems is more complicated:
Le Revolver à cheveux blancs. It could easily be dismissed as a marvelously
successful case of automatic writing, and it may indeed have come to Breton spontaneously. On the other hand, his friends mention that he chose
his titles very carefully and significantly. *Revolver* could refer to the pure
surrealist act mentioned in the Second Manifesto—the act of intense protest. *Cheveux blancs* could refer to the White Work in the evolution of
the Great Work. The emblem of the White Work was the crescent moon,
and its light was likened in its shimmering to white hair; the "white" stage
of the Great Work represented the work of youth, imperfect but more
available than the subsequent phases of the Great Work. Thus in a sense,
Breton's title could be said to combine protest and magic, and the half-
open door of revelation. In fact, the reader, coming face to face with these
poems, the largest of all the collections, can expect not total comprehension but partial recognition of Breton's meaning: the provocation of imagination and sensuality, and a suggestion of the personality of an unusual
man. In his own analysis of Raymond Roussel's hermeticism Breton says:
"Whether one likes it or not, this half-deceptive, half-engaging attitude is
rigorously conforming with that of the hermetic philosophers. . . . All
occult literature teaches that this secret is not forever hidden." [12] Rather
than give the reader what could be only a subjective and therefore arbitrary interpretation, I shall attempt to single out some of the emblems,
their scope, and throw light on the composition of the poems.

Various devices are used to suggest the metamorphosis latent in the
imagery. First of all, the distinct divisions separating animal, vegetable,
and mineral worlds are broken down, and a fluid passage occurs from one
to the other as the barriers are dissolved. "The smoker puts the last touch
to his work he seeks unity between himself and the landscape." [13] "The
seasons raise knot by knot their net shining with the live water of my
eyes." [14] The unity is strikingly expressed in the image: "A musician is
caught in the strings of his instrument." [15] A parallel of this mingling of
the three kingdoms occurs often in the paintings of Breton's artist friend,
Max Ernst. The physical elements, such as sun, wind, air, and water, act
as conjunctions between these various forms of existence. The most important among the key expressions on which the alchemy centers are all
the words that suggest fire, for it is indeed the most basic agent of transformation. Heat, high flame, lightning, burning coals are some of the
variations. Light in its various forms, such as flares, lanterns, beacons, astral
illuminations, as well, of course, as the sun, are variations of the fire image.
"The sand is nothing but a phosphorescent clock." [16] Fire and its wide

range of designations has the hermetic function in Breton's poetry described by Fulcanelli: the fire in the world outside is prolonged into the fire in us, making us aware of what the alchemist calls our "ignited nature"; [17] and Breton: "Flame of water lead me to the sea of fire." [18]

The other important image is that of water in all its variations, with rain as an almost divine manifestation; we have already noted this in *Poisson soluble*. Fountain is another image nucleus, with hermetic implications as it means source and the mysteries of creation. If fire transforms, water illuminates in turning the opaque into something translucent and transparent. Ice, mirror, glass, and crystal are substances resulting from transformation in which fire and water play a role. (In view of the innumerable examples of crystal images, Breton may have derived his love of crystal from his father who was at one time a glassblower.) In the hermetic sense "translucent" is another way of saying "spiritual." To quote Eliphas Lévi: "spiritual and corporal are simply terms which express the degree of tenuity or density in substance." [19] The adept reaches the translucent while the crowd lives in opacity. When the imagery of Breton assumes a translucent character, he is indicating its "spiritual" or "pure" nature.

In the world of correspondences the simile most faithfully translated the parallel between the material and its spiritual counterpart. Quite to the contrary, Breton tells us that *comme* does not mean "such as." Things and beings are not *like* other qualities or states; through the alchemy of the Word they *become* something else, and the metaphor through which they are transformed draws them not from parallel spheres but from forms that are logically unrelated. The analogy in the hermetic sense in which Breton views it is not a correspondence but is reached through an acceptance of the antinomies. To quote Eliphas Lévi: "harmony consists of equilibrium, and equilibrium subsists by the analogy of contraries." [20] Analogy as the evidence of the unity of all things is also "the sole possible mediator between the finite and the infinite." [21] The search for analogies, where most eyes see irrelevance and absurd connections, is Breton's adherence to the hermetic ideal: "Analogy yields all forces of Nature to the Magus; analogy is the quintessence of the Philosopher's Stone, the secret of perpetual motion—the key to the Great Arcanum." [22] Breton, like the Magus, aspires through his poetry to the "overcoming of the antinomies." It is a mystical dialectic parallel to the social one Breton espoused through reading Hegel.

For André Breton the same life element penetrates all the ramifications of form, without overflowing into the supernatural. The state of mutation and fusion is produced by the sharpening and integration of the senses and the images they conjure up. Breton alerts the senses with a beacon light, to borrow his metaphor, and plays on all of them. One image flows into another, or several images are produced simultaneously: a subterranean passage unites all perfume, colors are diffused, sounds often are undetectable by human ears, their muted rhythms perceptible only to touch. A cluster of these can be gleaned in Le Revolver:

> Les journaux du matin apportent des chanteuses dont la voix
>   a la couleur du sable sur des rivages tendres et dangereux

> (The morning newspapers bring singers
>   whose voice has the color of sand on tender and dangerous shores)

> . . . des mains plus blanches que la corne des étoiles à midi

> (Hands whiter than the horns of stars at noon)

"Les Ecrits s'en vont"

Les réverbères mouillés bruissent encadrés d'une nuée d'yeux bleus

(The street lamps, moist, make sound, framed in the nebulae of blue eyes)

"Le Sphynx vertébral"

> L'air de la chambre est bleu comme des baguettes de tambour.

> (The air in the room is blue like drumsticks.)

"Le Verbe Etre"

The result is a universal conciliation which even touches such concepts as presence and absence, maneuvering a complicity. The primary quality of life becomes the awareness of the inner rhythm produced by the unrelenting molding of forms. The wider the radius of recognition of the interrelation, the more intense the life experience. And death is simply the prolongation of the radius beyond comprehensive limits. The process can also be reversed whereby resurrection may occur on a purely material basis. The poet's work thus envisaged is in a constant state of flux, producing unexpected transfigurations as they pertain to all the principal meditations of man: life, love, time, death, destiny, and social concern.

Life is ubiquitous and unconstrained. It is dynamic and ever in transition, leaving its imprints in the same places as death; it is tangent to death rather than its antithesis. Form is a variable of life and not a determining factor. Life is an ever-restless aspiration toward transformation, which can make the earth more translucent than water and let the metal ooze out of its shell. Such are the generalizations one can derive from the galaxy of images expressed by the brisk verbs suggesting change—such as "cutting," "escaping," "throwing," "flying," "digging," "overthrowing"—or those that express penetration, diffusion, radiation, seepage, flow, and all the fluids ranging from the blood of man to the sap of the tree. Words like *cosse*, *cogne*, *écorce* suggest the soluble confines that the life force is constantly breaking through. To produce a powerful metaphor the long arms of the analogy do not merely touch but bear one on the other, and the inter-action is expressed by the skillful manipulation of the verb at the center of the image. This constant *becoming* rather than static *being* makes vitality the primary poetic awareness.

Looking at particular poems, we can see how the early ones such as "André Derain," "Forêt-Noire," and "Pour Lafcadio" have the fragmented, collagelike automatism associated with Dada; and indeed they date from the *Mont de Piété* collection from 1919, the only year when Breton was truly functioning under the Dada influence.

In "Il n'y a pas à sortir de là," dedicated to Paul Eluard, Breton begins with "Liberty color of man" which was twenty years later to inspire Eluard's war poem on the multitudinous aspects of man's longing for liberty. But whereas Eluard's poem on liberty is circumstantial, Breton's liberty is nonspacial. It is all interior and contains in latent form most of the ingredients that become the mark of his later poetry: the seemingly disconnected vision, which in effect is one of subconscious associations; displacement of the stars, in expressions such as "rivers of stars," combin-ing the element of light and water; the images of eroticism of the "naked young girl" and her mingling with natural elements; the caprices of chance; and the notion of a hereafter produced by metamorphosis and crystallization.

A more hermetic and intriguing poem is "Au Regard des divinités" in which at each reading one can discover new meanings. A series of images transmits what Breton calls in the first page of *L'Amour fou* "states of perfect receptivity." In those same first pages he tells us that he often imagines in a stage setting a series of phantom figures bearing keys. "Au Regard des divinités" contains the first of this series of key bearers, "her-alds" of news brought to the poet. Another element of invocation is a sealed letter.* The *débarcadère* of the first line is the point of departure for his imagination:

Un peu avant minuit près du débarcadère

---

* "La lettre cachetée aux trois coins d'un poisson" becomes less mystifying when one sees the poem surrounded by the drawing of a fish in the private printing in Mme Collinet's collection. The fish is made to look like a triangle: the two sides of the head and the point of the tail make the three points of the seal.

The woman, as in all hermetic concepts, is the intermediary between the visible and the invisible:

> Si une femme échevelée te suit n'y prends pas garde.
> C'est l'azur.

And the third element, the vase, dispenses, according to the hieroglyphic meaning attached to it, the fire of the wise—that is, again the symbol of invocation. It is *in* the tree—that is, in nature:

> Il y aura un grand vase blond dans un arbre.

And just before midnight it is the thought of light and azure that haunts the poet. We have here the conciliation of antinomies: darkness and light. The image of the geyser combines in its movement the surge of water and plant (fern)—a marriage, a fusion of the movements of two different elements:

> . . . Le geyser brun qui lance au ciel les pousses de fougère
> Te salue.

The next part combines the erotic images of *la belle:* the cloud she creates, the work of the night, the dream, the illusions. The white fathers and the heralds are the obsessive image which reappears in *L'Amour fou:*

> Voici les Pères blancs qui reviennent de vêpres
> Avec l'immense clé pendue au-dessus d'eux.
> Voici les hérauts gris; enfin voici sa lettre
> Ou sa lèvre: mon coeur est un coucou pour Dieu.

The last stanza is a battle between time and eternity, a determination (*montre-bracelet*) on the finite level of the mystery of the night and of love and of the recognition of the unity of happenings. "Sur le pont à la même heure" gives the impression of the simultaneity of events. It is a pursuit of the secrets of the night, interchangeable as in a hermetic rebus:

> L'éternité recherche une montre-bracelet
> Un peu avant minuit près du débarcadère.

The words *pont* and *débarcadère* create the state of fluidity and fusion. The poem explains the power that night possesses to light the imagination, to arouse love, to bring the poet closer to the secrets of the universe.

There are less cryptic poems in *Clair de terre,* which give intimations of Breton's more affirmative attitude. "Plûtot la Vie" tells—in rational statements which, supported by automatic images, carry a certain unity of theme to the end—of his love of life despite its scars and betrayals and its waiting rooms that are only blind alleys, his choice of life over books, long life even if unfavorable, life of presence, "nothing but presence," mingled with the presence of woman.

Plutôt la vie que ces prismes sans épaisseur même si les couleurs sont plus
    pures. . . .

Plutôt la vie avec ses draps conjuratoires
Ses cicatrices d'évasions
Plutôt la vie plutôt cette rosace sur ma tombe
La vie de la présence rien que de la présence. . . .

Le soleil a beau n'être qu'une épave
Pour peu que le corps de la femme lui ressemble. . . .

La vie comme un passeport vierge. . . .

(Rather life than the depthless prisms even if their colors are more pure. . . .

Rather life with its conspiring paraphernalia
Its close-call scars
Rather life than that rose-window on my tomb
A life of presence nothing but presence. . . .

What if the sun is only flotsam
As long as it bears the semblance of a woman's form. . . .

Life like an unmarked passport. . . .)

                                         "Plutôt la vie"

"Mille et mille fois" contains perhaps the first images of Breton's love of woman and his association of the sexual experience with the most intimate states of receptivity of the forces and sensations of the earth. "I undid the sky like a marvelous bed"; the signals of love have mystic numbers, and the topography of love is parallel with that of the earth. Love is associated with the signal flares of the universe.

"Aigrette" is notable because in its title it brings into view a bird that appears to Breton particularly emblematic, with its resemblance to the sacred ibis and to the phoenix. The poem begins with a series of miracle images; again the miracle of the physical world—sun rising in the dark of night—with the miracle of love. The ermine, emblem of the abyss, of chaos, subject of meditation of the wise men, is confronted by a priest with blindfold. At the end of the poem of imponderables Breton plays on the word *mèche*—just as in a hermetic rebus—with its double meaning of hair and fire; and the digging of a tunnel under Paris which he wishes his train could enter, introduces the thought that he might make a breakthrough into the sacred mystery.

"Tournesol," which in *L'Amour fou* Breton himself identifies as his prophetic poem about his meeting with Jacqueline, was according to him a purely automatic poem at the time of its creation. In explicating the poem in terms of certain metaphors but without explaining the intention behind them, Breton gives the best example of the manner in which his poems might be interpreted. Unfortunately in the absence of such clues we can only conjecture about the other poems and, through the number of possibilities and the distance of the poles of his metaphors, suggest their provocative or illuminating power. Perhaps, indeed, the farm in the heart of Paris whose windows open upon the Milky Way is the more cosmic and phantasmagoric if we do not know that Breton was, as he revealed eleven years after writing of it, referring to the flower market set up at night in Les Halles in preparation for business in the morning. Again, as in the case of "Aigrette," *Tournesol*, the sunflower, is mystical in its radiative power and its sudden and solitary apparition, and in this case in its identification with the statue of the revolutionary fourteenth-century leader, Etienne Marcel: he, like the black eye of the sunflower, beckons to the poet.

> Je ne suis le jouet d'aucune puissance sensorielle
> Et pourtant le grillon qui chantait dans les cheveux de cendre
> Un soir près de la Statue d'Etienne Marcel
> M'a jeté un coup d'oeil d'intelligence
> André Breton a-t-il dit passe.

From "Au Regard des divinités" to "Tournesol" we have the sense of the aleatory movements of the young poet in Paris, a Paris of statues, but also not devoid of nature's vegetation, inert but not insensitive to the poet's heart teeming with desire. It is a perpetual wandering through forbidden zones.

The next poems, those that were written at the same time as *Nadja*, *Les Vases communicants*, and *L'Amour fou*, reveal the same preoccupation that dominates these books. Whereas Ronsard evoked the diversity of his loves, Breton, in a similar state of flux from wife to mistress and then to second wife, here as in other aspects of his vision seeks unity: the universal essence of woman over and above the miscellany, eventually crystallized as Elisa in *Arcane 17*.

The unique love changes in terms of the person it embodies but does not change face; it is linked with the phases of nature, expressed in terms of sun, plants, and sea, and the movements of the elements; not in terms of form, as has been done so often in love poetry before, but in terms of similarity of effects. The mystique of sexuality has rarely been captured so extensively and explored so deeply in modern poetry or so intensely expressed—"I have found the secret/of loving you/Always for the first time" (*L'Air de l'eau*)—thus turning what in someone else might seem a restless instability in love, into an uninterrupted identification.

Breton restores the role of Eros to poetry, and woman plays the same roles as nature itself: she is part of the unfathomable, magnetic, provocative, illuminating the world around him, a force, a metaphor of contradictory images which envigorates rather than appeases the senses. She is a product of miraculous chance, a medium through whom the poet grows closer to the unity he seeks between his inner world and objective reality, through whom he understands better the purity of the mountain snow, the soaring of the birds, and the convulsions of earthquakes. Love is power for Breton, and it is always power for good, as sin is never associated with sexuality. The story of Adam and Eve is an antiquated myth, and the act of love is on the contrary an evidence of the survival of the golden age as if Eve had never been tempted by the serpent, and she had enjoyed the apple. To Breton love does not consume itself; it is like his *débarcadère* leading to the sea, to the fertility of imagination, to the larger embrace of the universe; it is a state of grace attained, similar to a religious ecstasy enjoyed; but because it is not totally understood, it leaves him in a state of wonder and bewitchment. Love is always reciprocal in his poems, and therefore no element of self-pity or frustration is engendered. Though Breton had many disappointments in his love life, there are no "lost love" poems, only poems of the glory of love, as part of the glory of life itself.

His most famous love poem is "L'Union libre," written in 1931 when he was between marriages. If, as some of his friends have suggested, it refers to his mistress—cited as the X figure who left him, and whose absence sent him in *Les Vases communicants* into a compulsive search for love—the title would indicate the "free love" he had enjoyed with X. On the other hand, the poem could refer to the essence of woman, in a universalized sense, as indeed both Jacqueline and Elisa say that Breton told them it was. To Elisa, his third wife, he said that when he wrote "L'Union libre," he was as heart-free as he had ever been in his life, and that is why he could crystallize his notion of love, identifying it not with an abstract ideal of woman but making a synthesis of her power and her beauty. In the second context as the eternal Eve, *ma femme* has an intimacy and power of generalization that are impossible to translate into another language, and gives the title "L'Union libre" a much broader meaning as the free association of images indicates.

The form of the poem reminds one of the Song of Solomon or of the description of the body of the Alétheia of Marcos. The reader of the poem must remember Breton's concept of the analogy: the parts of the metaphor that seem so distant from each other actually lose their antinomy when we think of them from the point of view not of *form* but of *function*, which is the basis of the association. The poem does not present a photographic picture of the woman but conveys the power she exercises on the poet; the erotic force of woman in the generic sense, totally departicularized, is defined in expressions that give spiritual and physical values; or, in the hermetic sense, run from opaque to transparent, from water to fire, from weighty to ephemeral, and relate the loved one to a broad scope of natural phenomena: vegetation, animal and mineral life, even to the bowels of the earth. The poem created the anatomy of desire and its consummation. It illustrated Breton's contention that "beauty must be convulsive." For every image conveys a sense of movement.

Love is penetrating like water, moving like air, solid like earth, and hot like fire. Heat is expressed by the hair that relates to kindled wood, to lightning, to a hot slate roof, to amber; movements relate, in terms of her body, to an hourglass, to a mill, a torrent, to the regularity of a clock and the irregularity of despair. There are unusual images of humidity and thirst, and liquid that quenches the thirst. There is the suggestion of the insatiability of love: the mariners who must repair the ship in order not to let the water in, yet who cannot quench their own thirst. There are images of penetration, of secretion, of resistance; reference to an asbestos lamp which does not burn itself, but serves to ignite and give light. Finally there is allusion to the element of pain in the very grip of physical love: masculine force and feminine delicacy: attraction, captivity, escape, embrace, tension, and release of energy. The eyes are reserved for the last because their power is greatest; they are, as in the case of the occultists, the visible evidence of the ignited nature of the human organism. Here, as elsewhere, Breton is telling us that what attracts him most in a woman are the eyes, both in the mystery they project and in their illumination. They are related to the four elements all at once, and the metaphors with which he designates them are drawn from these four levels. Love is a magnetic process which draws the lovers into a conjugation with the varying forms of the earth. Instead of being raised above the material framework, here, on the contrary, they seem to become more entrenched in it, effecting an intimate communion with the earth. What is extraordinary is that with all the erotic precision of his vocabulary Breton manages to avoid the scatological generally associated with poems of this nature, and instead leaves an impression of purity.

To grasp some of the more obscure metaphors, one must recall that Breton detested the preposition *comme*, the usual linking word of the simile, and replaced it with *de*, which at the same time replaces the usual juxtaposition by the ancient alchemic notion of "one in the other," or the rebus. The power of the feminine is precisely for him the ability to provoke one image out of another. The expression "hair of kindling wood" really means that he sees the image of the kindling wood *in* her hair; the most powerful of the images have precisely this quality of passing beyond the barriers of analogy to a state of metamorphosis.

If we remove the *de* and remember the notion of "one in the other," we get in "L'Union libre" images such as these:

Ma femme à la taille de loutre entre les dents du tigre
Ma femme à la bouche de cocarde et de bouquet d'étoiles de dernière grandeur
Aux dents d'empreintes de souris blanche sur la terre blanche
A la langue d'ambre et de verre frottés
Ma femme à la langue d'hostie poignardée. . . .

Ma femme au cou de Val d'or
De rendez-vous dans le lit même du torrent. . . .

Ma femme aux yeux de bois toujours sous la hache
Aux yeux de niveau d'eau de niveau d'air de terre et de feu

(My wife whose waist is an otter between the tiger's teeth
Whose mouth is a cockade, a bouquet of stars of the largest magnitude
Whose teeth are the marks of a white mouse on white ground
Whose tongue is polished amber and glass
My wife whose tongue is a sword-slashed prey. . . .

My wife whose throat is the golden grape
The rendez-vous in the torrent's bed. . . .

My wife whose eyes are the woods always at the mercy of the axe
Whose eyes are the water level, and the level of air, of land, and of fire)

The last line gives us the key to the alchemic character of the poem in its enumeration of the four elements governing the universe of the al-

chemists and of the occult philosophies that had such a profound influence on Breton's own notions of life, love, and poetry.

In the collection of *L'Air de l'eau* there is a more subtle metamorphosis.
When the poet says "world in a kiss," it is not a new world but a fuller
possession and a more concrete apprehension of the already familiar one.
The loved one, in this case the miraculously encountered Jacqueline, like
a magnet draws to herself plants, insects, rocks, precious stones. On the
surface it is the theme utilized by both Baudelaire and Verlaine where
the beloved is compared to a beautiful landscape. But in the case of Breton, love is a transformer almost in the technical, mechanical sense of the
word. The loved one does not evoke but actually produces "the far-off
country," new suns, volcanoes steaming with snow. Jacqueline becomes
co-ordinated with all the pulses of physical nature and enters into the
fibers and the sap of the world around her.

Ta chair arrosée de l'envol de mille oiseaux de paradis
Est une haute flamme couchée dans la neige

(Your flesh sprinkled with the flight of a thousand birds of paradise
Is a high flame lying in the snow)

Tes bras au centre desquels tourne le cristal de la rose des vents
Ma fontaine vivante de Sivas

(Your arms in the center of which turns the crystal of the rose of the winds
My living fountain of Sivas)

J'eus le temps de poser mes lèvres
Sur tes cuisses de verre

(I had just time to place my lips
On your thighs of glass)

She is the medium through whom the poet satisfies his yearning for the
golden age. In one of these poems the erotic act is cadenced with ice, fire,
and darkness, is freed of all evil with the appearance of a blossoming apple
tree on the high seas. The meaning in terms of a conventional love poem
would be, I suppose, that the love act transposes the poet to the threshold
of a lost paradise, and that original sin is erased in the vision of "second
sun of canaries": a new apple tree attired in pure blossoms. Vision would
thus have proceeded from substance to essence and to quintessence. But
no such gradation seems intended here. First appear the images resulting
from the alchemy of love; then they are traced back to the generating
force and the source of light—thus encompassing the entire magnetic field

of operation. Jacqueline suggests that Breton may have been thinking of the projected trip to the Canary Islands, which took place shortly after. However, it is also likely that here as in so many other poems he again uses the hermetic emblem that announces the golden age: the magic polychrome of the double rainbow, the glow of new skies, and the chance of a new earth.

In a letter, Jacqueline explained to me the circumstances of the writing of the fourteen poems that compose this canticle to love.

> L'Air de l'eau was written very shortly after my meeting with André in about one week, which he spent in the outskirts of Paris, at the edge of a little river. I don't remember the name of the place, but he knew it well and loved it, and knew that it was propitious to him. . . . This poem is entirely about me, or better about us; he went off by himself, circumstances having prevented me from following him, at that moment. I think, however, that it is clearer to say that he preferred being alone to write it just as he stopped suddenly in our walk across Paris the night of the "Tournesol," detaching himself as if better to note what was true . . . After having written L'Air de l'eau he came back and read it to me, making a commentary of it, explaining each sentence. But later I have heard him say that he had all sorts of reservations about analysis of what did not become immediately evident in his own poems, as one cannot autoanalyze oneself completely. It must also be remembered that automatic writing was over for him at that period and although always spontaneously born, each sentence was worked over, endlessly, as a thing that is foreseen and at the same time outlived.[23]

The letter indicates the feverish rapidity with which the poems were written. Jacqueline always speaks of them as one, always using the word in the singular, and indeed the poems flow one into the other without separate titles. They suggest a continuity, within which the breaks are simple pauses, as if to allow the poet to catch his breath. The other thing to be noted is Breton's solitude in the act of creation as if to distill the experience, and even in circumstances so totally involved in a single and intense love as in his marriage to Jacqueline, the need to create the distance and objectivity of absence to universalize it. Significantly, as Jacqueline notes, the automatic period was over, and there was in these poems an element of conscious effort: casting and recasting, analysis, interpretation. Jacqueline's letter reveals the evolution in the poetics of Breton, from the automatism of "Au Regard des divinités" to a more consciously contrived series of images. Yet Breton felt that even the product of deliberate effort should possess the character of open communication, be responsive to the arbitrary subjectivity of the recipient. This is the only sense in which we can approach the poems of Breton. If the explanations he gave to Jacqueline remain irrevocably sealed in the abyss of her forgetfulness, perhaps it is just as well, for the images that were reflected in the brook that Breton contemplated in a cold December carry in their ambiguous but starkly concrete impact a fund of meaning that explanation would polarize into a single direction and create "frightful mental limits," to borrow his own line in "Monde dans un baiser."

But Jacqueline's account of the circumstances helps explain perhaps the preponderance of water and snow images. However, these elements are so intricately amalgamated into the qualities of the beloved as to evoke adventure and passion. The poems are, as Jacqueline suggests in her letter, the survival of experience. Where so often romantic poets confided to nature their sorrows of love, Breton imparts to mother earth his joy and exaltation. Hermetic expressions—such as the crystal of the rose, the living fountains of Sivas, the great celestial Turtle, the phosphorescence, the fire that becomes man, the magic salt, the mystic bird, the metal that is liberated from its form, the marvelous stones, the magic coincidence—create the enchantment of a fairytale atmosphere. Perhaps the most resplendent image is the unusual "Spath of Island," which is a calciferous crystal, transparent and capable of double refraction. The two transfigured beings move within vegetation like a labyrinth but which has grown transparent, allowing their reflections to penetrate each other.

The images have self-contained movement, a sense of becoming, even more so than in the previous collections of poems. "Your existence the giant bouquet that slips from my arms":

Cette précipitation l'un vers l'autre de deux systèmes tenus séparément pour
    subjectifs
Met en branle une série de phénomènes très réels
Qui concourent à la formation d'un monde distinct

(This precipitation one toward the other of two systems considered separately
    as subjective
Puts into motion a series of very real phenomena
Which confer to form a distinct world)

Pour me permettre de t'aimer
Comme le premier homme aima la première femme
En toute liberté
Cette liberté
Pour laquelle le feu même s'est fait homme

(To permit me to love you
As the first man loved the first woman
With complete liberty
That liberty
For which fire itself turned into man)

Many of Breton's surrealist colleagues were to write of their eternal
loves: Eluard's Gala (who left him for Dali); Aragon's Elsa (the most
enduring of the loves consummated under the aegis of surrealism), and
the women loved by Péret and Desnos have been immortalized in the
poets' writings. What distinguishes Breton's love poetry from the others,
equally intense though many of them are, is that none surpasses in so
many ways the subject of the erotic and the particular. The power of
infiltration that Breton gives the erotic experience in these cryptic poems
—teasing in their seeming naïveté but imponderable in their cosmic
frame of reference—generates meaning and feeling beyond the immediate
subject, suggesting in a million ways how the human embrace extends itself to a more intimate contact with this earth.

Finally the notion of death itself enters into Breton's alchemic vision
of the universe. If human love produces a greater love of the earth, this
intimacy with physical nature makes the transition from life to death part
of the great metamorphosis and easier to accept. "La Mort Rose," for example, concerns the passage of the couple from one state into another in a
double metamorphosis: that of the beings and that of the earth. The beloved's hair mingles with the sun, and her hands are projected into a peach
tree in bloom. The echoes of voices linger in the landscape, and her footsteps are entrapped in the moss. But the earth changes in form and texture
as well, as the comets burn down the forests tenderly, the horizon is enlarged, and rivers overflow. The two transfigured beings move within a
vegetation grown transparent and penetrate into each other's dreams and
probe the depths of each other's tears.

Mais la peur n'existera déjà plus et les carreaux du ciel et de la mer
Voleront au vent plus fort que nous
Que ferai-je du tremblement de ta voix
Souris valseuse autour du seul lustre qui ne tombera pas

(But fear will no longer exist and the windowpanes of the sky and
    of the sea
Will fly with the wind with more force than we
What will I do with the trembling of your voice
Mouse waltzing around the only luster which will not wane)

"Fôret dans la Hache" contains an image of death in which the soul disappears. The body becomes a transparent cavity in which doves and daggers fly. From this dwelling of the poet's consciousness, the soul has been banished and with it the notion of duality; the physical world is freed of its arbitrary laws. He retains a sense of heat and cold, but the colors of the spectrum have been amalgamated, and his body is inhabited by living forms, his brow is covered with crows, his eyes are made of mistletoe, his mouth is a dead leaf, and he takes on the characteristics of glass. Death is tangent to life rather than its antithesis. It annuls the barriers between colors, the elements, and the species.

The hermetics thought of death as the tearing of a sheet, according to Eliphas Lévi. The image has both a poignant and a triumphant form in Breton's "Vigilance," where he identifies death with the process of dissolution and integration:

A Paris la tour Saint-Jacques chancelante
Pareille à un tournesol
Du front vient quelquefois heurter la Seine et son ombre glisse imperceptible-
    ment parmi les remorqueurs
A ce moment sur la pointe des pieds dans mon sommeil
Je me dirige vers la chambre où je suis étendu
Et j'y mets le feu
Pour que rien ne subsiste de ce consentement qu'on m'a arraché
Les meubles font alors place à des animaux de même taille qui me regardent
    fraternellement
Lions dans les crinières desquels achèvent de se consumer les chaises
Squales dont le ventre blanc s'incorpore le dernier frisson des draps
A l'heure de l'amour et des paupières bleues
Je me vois brûler à mon tour je vois cette cachette solennelle de riens
Qui fut mon corps
Fouillée par les becs patients des ibis du feu
Lorsque tout est fini j'entre invisible dans l'arche
Sans prendre garde aux passants de la vie qui font sonner très loin leurs pas
    traînants
Je vois les arêtes du soleil
A travers l'aubépine de la pluie
J'entends se déchirer le linge humain comme une grande feuille
Sous l'ongle de l'absence et de la présence qui sont de connivence
Tous les métiers se fanent il ne reste d'eux qu'une dentelle parfumée
Une coquille de dentelle qui a la forme parfaite d'un sein
Je ne touche plus que le coeur des choses je tiens le fil

(In Paris the tower of St.-Jacques swinging
Like a sunflower

Bumps its head at times against the Seine and its shadow slides imperceptibly
    in the midst of the tugs
At that very moment tiptoeing in my sleep
I veer toward the room where I am asleep
And I set fire to it
That nothing may remain of the promise drawn from me
The furnishings then make way for animals of the same size that look at me
    fraternally
Lions in whose manes vanish the chairs
Sharks that gobble up in their white bellies the last shuddering of the sheets
At love time and blue-eyelid time
I see myself burning as my turn comes
I see that hidden cove of solemn nothings
That once was my body
Pecked by the patient beaks of fiery ibises
When it's all over and invisible I pass under the arch
Heedless of the passers-by of life whose dragging footsteps I can hear far away
I see the sun's rays like fishbones in the rain-drenched hawthorn
I hear the human sheet torn like a great leaf
Under the nail of absence and presence which are mere subterfuge
All crafts fade away of them remains but a perfumed lace
A shell of lace that has the perfect form of a breast
I now touch the heart of things I hold the thread)

If natural phenomena become symbols that man is called upon to
decipher, they do not represent abstract notions but are in reality outbursts
of that matter which can take all kinds of varied forms, and from which
we can never be separated according to Breton, not even in death.

As in terms of love, so in terms of the death experience, Breton's poetry
envisages the universe as a source of light: efflorescent and phosphorescent,
benign, ever in movement, the heartbeats of man following the cadence of
its great convulsions, the eyes of man spying and reacting to the beckoning
of a world in which there exists for Breton nothing inanimate. If the unfathomable with which he is ever confronted, suggests a mystery and an
Arachnean destiny for man, the poet Breton finds nothing foreboding in
nature, nothing strange, nothing particularly exotic, for he never lets go of
the thread that leads him toward the aurora borealis, strangely identifiable
with the light captured in a woman's eye.

X

SURREALISM
AND PAINTING

"Nothing of what surrounds us is object, everything is subject."
—*Le Surréalisme et la Peinture*

Of all the activities of André Breton in the domain of the arts his role in the evolution of painting in the twentieth century is the most extraordinary. Neither Eluard, Aragon, Desnos, Péret, nor Artaud had the continuous involvement in the life and work of the artist that Breton maintained from the early twenties to the very end of his life. If it in turn supplied him with his major source of livelihood, this is not surprising in view of the number of artists he discovered and brought to recognition and prominence through the many expositions he organized and supervised. He was himself a man of absolutely no talent in terms of performance in the plastic arts; but he marveled at the creativity of the painters. His knowledge of art history was vague in contrast with his wide reading in history, literature, religion, politics, psychology, and philosophy. Yet his influence on artists was even greater than on writers, and more immediate. Not only did he channel many artists' vague aspirations but he verbalized their intentions as they could never have done themselves.

Rebellion against formalism in art was already an old story when Breton came upon the scene, and the metaphysical concerns of the artist were already recognized before he wrote any of the articles that constitute *Le Surréalisme et la Peinture* (1928).[1] In *The Cubist Painters* Apollinaire had pointed out that in his craving for orphic expression of the universe the artist had been trying to represent the fourth dimension in painting. And Apollinaire was not the first poet to associate himself with the artist. Before him Baudelaire had tried, through the critique of his salons, to give romanticism a more graphic and distinguishing definition than art criticism had been able to do. In fact, Baudelaire was the first to acknowledge that romanticism had come of age in France through painting rather than through poetry; in the middle of the century the poets were still groping through a so-called second generation to find truly distinguishing features, to become liberated from classical formalism. But Baudelaire wrote of art very subjectively, as each painter impressed him. Apollinaire, on the other hand, tried to classify the new art, and his groupings have proved clumsy and arbitrary; they are really interesting not for what they contribute to the understanding of the cubists but for the light they throw on his own concepts and poetic principles. Breton, in fact, was to attach little importance to Apollinaire's art criticism, which he found disconnected and unadventurous; he suggested that Apollinaire had died in time to save himself embarrassment for his default in this domain.

Breton calls all art criticism "a complete failure" [2] because he sees the art critic as one who describes *form* rather than content, one who generalizes on the trends and attainments in the field of technique rather than seeks sources for new inspiration. For him the true art critic is one who views art from the point of view not of the finished product but of its *genesis:* the psychological vantage point of the artist, his notion of reality, his choice of subject, the means rather than the degree of execution of intent, not the finished product but the process of creating the structure, not its relation with other art, but its contingency with life, as a product not of the hands and the palette but of the mind's labyrinth. Art for Breton involves an even more alchemic operation than poetry, and the artist is the true magician among men. Art is not for aesthetic pleasure, but a rebus holding many meanings; it is an undefined substance, containing the power of fire, serving for the viewer as a source of meditation and of psychic renewal. Art is an education in life, a cult that comes closest to replacing the religious in modern times. Since Breton could set no example through personal performance, his role was to recognize potential in the artists of his time and to supply the inexhaustible resource of enthusiasm which he possessed, and which ignited artistic genius in others. In fact, with the burning regret of not having been an artist himself, he was bitterly intolerant of those who, possessing "the magic power" of transforming reality, used it merely "for the conservation and reinforcement of what could exist without them." [3]

Early in his career he had chosen to settle among the artists in Montmartre rather than among the poets of Montparnasse, realizing possibly that there was more latent dynamism among those who could channel their creativity through painting than among those who did it through poetry; or rather that poetry in the modern world could better reveal itself through the pictorial emblem than through the word. The alchemy of the Word that Rimbaud had desired was not as powerful a transformer as the alchemy of the object. Never has a literary man been so totally surrounded by artists or exercised on them a deeper impact than on writers. Where Mallarmé sought more intimate relationship between the musical composer and the poet, Breton effected an identification between the artist and the poet, an association that was to have perhaps more benefits for the artist than for the poet; as a more universal medium it reached a level of truly international language recognizable over and above ethnic barriers. In truth, whereas the majority of poets in the surrealist coterie were French, the artists represented a much broader and less monolithic spectrum, from Eastern Europe to America. To name them would involve a roll-call of the artists represented in the world's museums of modern art. It would be safe to state that no major artist loomed between 1925 and 1950 anywhere in the world who had not first come in contact with Breton or felt the impact of his metaphysical thought, although in many cases the relationship may have been of short duration.

Le Surréalisme et la Peinture was a product of the same creative years that produced his major collections of verse and his semiautobiographical writings which have been viewed in the preceding parts of this study. In these creative years, from 1923 to 1936, Breton delved simultaneously into many areas: poetry, art, politics. The varied nature of his preoccupations between his thirtieth and fortieth years was not an indication of diversification or indecision; rather, it pointed to a certain unity in his mental activities. The arts were expressions of man's ceaseless effort to comprehend the world through which his passage was so brief but so engrossing. The practice of an art was as much a part of the total involvement in life as the creation of social relationships.

The earliest series of surrealist activities at the rue Fontaine and in the cafés had to do with automatic writing and psychic and erotic analysis. With the arrival of artists such as Max Ernst and Man Ray, and a few years later of Miró, Salvador Dali, René Magritte, Yves Tanguy, and Marc Chagall, the group turned more and more to automatic drawing and to the questioning of the psychic function of the object—what Max Ernst was to call "the crisis of the object." After Breton took over the editorship of the magazine, La Révolution surréaliste, he began contributing articles on the artists whom he had discovered, and who had worked with him in the laboratory that his home had become. These articles were later collected in a volume, Le Surréalisme et la Peinture, that is "Surrealism and Painting"—not exactly the same thing as "Surrealist Painting." The distinction is important and once more points up the fact that Breton thinks

of surrealism as a generic label defining a mental attitude, and that any
art form related to it is a subdivision of it.

Since he is more concerned with the mental orientation than the art
forms it produces, it is not surprising that there is no discussion of technique in this book. Nothing that Breton says relates to the scale of values
by which an artwork was previously judged.

Much of the book consists of the prefaces he wrote for the many
expositions he organized. It is the high pitch of his enthusiasm that constitutes the unifying factor of the work. There is actually no "criticism"
but rather a series of approbations. In rejecting historical criticism he
denies antecedents for the modern artist—unlike his list of presurrealist
writers in the First Manifesto. He feels that no one has done for art what
Lautréamont, Rimbaud, and Mallarmé did for poetry: that is, no one has
prepared the ground for new mental operations and new objectives. He
relates, in the 1945 augmented edition of *Le Surréalisme et la Peinture*,
that when in 1929 Dali joined the surrealists, his techniques were "ultra-
retrograde" and heavily influenced by Meissonnier, which burdened his
natural ingenuity. Surrealism liberated him for a while, says Breton; but
after 1936 when Dali officially left surrealism, he is supposed to have reverted to his academic tendencies.

Art as Breton conceives it starts with Picasso and Chirico: the former
with his invention of tragic toys for adults; the latter with his creation of
an atmosphere, a climate as the natural background for human expectancy
and receptivity of marvelous, objective chance encounters. Perhaps nothing
had quite affected the young Breton in his earliest years as a poet in Paris
as the sense of the *insolite* in Chirico's early paintings: the objects left
with a provocative casualness in deserted streets, each suggesting to the
viewer a whole range of possible metaphors. Breton saw in Chirico's canvases hermetic and metaphysical landscapes at their purest, which helped
him crystallize the very notion of surrealism. Not only he but the whole
coterie of the young surrealists became enchanted by Chirico's metaphysical derangement of the visual field. But soon monotony and sterility set
in with repetition of these inscapes, and Breton felt that they became a
channel of escape rather than of revelation. His impatience with Chirico
coincided with the period when he and Aragon, in *Nadja* and *Le Paysan
de Paris*, respectively, were becoming more interested in crowding the
streets of Paris with objects and happenings than in leaving them simply
in a state of vacuum, waiting for the unusual to occur. One might say that
Chirico's canvases were like stage settings for *Waiting for Godot*. Empty
arcades are intriguing in their initial impact—just as protest is a stimulation threshold for rebellion—but when nothing comes out of them, they

revert to the role of *décor*. Consequently, if Breton's criticism of Chirico becomes harsh, it is indicative of both his deep disappointment in Chirico's lack of progress in the labyrinth and his own belief that the darkness is fascinating only as a prerequisite to illumination. He describes with his well-known verbal cruelty the sense of fatigue that sets in as this potentially most creative of early twentieth-century artists eternally repeats his early work. It is, he says, like men "who dare speak of love when they have already ceased to love." [4] He deplores the waste of talent: "he has done nothing for the past ten years but misuse his supernatural power." As in all of his subsequent condemnations of fellow artists, Breton suspects that Chirico has sold himself short for venal reasons: "the bowl of bouillon which interrupted the dream." Breton's quarrel with Chirico, as it was to be with Dali and a number of others, was motivated by his phobia about the commercialization of art, what he called "the grotesque and stinking beast which is called money."

In contrast with Chirico's default, Breton sees Picasso keeping pace with the times, consolidating his initial breakthroughs, maintaining his leadership as he bridges the gap between early rebellion to reconstruction of the premises of art. Breton notes the inadequacy of the label "cubism" to describe what Picasso has done for art.

The third beacon is Man Ray, who demonstrated in his relationship with the surrealists that photography, which had seemed to stand for the imitative in the plastic forms, was capable of joining the artist in demolishing the techniques of representation: "to make photography serve purposes other than those for which it appeared to have been created." [5]

The first and most fundamental statement that Breton makes is that "The eye exists in a savage state." It is the opening sentence of his book. The word *sauvage* in its French connotation has a much broader significance than in English and does not necessarily mean "barbaric"; much more accurately it denotes "primitive," "unrestricted," "natural," and etymologically speaking "free." What lends this series of articles a certain unity is the fact that Breton illustrates the freedom of the eye achieved by modern artists; it is a liberation from the trite associations with which civilizations, one after the other, have encumbered our perceptions of the exterior world. As in verbal expression Breton wanted to narrow the distance between sensation and representation, he thought that the artist should work in the same direction to shed established and ingrained visual impressions with which the eye is burdened, and to establish a new "scale of vision."

The mind of primitive man, on the other hand, was more free, and his observation of reality, therefore, proceeded according to the following states: concrete relationship with his personal subjectivity (usefulness of the object to his own needs) and personal choice of relationships between objects, according to his position and gravitation in the exterior world. For Breton the metaphysical purpose of art (which has no connection with the euphoria produced through decorative art) is to restore to the domesticated eye some of the "savage" state it has lost so that it may achieve "the nondistinction more and more firmly established of sensory functions and intellectual functions." [6] His relationship with an art in which he was not adept according to traditional qualifications is based on the fact that he was able to establish guidelines for the artist, as he had for the poet, to understand the primitive mind, a subject that has equally intrigued sociologists, anthropologists, and psychologists such as Lévy-Bruhl, Lévi-Strauss, and Jung. Breton observes in *Point du Jour* that:

> All the experimentation in progress would be of a nature to demonstrate that perception and representation—which seem to the ordinary adult to be opposed one to the other in such a radical manner—should be deemed only the products of dissociation of a single, initial faculty, whose eiditic image finds response and of which traces are found in the primitive and in the child. It is this state of grace that all those whose concern it is to define the true human condition, are trying more or less confusedly to rediscover. I say that only automatism leads to it. One can, systematically and sheltered from all delirium, work to eliminate the necessity and value of the distinction between the objective and the subjective.[7]

In *The Savage Mind* Lévi-Strauss says: "Images cannot be ideas but they can play the part of signs or to be more precise, co-exist with ideas in signs, and if ideas are not yet present, they can keep their future place open for them . . . they are permutable, that is, capable of standing in successive relations with other entities." Breton goes further than Lévi-Strauss. The latter limits the permutability of symbols to a closed system and relegates them to a range somewhat inferior to that of concept, whereas Breton aspires to a notion of art which would essentially be myth-creating on a level free of specific cultures and therefore with an open end, leading to infinite provocations. In avoiding abstraction the artist renders himself capable of transfiguration, and objects become infinitely mutable and capable of spontaneous generation. Lévi-Strauss's criticism of painters—"the problems which painters have set themselves . . . amount to little more than a game of technical refinement" [8]—suggests that he did not recognize the common premises from which he derived his concept of myth, and Breton his revolutionary notion of art; both of them had studied under the same masters. But the work that Lévi-Strauss has done on the "savage mind" should make it infinitely more possible for modern man to understand the broader franchise of modern painting proceeding from the same base.

Breton proclaimed the primacy of the eye over all other senses of man and so implied the primacy of the artist, whose work is dominated by vision, the "*regard*" that relates everything to the universal rainbow. He also observed that whereas in language we have classifications of meaning or function, we have made indiscriminate use of vision and failed to establish a scale of nuances and degrees of power. He of course was implying the importance of *mind* in the operation of art: the artist in Breton's scale of values is a thinker before he is a technician.

He asserts that everything is subject and nothing is object in art: "Nothing of what surrounds us is object, everything is subject." [9] In other words, the efficacy and success of a work of art is dependent on its reflection of the process of transfiguration that has taken place when the sensory data have been submitted to the psychic process of analogical association in the mind of the artist. The artist has achieved meaning by the disposition of things according to the laws of objective chance, which are out of his range of control, but whose manifestations can assume meaning by the interpretations that his mind gives to them. Because the resulting work of art is more graphic and concrete than the verbal one arrived at by the same process, and where words replace the objects, Breton succeeds in making his distinction between reality and surreality much more clear in his meditations on painting than in his other works. Not only is the frontier between the real and the surreal more clearly and systematically defined in the case of the artist than of the poet, but also it is clearly stated that the real contains the surreal.

> All I love, all I think and feel, leads me to a particular philosophy of immanence, according to which surreality would be contained in reality itself, and would be neither superior nor exterior to it. And reciprocally, for the container would also be that which is contained. [10]

He could not show the distinctions and illustrations quite as clearly in the case of writing; perhaps this is why, although he was concerned all his life with commentaries on art, he never really went into poetry criticism.

His only classification of the art works he observed and commented upon was according to the degree of knowledge of the surreal they contained or were able to convey. First and foremost among these is what he calls the "irrational knowledge of the object." In this respect, whatever his disapproval of Salvador Dali's personality and behavior, Breton always affirmed the fact that the painter's benign mental unbalance, coupled with his "first-rate" intelligence, contributed more than anything else to the revelation of the nonrational functions one could attribute to objects. "During three or four years, Dali will incarnate the surrealist spirit and will make it shine with all its fires as only could be done by one who had not participated in the sometimes thankless episodes of its gestation." [11] It was particularly Dali's open, uninhibited ability to communicate the paranoic vision, to give the free spirit the rigor of artistic discipline, to catch the free play of association out of his mental aberrations and to channel it into systematic, conscious artistic realization, that captivated the surrealist coterie. "It is perhaps with Dali that for the first time the windows of the mind are wide open." [12] Breton and Eluard were to try the same type of operation verbally in *L'Immaculée Conception* by simulating artificially the operation of the erratic mind by their own rational ones, which naturally demonstrates nothing better than the inability of the normally keyed mind to assume the volatility of the deranged. Breton never ceased to express his admiration for Dali's power to implement all the possibilities of the innately savage mind and eye, which he so hoped to see infusing the work of art in all its forms; he admired in Dali the rare ability to catch the sparks of coincidence between natural necessity and logical necessity, which objective chance generates and which vanish too quickly for most people to note them. He perceives Dali's play of superimpositions, of phantom figures, his natural and prolific automatism channeled through impeccable techniques, his ability to transform a superb and totally obsessed narcissism into a "superego" with a detached, objectivized, and therefore humoristic and universal character.

The example of Dali was the most sensational of those with which Breton illustrates in his series of articles the common characteristics that connected a number of artists: the change of intention of the object, the function of "turning it away from its intent." The earliest of these innovators was Marcel Duchamp with his "readymades"; but a greater variety of result was achieved in Dali, Man Ray, Victor Brauner and others, as Breton's dominant personality hovered over them, orienting their creativity.

The juxtaposition of objects was another characteristic of surrealist activity among artists. Breton's experimental activities in the company of artists such as Max Ernst demonstrated to him that in truth automatic juxtaposition was not so important as the recognition of new relationships. As he says in his article on Tanguy: "Seeing and hearing are nothing, recognition (or the lack of it) is all." [13] The power to bring to awareness occult relationships is in Breton's sense apocalyptic art. In Chagall, who never was officially a surrealist, Breton recognizes this superb power of pictorial metaphor whose hypnogogic character is equaled, he says, only by Rimbaud. The great contribution of Max Ernst in this respect was his erudite probe of the substance of objects and of their relationships to each other, in order to transcend the particular work of art in which these phenomena were observed or revealed and to generalize about the crisis of the object, which he thought symptomatic of the crisis of modern times. Some of the artists had gone along instinctively with these experimentations, without intellectual conviction or orientation. But in the case of Max Ernst there was indeed a conscious identification of the artist with the poet. Ernst matched Breton's meditations on art with his own, such as *Beyond Painting* in 1937, focusing on the same metaphysical problems as had been raised in Breton's writings about poetry and painting. Of this parallel Breton was keenly aware: "I like to reassure myself that he [Max Ernst] suffers from the same things as I, that the obscure cause to which we are dedicated is no more won for him than for me. What moves him, moves me, and what reaches up to him sometimes surpasses me." [14]

Another channel for surreality in painting was the creation of new objects or beings, which indeed would forewarn of the creation of new myth emblems. The unwonted characters of Victor Brauner, the Great Masturbator of Dali (whose original inspiration had been Chirico's Vaticinateur), were a distinct contribution of modern art. It was in the creation of phantom objects that Breton felt he could participate in art activity as a nonartist; this is the purpose of his poem-objects which he defines in *Entretiens*: "a composition which tends to combine the resources of poetry with those of the plastic arts in speculating over the power of reciprocal exaltation." [15]

The figures created by Giacometti, Magritte, Miró, Man Ray, and, of course most of all, Dali contributed to an atmosphere of daily magic which was a fundamental characteristic of surrealism in the art forms. In this context Magritte is the least automatic according to Breton but also among the most successful in revealing the character of strangeness in the midst of ordinary objects confronting each other in unexpected encounters.

The passage of the dream into reality was the parallel in painting of dream transcription in verbal surrealism. The illustrations here are many, whether we refer to the work of Ernst or that of Chagall, or the many later surrealists such as Wolfgang Paalen, Wifredo Lam, Matta, and Archile Gorky, all of whom found their way into Breton's influence and into his book. And with the dream must be mentioned the nightmare which often transforms reality more dramatically than does the benign oneiric vision.

All these illustrations of processes bring into focus the new role of the painter as a seeker of knowledge, like the old magician and the new scientist: not simply to express the world apparent to all eyes, but to clarify the relationships of man with the universe; not to communicate our impressions but to present the results of these impressions in concrete form—that is, the metamorphoses that occur when the psychic mechanism acts upon exterior data. That is how by departing from the same scientific formation but relating to quite different fields of mental activity and subject matter, Breton finds himself approaching the scientific philosopher, Gaston Bachelard. In the close approximation of his notion of surrealism with that of Bachelard's surrationalism, the common ground is the search for knowledge of man—on the part of the poet, the painter, as of the man of science—in the discovery of conciliations behind apparent contradictions.

> Reason today proposes as its objective more than anything else the continual assimilation of the irrational, assimilation in the course of which the rational is constantly called upon to reorganize itself, both to reaffirm itself and to grow. It is in this sense that one must admit that surrealism is necessarily accompanied by a *superrationalism* which supports it and gauges it.[16]

Breton sees a common purpose in "the search for experience." Reason will trail behind. Breton's description of the nature of reason is ambivalent, suggesting blindness and illumination at the same time: "with her phosphorescent band tied around her eyes." The search for knowledge, then, becomes the primary objective of the man in the arts rather than the discovery of new means of expression. Here Breton betrays again his early scientific training as he attributes to the arts the disciplines and aspirations germane to the man of science.[17]

In terms of "pure" surrealism it becomes evident that at the time of the compilation of *Le Surréalisme et la Peinture*, Breton considered Miró's and Tanguy's the most purely representative of surrealist aspirations. He makes a very significant observation about these two painters, who might appear to the naked eye more abstract than surrealist, about their confrontation of reality: that the simplification which occurs in their style—the distances their objects assume from recognizable reality—is not a rejection of reality as in earlier abstract art but a field of recognition of line and color and of their generic symbolization that most other mortals have not reached. The "pure imagination" of Miró is a level of creation that may spell the void for the ordinary powers of sight in the viewer, but his objects are more open as signs and less narrowly representative of objects in our current use; we are less likely to recognize the functions of his objects dependent on our specific culture than we are in any other artist's.

As for Tanguy, he is perhaps the artist that Breton would have liked to be, for Tanguy puts into reality all the dreams of Breton. Also of Breton origin, with an equal dose of natural mysticism and propensity for the dream, but with less academic discipline, possessing the free associations that Breton would have liked to be able to acquire, less intelligent in the accepted sense of the word, but thereby more intuitive and spontaneous, he focuses a truly primitive eye on the cataclysmic world. His was the ability, says Breton, "to yield to us images of the unknown as concrete as those which we pass around of the known." [18] Suspicion surrounds everything Tanguy looks upon, and he suggests the aurora borealis that Breton envisaged in his dreams. He destroys terrestrial gravitation to an extent that as Breton perceives: "the ball of feather weighs as much as the ball of lead." His paintings are "the preferred site of obscure and superb metamorphosis, the first nonlegendary glimpse of the considerable area of the mental world which exists at the Genesis." In his very indictment of the world as it is, he achieves through the power of metamorphosis the apocalypse and the lights, never before used on a canvas, of a new sun with a new spectrum. Tanguy is the realization of *Clair de terre*, dreamed by Breton, reflection of our banal earth as a new habitat. If indeed his is a notion of the concrete world, the notion of the concrete has undergone as much revision as the notion of reality.

Through the examples closest to him and dearest to him, Breton in *Le Surréalisme et la Peinture* defines the tenets of surrealism in painting as he does of poetry in the First Manifesto. They have much in common, but most of all, a common approach to art: the exploration of the psychophysical field: "A work cannot be held to be surrealist unless the artist has forced himself to attain the total psychophysical field (of which the conscious aspect is only a weak part)." [19] Painting, then, under the sponsorship of André Breton assumes a role among the essential postulates of effective living in the modern world, whether it refers to man the painter, or to man the receiver of the painter's message. The connection is intimate, and the contribution of the recipient is deemed almost as significant to Breton as that of the giver of sight, perhaps in his mind compensating a little for the frustration of not having been an artist himself.

Among the artists closest to him in his last years were the American, Alexander Calder, the Latin American, Matta, and the Czech, Toyen. It is significant that their art is so different, one from the other, yet they have a common character, a mystique that relates them to surrealism. In Matta he finds the ceaseless questioning of nature: "No one has proved himself more jealous to gather the living substance." [20] He describes Matta as a poet rather than an artist, a *voyant* in terms of poetry as conceived by Rimbaud: "Matta is the one who has best maintained the star, which is no doubt the best road to lead to the supreme secret: the mechanism of fire." In Calder, Breton sees the substantiation of the active role and protean power of objects, their relation to emptiness and fullness of space, the metaphysics of movement "no longer figurative but real, [it] is miraculously restored to concrete life, and restitutes for us the evolutions of celestial bodies and the tremor of leaves as well as the memory of kisses." [21]

It is interesting to note that, in his introduction to Toyen's exposition in 1947, Breton has not changed his criterion in twenty years: what he accepts as surrealist in the Czech artist is the sense of magic, her ability to "advance with a true step into the night of the Apocalypse." [22] Toyen, citizen and refugee from Prague, which Breton calls "the magic capital of Europe," had in her eyes "the beaches of light." It was in Czechoslovakia that Breton had received more encouragement than anywhere else in Central Europe, and when that country fell as the first victim to Nazi German demagogy, Breton never forgot that "Czechoslovakia was more avid of liberty than any other land." Toyen represented in her art that sense of liberty and the prolongation of the surrealist objective to pursue through the arts, in the midst of all kinds of obscurity, the thread of Ariadne, to question, to risk total loss of identity in order to rediscover oneself. For him she is indeed Ariadne. In her he recognizes the gnostic forces without which no one in Breton's opinion can qualify as an artist.

Art critics generally seek unifying trends in the works they view in an effort toward classification and labeling, but Breton creates a unity by the motivation and orientation he provided for artists of disparate origins and totally unlike personalities. Even more than it was true in the case of the poets that came in contact with him, he was able to drive the artists toward metaphysics, toward a common basis of communication that over and above their varied techniques related them to surrealism. Surrealism in painting is the permeation of the surrealist mystique into individual techniques of artists whose resemblances would otherwise be minimal. One has but to view an early painting of Chagall, so imitative of Utrillo, to observe that each painter coming in contact with Breton achieved a projection of the inner self which did not occur previously. Their recognition of this is attested by the number of gifts they made of their canvases to Breton, whose collection, now partially owned by his first wife, is composed of masterpieces, many of which are superior to those in museums of modern art. These artists gave him their best, and almost each one capable of painting a portrait has left his interpretation of the face of André Breton.

XI

THE POLITICAL
ADVENTURE ON
TWO CONTINENTS

"One can say without exaggeration that never
has human civilization been menaced by so
many dangers as today."
—*Pour un Art révolutionnaire indépendant*
(25 July 1938, Mexico)

If Breton's role as a rebel in the total experience of life was first manifested in experiments with psychic breakthrough, and in the application
of revolt to art forms, in the probe of the phenomena of eroticism and
objective chance, the fifth decade of his life was mostly marked by political concerns, which, more than any other factor, were to determine the
events of his personal existence.

Of course Breton had previously participated in political manifestations,
but the political applications of surrealism did not so totally preoccupy
him as in the years between 1935 and 1946. Actually, as he points out
himself, the first political action of the surrealists had been a protest
against the French colonial war in Morocco in 1925. As he states in *Entretiens*, every new writer or artist who joined the group after its initial
formation was attracted to it because of his alienation from a "world
that scandalized us." [1] That is why the motto of the first surrealist magazine, *La Révolution surréaliste*, is: "It is necessary to reach a new declaration of the rights of man." Action for Breton is mental and verbal; the
effectiveness of a protest lies in its power of provocation. Again, espousing
as always unpopular causes, Breton committed his protest to immediate
ineffectiveness. "Success" as judged by the world was never his, since
success means being in tune with the ways of the world; and Breton's
basic character in the world of his time was his antagonism, his nonconformism with the world, his quality as nonrepresentative writer in the

society of his time. The protest against French imperialism was his first bid for unpopularity.

The basis of his political thought was Hegel, with whose philosophy he had come in contact as early as 1912. He followed the path from Hegel to Marx and Engels through their writings that appeared in France in the 1920's and 1930's. He mentions in *Entretiens* that he was particularly impressed by Trotsky's commentary on Lenin, which he published in the fifth issue of *La Révolution surréaliste*. But the notion in communism that had most fired his imagination was in Marx's commentary on Feuerbach: "Philosophers have only interpreted the world in different ways, but the question is to transform it." Breton felt from the very beginning that Rimbaud and Lautréamont could help transform the world as well as any political prophet, because without the liberation of the mind there could be no real liberation, and mere economic freedom, leaving an intellectually impoverished human condition at status quo, was to him a poor victory. What angered him most about the existing system was the fact that it imposed psychological as well as economic barriers by binding man to concepts of duties and constraints that had outlived their usefulness. The most important of these were "fatherland," "family," and "religion": for them he would substitute a broader notion of union, a freer concept of the attraction of humans to other humans in their social condition.

First of all, Breton could not bring himself to accept the notion of a purely French cultural legacy, because he felt that France, like her neighboring countries, shared a common European legacy: "It is a shame that we are obliged today to remind anyone that we are concerned with a universal legacy which makes us tributaries as much of the German as of any other." [2] He felt that the measure of greatness of philosophers and poets had been in direct relation to their ability to transcend purely circumstantial and ethnic problems. He himself felt closer to the spirit of Hegel than to that of Voltaire although his education had been French. In this notion of the common pool he found support in modern psychology which had revealed a psychic depth beyond the *moi* in the *soi*, suggesting a melting-pot quality in the substrata of the collective human heritage.

Breton was greatly influenced by Marx's reconciliation of English and French philosophers of the seventeenth and eighteenth centuries with the Germans, Feuerbach and Hegel. With Engels he espoused the notion that truth is not an independent entity but a continuum inherent in the very process of acquiring knowledge. Breton's political thought is largely based on his reading of an anthology of German dialectical thought, which first appeared in the 1920's in France and to which he often referred: Karl Marx, Friedrich Engels, *Etudes philosophiques: Ludwig Feuerbach, Le Matérialisme historique, Lettres philosophiques, etc.*[3]

Marx's and Engels' interpretations of the philosophical heritage of the West have precisely this in common: when ideas become congealed and static, their truth is compromised. This was indeed to be the gauge of Breton's value judgments as he first applauded and then rejected the affiliations of dialectical materialism under the Soviet regime of the 1930's.

In attacking the notion of patriotism, Breton insisted time and again on the oneness of Europe. He did so not because he placed Europe above other portions of the world, but the notion of Europe as a "fatherland" was only a preliminary step to the notion of one world. Breton's wild and utopian aspiration is what for one brief moment he was to see crystallized much later in Garry Davis' concept of "citizen of the world."

As for the notions of "family" and "religion," Breton's violent rejection of them can only be understood in so affectionate and mystical a man as he, in terms of their institutionalized character. Gide before him had said "Families, I hate you"; and Voltaire had declared long ago the tyranny of institutionalized religion. To Breton these two institutions were dangerous because they precluded personal choice and involved, therefore, neither personal affection nor individual mysticism. In his attacks on these groupings it is the mechanical aspect of the adherences that he was disapproving. In their true sense "family" and "religion" should be concepts that are not handed to us at birth as congealed realities, but ones which are part of the dream that we would bring into concrete being in the personally managed events of our own life. Here Breton agrees with Marx that man must be judged not as a product of his environment but as one who acts upon circumstances and creates his own destiny.

Another common ground of Hegel and Marx that Breton adopts—and it marks his thought consistently—is the notion of history, which he views in terms of dialectical materialism. He does not accept history as the account of a chain of extraordinary events; what is called "great" in terms of history is, he believes, in fact the arbitrary selection of these events by the witnesses of their own time. Instead of making use of perspective gained by the passage of time, future generations have automatically accepted the chain passed down by these myopic viewers. In the artificial emphasis on "great" men and "great" events, *conflict* and *contrast*, the confrontation of opposing forces stand out, and the continuous evolution of the social psyche which eliminates apparent contradictions is lost from sight.[4] For Breton, national "histories" are sources of vile misrepresentations and errors of judgment, and the age of a true humanism cannot come until history is viewed nonnationally and measures the steps of the social evolution.

As for religion, again in line with communism, he views it as an institution at the service of bourgeois society which it helped strengthen by giving solace to the economically exploited with the promise of a better world in the hereafter. He believes that the mystic propensity, which he considers an integral part of human consciousness, should be canalized into a better comprehension of immediate reality and should contribute to the liberation of the mind from fixed emblems of reality.

Thus Breton had much in common with Marxist politics; yet some aspects of communism as it operated in Russia and in the Communist Party in France in the thirties kept him in a constant state of anguish, making his political protest a two-edged affair. On the one hand, he attacked French imperialism, "France armed to the teeth," slogans such as "He who wants peace prepares for war," [5] the bourgeois exploitation of the salaried workers of the world, and the tyranny of organized social allegiances which are the product of bourgeois society; on the other hand, he found as much to attack in dialectical materialism as practiced by the Soviet regime and in the proliferation of communism in other parts of Europe.

The main target of his attack was the plight of the artist under Marxist society in its contemporary form—that is, the artist's lack of independence. Although the second major magazine of the surrealists had been called Le Surréalisme au service de la Révolution, Breton's notion of the "service" of the artist to society in any form was not conceived in terms of a political commitment dictated by the Presidium.

As we have already noted, he thought of journalism as the extreme opposite of creative writing; while the former was geared to the direct reporting of ideas and emotions, the artist was creative precisely in his capacity for indirect statement, which was the process by which subjective emotionalism became transformed into codes of expression that had a richer basis of meaning than the immediate event and emotion.

In 1926, Légitime Défense had been Breton's protest against the director of the socialist newspaper, Humanité, Henri Barbusse, who had asked him to put his pen at the service of the proletarian cause. In 1932 in Misère de la poésie (whose title was no doubt inspired by Marx's Misère de la philosophie) he had drawn an even finer distinction between his defense of Aragon's freedom of the press and his dismay at the quality of the particular piece of writing.

Breton's confidence in the eventual alignment of artistic revolution with political revolution seemed to weaken as the years passed, first to cause him perplexity and eventually to bring him to a state of frustration and despair. The addresses he gave on this subject during his visit to Prague with Paul Eluard, at the invitation of Vitezlav Nezval and Karel Teige, before the group known as *Front Gauche*, stress particularly the need of the artist to come to grips with the impacts of political revolution that extend beyond political action and involve the very fibers of man's psychic mechanism if life is indeed to be transformed. Otherwise, under the guise of a new regime, the revolution will turn into involution, nurturing the same basic flaws of the old regime. He sums up the situation in "Position Politique du Surréalisme": "We are living in an epoch when man belongs less than ever to himself, when he is justifiable for the totality of his acts no longer before his own conscience, but before the collective conscience of all those who want to put an end to a monstrous system of slavery and hunger." [6] Then he must be supported by an avant-garde art that is willing to shed all the earmarks of bourgeois literature. The dilemma Breton voiced in Prague—and which he had faced in embarrassment in Paris in the *Affaire Aragon*—is precisely this: why cannot the Marxist revolution understand its parallelism with the surrealist revolution? The surrealists, as Breton saw it, were faced with the dramatic choice: to renounce their newly acquired techniques, which in the arts express the crisis of the human psyche, or to give up trying to "collaborate on the plane of practical action in the transformation of the world." He asks the Marxists plainly and squarely: "Is there an art of the Left capable of defending itself, I mean, that is capable of justifying its 'advanced' technique by the very fact that it is at the service of a leftist state of mind?" If the Communists did not accept surrealism, as seemed more and more obvious each day, what other alternative could they offer those of their comrades living in the West "in open conflict with the immediate world that surrounded [them]"?

Perhaps Breton expressed the mingling of the poetic and the political consciousness best in a metaphor as he gazed out of his window at a rainbow and viewed the poet's grasp of politics as akin to his comprehension of the total spectrum arching across the sky and burying itself deep within the fathoms of the earth's horizon. The word of the poet must express at the same time over and above the sea of abstraction beauty and mystery, even fear. The writer must be allowed his reservations, his criticism, as well as his liberty to create new forms. Breton finds support in Lenin's statement that "Everyone is free to say and write what suits him." He objects to "the frenetic need for orthodoxy," which he discerns in Communist circles, and to which he refuses to subscribe.

Despite the hopes he had at first placed in the proletariat as potential trailblazer in the realm of the arts, Breton is faced with the unhappy paradox that revolutionary art was better nurtured in bourgeois society than under Communist regimes. "The political milieus of the Left can appreciate in art only the sanctified forms of art, and primarily the obsolete." In fact, he cannot declare, as many of his colleagues were willing to do, that there is a proletarian literature. There is in effect, as he sees it, a propagandist literature under a proletarian regime that adopts the simplistic forms of realism generally discarded in capitalistic countries some decades earlier as too regressive. "To put poetry and art to the exclusive service of an idea, however enthusiastic one may be about it, would be to condemn them quickly to immobilization."

He placed then the possibility of a truly proletarian art in the period that he called "post revolutionary," when the working classes would have acquired the education and leisure to perform as artists, to represent not an inferior imitation of the bourgeois arts but something distinctly characteristic of themselves. In the meanwhile, in a period of transition the role of the revolutionary artist, who is a product of bourgeois society, is to "serve" members of the working class by subtilizing their minds, by freeing their powers of imagination, by making them aware of the linguistic potential.

In terms of action what is Breton's involvement in the political drama? His point of departure is a sense of keen urgency. As early as 1929 in his "Lettre aux Voyantes" he had himself done some looking in the crystal ball and had predicted World War II: "There are people who claim to have learned something from the war; just the same, they are less advanced than I, who know what the year 1939 has in store for me." [7]

All of Breton's political positions in the years preceding World War II are structured on the basic premise that the status quo is untenable, that in fact it does not exist, that Europe, and by extension the entire world, is in "a state of social rupture" indicative of the existing state of failure in bourgeois society. He considers his age a time of "a veritable crisis of judgment, as a function naturally of the economic crisis."

His own aspiration was to find a midway position between two equally demagogical attitudes, as he considered the powers of the East and of the West to be. He had a series of frustrations, as he first joined the Communist Party and then quickly separated from it. As he could not bring himself to collaborate with the official organ, L'Humanité, so he could not work with the group of Clarté, directed by Naville, who between 1930 and 1939 was one of the directors of the French section of the Fourth International.

Yet with all his disappointments Breton could not turn his back on politics. He was far too aware of Engels' criticism of Feuerbach; Engels had deplored the philosopher's incomprehension of the significance of the year 1848. According to Engels, although Feuerbach's ideas were fulfilled in the political actions of 1848, he could not free his mind from abstractions and come to grips with the living reality.[8] Breton had a fear of abstractions; he wanted to be in the field of action.

When the Nazi *Putsch* occurs in 1934, Breton organizes an all-night protest on February 6; out of the meeting comes the text "L'Appel à la lutte" which by February 10 had ninety signatures of French intellectuals calling on world syndicalism to effect a general strike against fascism. To get the support of Léon Blum, the incumbent leader of the *Front Populaire*, Breton visits him in his luxurious apartment on the Ile St. Louis on the Seine, in the heart of Paris. Characteristically this political leader, who had a basically literary background, can communicate only in terms of literature with a man who, though on a political mission, represents essentially art not politics. Breton gets no support from Blum. The bourgeois friend of the proletariat cannot see a literary man in the context of political action. He does not take the poet's desire for political action seriously. Breton then organizes the Committee of Vigilance of Intellectuals, which, as is the nature of committees, remains restricted, the symbol of a mystique for action rather than a source of action itself. When subsequently Breton tries to organize an Association of Revolutionary Artists and Writers, he is stopped by Aragon. The latter was sojourning in the Soviet Union at the time and had already, unlike Breton, a tremendous influence in Communist circles by his very orthodoxy; he wrote asking Breton to desist from forming an organization that was too much like the already existing Soviet organization of practically the same name.

Breton's hope, then, was to read a forceful statement at the impending meeting in Paris of the Congress of Writers for the Defense of Culture in 1935 under Communist sponsorship. Unforeseeable circumstances, which demonstrate Breton's impulsiveness and lack of political acumen, took this opportunity away from him. The major event has often been described in histories of surrealism and in Breton's own article "Du Temps où les surréalistes avaient raison." One day, on the eve of the Congress, he accidentally meets Ilya Ehrenburg on a street in Paris—no doubt Breton was on an aleatory excursion—and he cannot suppress an act of violence: he slaps the Russian writer in the face to express his contempt for the latter's having made disparaging remarks in print about the surrealists and for having vilified Breton's own character by saying that he was living off his wife's dowry. Breton claimed that at the time he was unaware of Ehrenburg's role in party organization. Had he known, would he have controlled his anger? It is unlikely in view of the spontaneity of Breton's character, his capacity for anger as for love. The fact is that as a consequence he is not permitted to read his text. Although by the intervention of colleagues in better Communist standing, the injunction is modified to permit Eluard to read the text, it is aborted when the lights are turned off at midnight. The event made Breton again dismally aware that the power to muzzle freedom of speech is as possible under Communist systems as under the bourgeois ones he had deplored in *Misère de la poésie*.

The speech that was scuttled deals with questions that were to come to a crisis thirty years later in the world at large. Its form had been used frequently by Breton: "a proclamation of a state of alarm." In this instance his nonpartisan integrity had been aroused by the recent Franco-Soviet pact, and as a result he had chosen to attack both West and East for the political maneuverings they carried on at the same time as they proclaimed the need for cultural rapprochement. In indignation he disavowed both France and the Soviet Union for their military alliance, intended to maintain the status quo of the Versailles Treaty, which he considered beneficial to France alone and iniquitous to all other parties concerned. He was furious to think that it was for war and not for peace that international alliances were soldered. In this speech, as elsewhere, the consistency of Breton's nonnational attitude toward political problems is eloquently precise; so is his dialectical approach to paradoxes. In this case the paradox was inherent in the desirability of a Franco-Soviet alliance and the unacceptability of its terms.

The union of artists must be projected not as a marriage of convenience at the pleasure of paternalistic governments, but as one in which both parties recognize each other's complementary qualities and see in them a basis for common future aspiration: "the affirmation of our unshakable faith in the powers of emancipation of the mind and of man which we have each in our turn recognized and which we are prepared to fight to have others recognize as such." [9]

But what did Breton, the man who despised war more than anything else in this world, mean by "we are prepared to fight"? The preservation of culture, in his opinion, involves the *action* of the poet and the *dream* of the politician in a reversal of their usual roles. For this reversal of roles he has the backing of Goethe and Lenin. Goethe called for action, Lenin exhorted the dream. The writer has an impact on future generations only as a transforming agent by the vitality that he instills in future generations, not as a spokesman for a particular political event of his time. Rimbaud the *communard* belonged to the France of 1871; Rimbaud the *voyant* is one of the assets that European culture can salvage from a society that Breton deemed in definite decline. Whereas so many humanists have considered the work of art as a representative token of a particular ethnic culture, for Breton the work of art, confronted from time to time with new agitation and new civilizations, will undergo as violent a struggle for survival as men on a battlefield; and it is not the typical that survives but the work of art that has a built-in transformer that from the old reaps the new. Breton exhorts the new nations—in this particular case the Soviet Union—not to accept what the politicians push down their throats as representative of the old culture of the West:

> On the intellectual plane, as it were, we can expect the propaganda services of the Quai d'Orsay to take advantage to unload on the U.S.S.R. the wave of insanities and stupidities which France makes available to other peoples in the form of newspapers, books, films, and tours of the Comédie Française.

As we have seen, Breton confronted the notion of patriotism with that of the universal patrimony of Europe, rejected the former, put his dimming hopes for Europe's salvation on the latter.

Deciding what was retrievable in that patrimony one must discard the purely representative works—which interpreted a certain way of life—and choose those that create a new way of looking at life. Preservation involves rejection; just as rejection implies preservation.

Historians of surrealism have viewed the muzzling of Breton's proclamation as a reprisal for his assault on Ilya Ehrenburg. Actually, for the Soviet regime, the incident may have come as a providential political face-saving excuse. Given the content of the two-edged indictment of what he suspected to be Machiavellian politics lurking behind the cultural fanfare of the congress, it seems obvious that in any case the lights would have been turned off on André Breton. Of his expulsion from the congress, Salvador Dali has this to say:

> Whatever else Breton may be he is above all a man of integrity and rigidity like a cross of St. André. In any sidelines and especially in those of a congress he becomes the most burdensome and the least assimilative of all "foreign bodies." He can neither run along nor stick to the walls. That was one of the principal reasons that forbade the surrealist crusade from getting inside the doors of the Congress of the

Association of Revolutionary Writers and Artists, as I had wisely foreseen without the least cerebral effort of any kind.[10]

In assailing both the nation sponsoring the congress and the one on
whose soil the congress was taking place, Breton had once more committed himself to his psychology of failure: in cursing both their houses
he was bidding for unpopularity at home and abroad.

Although thereafter Breton never again involved himself with Soviet
communism, it was not to be the last time he attacked Stalin's regime.
It continued to receive equal rank with French politics as anathema to
all that surrealism stood for in his judgment.

His next series of vituperations were provoked by the Moscow trials of
1935 and 1936. In the questionnaire he filled out for *Contemporary Authors* in 1962 he stated as one of the highlights of his career the stand he
took against the trials: "I flatter myself to have been one of the very first
French writers to have denounced the scandal of the 'Moscow trials.'"
In a declaration read at a meeting of the surrealists on September 3, 1936,
called "The Truth about the Moscow Trial," he called Stalin "the great
negator and the principal enemy of the proletarian revolution, . . . he
undertakes not only to falsify the significance of men, but to falsify
history—and as the most inexcusable of assassins." It was one of the
greatest disillusionments of his life to see revolutionary action fall, as he
thought, into as deep a corruption as Western politics and the leaders
of the revolution reveal themselves as "traitors and dogs." [11] Backing his
statement were a number of surrealists, including Georges Henein, Maurice Henry, Georges Hugnet, Marcel Jean, Yves Tanguy, but of the
original group there was only Benjamin Péret; Eluard's and Aragon's
names were missing.

As the war approached, Breton predicted its gigantic proportions. He
declared in 1937: "the world risks becoming one big conflagration." [12]
He appealed to England to act as arbiter in "the latent conflict of the
two *miserable* nationalisms of France and Germany, ready once more to
have their peoples tear each other apart like dogs." [13]

He looked with a mixture of apprehension and hope toward the Spanish
Civil War: "in the eyes of the men and women fallen in July 1936 before
Saragossa may well be reflected the whole future." [14] Thereafter the official
surrealist group identified as the purest line of revolutionary action the
Loyalist cause in Spain. Breton gives in *Entretiens* the picture of Benjamin Péret before the "door" of Barcelona, "gun in one hand and with
the other caressing a cat on his knees." [15] But Breton could not join his
dearest friend to fight for the Loyalist cause. He tells us in *L'Amour fou*

the deep inner struggle he had to face at that time between his intense political commitment to the Loyalist cause, which would have led him to join his friends in Barcelona, and his personal sense of responsibility at the birth of his daughter at that moment, which made it imperative for the first time in his life to think of a regular means of livelihood. Paradoxically, the man who condemned the bonds created by "family" conceded the priority that a family—of his own choice—had over his actions. Instead of going to Barcelona, he applied to Jean Giraudoux, then minister of the Foreign Office and Cultural Services, to send him somewhere as cultural ambassador. Breton never commented on the logic of such a request: that for the first time of his own volition he was ready to represent his national culture in a foreign land in an official capacity. The ambivalence of the position can in fact perhaps be clarified by a scrutiny of the list of writers and artists he chose to lecture on to "represent" France when after much delay he was given in 1938 a choice between Czechoslovakia and Mexico.

He chose Mexico primarily because Trotsky had gained political asylum there following his exile from the Soviet Union. According to Jacqueline, when the Bretons arrived in Mexico they discovered that no arrangements had been made to lodge them. They would have found themselves stranded without any resources had not Diego Rivera come to their rescue and offered the hospitality of his home. Breton's first act was to arrange through him to meet Trotsky. Breton's enemies had forewarned Trotsky of his arrival and pronounced Breton a "subversive" against subversive ideologies. Former friends, Tzara and Aragon, now orthodox Communists, had let it be known that Breton was against Stalin's intervention in the Spanish Civil War and against the Front Populaire in France. This was true, but what balanced his paradoxical position in politics was the fact that he was equally if not more opposed to Franco's regime against which foreign Communist forces were sending their aid. The tremendous despair that marked Breton's view of Europe was due to the lack of any real choice between two supposed alternatives. It was a political situation from which there was no exit. As he saw it, either choice would lead to disaster; it was a betting game in which Europe stood to lose, no matter which way the dice fell. The man who could have offered Europe a real choice had been eliminated; Breton had looked forward to meeting Trotsky because he had felt for a long time that the Communist revolution had made a tragic mistake to reject the leadership of Trotsky, the "immortal theorist of the permanent revolution." [16]

Breton found Trotsky in his peaceful Blue House in Coyvacan, faithfully guarded by Mexican police against snipers and vengeful revolutionaries. They hit it off extremely well, with Rivera serving as intermediary. Breton's description of the political giant in chains resembles strangely the description one could have made of Breton himself a few years later in his walk-up apartment in Greenwich Village: the unmutilated freshness of childhood combined with the highest degree of mental tension, an electrifying personality possessed of animal magnetism, yet mild of manner, unpretentious in his reception of a man as intransigent as himself. While in his official capacity Breton gave lectures on poets such as Mallarmé and on artists such as Courbet, he was in constant dialogue with Diego Rivera and Trotsky in the search for a broader perspective for the Left, what was to be the nucleus of the New Left.

Breton was so little known in Mexico that he soon became identified as the mysterious stranger, the foreign agent, the fascist doctor, Mr. X. He made exploratory excursions in the countryside with Rivera and Trotsky. They took an 800-kilometer anthropological trip across Mexico to Guadalajara. There is no transcription of their discussion. One dreams of what a tape recorder might have preserved of the conversation of these three men about the origins of civilization and of man's everlasting struggle between his expression of the art vision and his involvement in self-destroying political action. The only written text that resulted from the dialogue was in answer to the question that preoccupied Breton in all his political considerations: what would be the legitimate and honest role of the artist in the new society? Trotsky had weighed the problem, and together they wrote a manifesto: *For a Revolutionary Independent Art.* When it came to signing, however, Trotsky withdrew his name and let Diego Rivera bear the responsibility of the second signature.

But whether coauthored by Trotsky or Rivera, the document contains the basic principles inherent in many of Breton's writings: in eradicating the dangers that beset the artist in bourgeois society, the proletarian state must not create new ones. If as Marx had said, "The writer . . . must naturally earn money to live and write but must not in any circumstances live and write to earn money," it also followed in Breton's thinking that the writer must not become a tool of a political system; his art is an end in itself and not a means either for economic solvency or for political apology. If freed from economic servitude he has to put his art to the service of political propaganda, he is indeed still in bondage. The artist must avoid all systems that are inimicable to his human dignity, whatever banners they wave or names they bear. He must try to maintain mental coherence in the face of outrageous distortions and repressions produced by organized opportunists. In this instance the condemnation is directed against the Stalin regime, which is considered as a betrayal of revolutionary communism in general. Disengaged but not self-centered, such is the image that Breton cherishes of the artist. He can accept neither an attitude of blind commitment to the ideology of the state, nor the detachment and indifference of one who lives merely for his art. His concern for the ethical problems that afflict the human condition transcends both personal and political considerations.

Breton returned to France on the eve of World War II, just in time to experience the full impact of the declaration of hostilities in September 1939, and to participate in the débacle he had so long foreseen and dreaded. Confronted for the second time in his life with a state of war, he donned the uniform of France again, but this time without the least semblance of protest: "I assumed then as best I could (but a little as if in a dream) the functions of physician at the school for pilots in Poitiers." [17] In this spontaneous allegiance to the call of his country he was acting like other surrealists. For Eluard and Aragon the concept of patriotism was to take the form of a burst of poetic lyricism and actions of national heroism. The theoretical refusal of national allegiance faded into thin air in the face of imminent danger to the national identity and the possibility of nonnational chaos. But once France collapsed in June 1940, Breton and many other intellectuals fled to the temporarily unoccupied zone, whose capital was Marseilles.

Completely destitute, accompanied by his wife and small daughter, he found asylum in Salon-de-Provence at the home of his friend Dr. Pierre Mabille, who had been in close association with him for many years in his studies of psychiatry and occultism; he had also been the family doctor of the Bretons and brought their child, Aube, into the world. Now he provided a temporary haven for them. But soon Breton was to join in Marseilles other friends such as artists Victor Bauner, Dominguez, Max Ernst, Wifredo Lam, and André Masson and writers René Clair and Benjamin Péret. The Bretons were lodged in an immense villa, "Bel-Air," as the guests of Varian Fry, and in a climate of tension the miracles of daily life were indeed the only ones they would count on. The surrealists resumed some of their group games in the pursuit of objective chance. But Breton's political situation was daily deteriorating. He had a close call when the emissaries of Pétain took him into temporary custody for questioning. His newly published *Anthologie de l'Humour noir* was removed from circulation by the censor, and he was not allowed to print his new long poem *Fata Morgana* even in a small edition at his own expense. His position was untenable; he was *persona non grata* whether the forces of fascism or of communism were to win, as he had spoken out loud and extensively against both. A political position such as Breton's had actually been viable only under the permissive bourgeois structure of prewar France which he had cursed most of all!

Unlike Aragon and Eluard, he could not join the marginal resistance movements since those underground forces were largely under Communist French leadership, and he was not to be trusted in time of war by the party he had so rabidly and dramatically repudiated in time of peace. On the other hand, were Hitler to win, Breton would be one of the first to be muzzled if not incarcerated, for as an archenemy of fascism, perhaps the most overtly critical among non-Jews, he had called the Nazis betrayers of the German heritage. It would have been no more tenable for Breton to live under the same sky as Hitler than for those who wore the star of David. There was no alternative for Breton but to leave France, which he did under the auspices of the American Committee for Aid of Intellectuals, to seek asylum in the United States between 1941 and 1946.

For this hospitality on the part of the United States and for the safe passage made possible by the superrich, under the guise of Peggy Guggenheim,* Breton was to be ever profoundly grateful; and it is to be noted that in subsequent political protests against the demoralizing characteristics of capitalist materialism, of which he could have found flagrant examples in the most materialistically evolved of modern nations, not once did he, unlike Sartre, make the United States the target of his attacks. He immunized, as it were, against attack the country to which he felt profoundly grateful, and where he eventually found unexpected happiness after being plunged into the deepest abysses of despair.

From Marseilles, Breton went to New York to a fifth-floor walk-up apartment on West 11th Street not unlike the one on the rue Fontaine, accompanied by his four-year-old daughter and wife Jacqueline. He was much troubled by the miseries of life in exile and poverty. It was at this period that I first met Breton, and was struck by the irrelevance of his personal situation with the premises of surrealism. Where was the freedom to dream, the nonslavery to life, the freedom of speech, the desire to transform life? Instead, the name "Breton" framed in an American letterbox, and under the skylight of an artist's mansard roof paced a powerful man trapped in a cage, muzzled by a language he could not speak, circumvented by a society he could not understand, caught in economic obligations to a wife and small child he did not have the means to support, reduced to a fearful reality that seemed forever to obliterate the possibility of the dream. He was Baudelaire's image of the powerful albatrosses brought down to earth by fishermen:

* She had sent the money to pay for the tickets of Breton and his family.

A peine les ont-ils déposés sur les planches
Que ces rois de l'azur, maladroits et honteux,
Laissent piteusement leurs grandes ailes blanches
Comme des avirons traîner à côté d'eux. . . .

Le Poëte est semblable au prince des nuées
Qui hante la tempête et se rit de l'archer;
Exilé sur le sol au milieu des huées,
Ses ailes de géant l'empêchent de marcher.

The only signs of another life now vanished were the surrealist paintings of his friends, which amazingly had accompanied him in his perilous journey and now lined the dismal walls of his home in exile.

Max Ernst and Yves Tanguy had also immigrated to America, but they were making a more permanent break with Europe, as they had both married American women; they are today listed by the Museum of Modern Art as "American" artists. Tanguy married Kay Sage, the artist and sculptor, with whom he lived in Connecticut until his death in 1955. Peggy Guggenheim was at that time Max Ernst's wife.

Breton found a job with the Voice of America, the O.W.I.'s "La Voix de l'Amérique en Guerre." With that another strange paradox was to enter his life. The man who had declared himself so forcefully and continuously against the role of propagandist, against direct involvement in government service, was obliged to take a job in which his function was to put, not his pen but his powerful, resonant voice and impeccable diction, to the service of propaganda. Observers noted how meticulously he read news reports over which he had neither editorial nor ideological jurisdiction. He read in an almost hypnotic tone, he a salaried worker, a tool, a medium, his voice employable, his thoughts of no consequence!

In the meantime he tried to relate to the artistic ambiance of New York. He contributed to the avant-garde little magazine, View, which ran an interview between him and Nicolas Calas. The interview started with the question: "Have you ever dreamed of Hitler?" Breton answered "No" but added that dreaming of Hitler, common among many people, was a symptom of a group psychosis which, if investigated, might throw much light on the obsessive public opinion that Hitler was an invulnerable superman. In another issue devoted to Marcel Duchamp, Breton contributed an article on his old friend who, in his comfortable position as Franco-American, had become something of a guide and sponsor to the disoriented Breton. Not only Breton's writings but those of his erstwhile surrealist friends found a natural medium in View. When Edouard Roditi translated a collected volume of Breton's poetry under the title of Young

Cherry Trees Secured Against Hares, it was published by *View* in 1946 and reviewed in *View* by William Carlos Williams. Yet it had been the editorial policy of the magazine to juxtapose in its pages many modernist trends. *View* had become the established center of the American literary avant-garde identified with Charles Henri Ford and his entourage. They generously opened their magazine to the rufugee writers and artists. But in speaking of those days Charles Henri Ford remembers Breton's less than total identification with *View.* Breton obviously could not bend to someone else's leadership—even if their objectives were compatible.

Breton joined forces with Duchamp, Max Ernst, and the American sculptor David Hare to organize a new review, *The Triple* V (multiplying the V that had become the emblem of Churchill): "V as a vow to return to a habitable and thinkable world, Victory over the forces of regression and death currently unleashed on the earth, but again V beyond the first Victory, . . . Victory over all that tends to perpetuate the enslavement of man by man, and beyond that double V, that double Victory, V again over all that is opposed to the emancipation of the mind." [18] How much good the review did to trigger interest in surrealism in its literary forms is highly questionable. Breton's collaboration in organizing an exposition of "Artists in Exile" did not particularly focus attention on him either.

The testimony of numerous witnesses to those years leads one to the conclusion that Breton's power of provocation did not catch on in America, and that his personal magnetism did not cross the language barrier. Perhaps a major reason for Breton's failure to stir enthusiasm was that America was at that particular moment depleted of its youth. Those who might have come knocking on Breton's door had quietly gone to war. On the other hand, he himself realized quickly that surrealism in America was already institutionalized and under the label of "art" had entered the orbit of the museums. As in the case of other orthodoxies, Breton shunned the orthodoxy of the museum mentality; in America as in France, if there was one thing that he was to maintain it was his independence of thought. In America he found three artists who could relate directly to surrealism: Matta, Alexander Calder, and Archile Gorky. And of American artists only Robert Motherwell has been able to express himself with noticeable empathy about Breton's philosophical orientation.

But *The Triple* V was to spell emotional disaster as well as intellectual dissatisfaction for Breton. It triggered his definite separation from his wife Jacqueline. Their marriage had become increasingly untenable as Jacqueline sought fulfillment as an artist in her own right and freedom from the precepts of surrealism. Breton saw her role in relation to himself quite differently: he demanded total devotion and subordination of herself to his love and his needs. With her knowledge of English, Jacqueline had been the intermediary between her monolingual French husband and the equally monolingual English-speaking David Hare. She left Breton to marry Hare, taking with her the child who was the being Breton adored above all else.

Now he was more isolated than ever. His intimates, according to Lewis Galantière, were George Duthint, the art critic, the anthropologist Claude Lévi-Strauss, who was also working for the Voice of America, the artist Kurt Seligmann (who shared Breton's interest in hermeticism), and "a long-legged young Greek educated in Paris" (obviously Nicolas Calas). One should add also Meyer Schapiro, the art scholar, who was his neighbor in Greenwich Village and one of the few Americans with whom Breton could speak freely in French.

But according to Galantière's observations, Breton, like a number of other exiled French writers, lived detached from the mainstream of American life. If some formed their own French clique within the political structure of the Free French Movement, "Breton ignored the official Gaullists" as well, according to Galantière. He became neither part of America nor part of the French colony in America. Although Breton had relentlessly pronounced his antipathy for nationalism and politically had tried to be nonnationalist, ecologically he belonged strictly to French soil. In America he was a stranger, unadaptable to language and to the particular climate of the World War II years. He loved to ride the open-top double-decker buses up Fifth Avenue and along Riverside Drive,* but in New York he could identify only with the Hudson River and Edgar Allan Poe. In the interview with Calas he explains how he related to the *paysage* through Poe:

> I like enormously what I have seen of the Hudson and its green islets —the Floating Island—which doubtless retain something secret and menacing from the books of my childhood. I was extremely pleased to become acquainted for the first time with that unique light of "apparition" which appears over the grass about five o'clock in the afternoon, and which bathes, to the exclusion of all others, certain poems of Poe, such as "Ulalume."

He also admired the American foliage: "Truly surrealist flora has been enriched as far as I am concerned, with a new species shown me by Kay and Yves Tanguy." He was to incorporate some of it in the imagery of his own last poems, written in America.

* As he told me a number of years later; Fifth Avenue was not yet a one-way street.

In the years 1943-4 Breton's tragedy in terms of personal and political disappointments was the deepest he was ever to experience. Yet, not one word of personal literature emanates from that state, and it is not until he has once more conquered the powers of darkness and veered again toward the North Star that he is able to translate the personal anguish and the moral victory into indirect verbal communication in both poetry and prose that represent one of his most luminous periods.

The objective chance that he had explored for twenty years came to his aid one day as he sat in the restaurant Larré's; it came in the guise of a beautiful and very sad woman, Elisa, who had lost a daughter, age seventeen, in a drowning accident after having lost her husband by divorce. Alone in the world, even as he was, she responded to his need, to his notion of love, always renewable, always as intense as the first time, always revising and completing the previous image, always giving a sense of the total and unalterable reality. With her he was to take the long journey to ancient Arcadia and on the peninsula of Gaspé, the closest place to the North Star, to reach the source of the aurora borealis, which in 1943 had graced New York for one brief moment. There he wrote the last of his analogical prose, *Arcane 17*, combining in the tapestry of symbols the great forces of eroticism and political destiny, the commitment of the human will to love and the social need for total fraternity. It was only then, in the light of a spiritual triumph over darkness and tragedy, that he could indeed speak of the sorrow that had overcome him in New York:

> When fate brought you [Elisa] to my encounter, the greatest shadow was over me. I understood when I saw you appear, when I heard your first words, that in a certain desperate course, vertiginous and unrestrained, of thoughts in which the mental machine is so strongly wound up that it comes off its bearings, I must have touched one of those poles which remain generally out of reach, activated by chance, that hidden bell which rings its extraordinary alarm for help. . . . A great part of the earth presented nothing but a spectacle of ruins. Inwardly I had to admit without resignation that all I held indefectible in the affective field had gone with the wind without my being able to know in what storm: there remained as a token a child . . . This child, by all that is unjust and severe in this world, had been separated from me, I was to be deprived of all her beautiful awakenings, which were my joy, which had made me lose—in losing her—the wonder of the daily contact with life, she was to be separated from me even more. I would not be there to help shape that young mind which used to come toward me shining like a mirror, so open. Inside of me there were also ruins, . . . And the thoughts by which man tends to keep

himself in firm rapport with other men, the thoughts were not spared
more than the rest. . . . The words that designated them, such as
right, justice, liberty had taken local, contradictory meanings. Both
sides had speculated so well on their understanding them in any way
they pleased, until they made them say exactly the opposite of what
they meant. Surely the military dictatorship found it to its advantage
to note the destruction of the semantic value, each day more meticulously so, destruction to which the most obtuse and the most cynically
venal sort of journalism was predisposed. Those who retained here and
there any concern for future significations . . . were forced into silence, put in a position where it was impossible for them to communicate with each other or even to count their number.[19]

To get a divorce from Jacqueline, Breton went to Reno, where he was
exposed to the Indian cults of mysticism which supported his belief that
all separations of humans along ethnic lines are arbitrary as far as basic
issues are concerned. The spirit of unity in all things and beings, the
need to find the miraculous conciliation between sensation and representation, between the antipodes confectioned by successive societies, was as
resplendently manifest in the gorges of the Colorado River as on the
snow-covered summits of the Alps.

While in the United States, Breton was to make one significant statement bearing political import; it was the speech at Yale University in
1942. When he was invited by Professor Henri Peyre to address a generation of youths preparing to go into the Army in the darkest moment of
the war, it is interesting to note how cursory was Breton's review of the
aesthetics and history of surrealism and how he plunged straight into the
sociology of literature. In this address as elsewhere he showed himself
plagued by the ambiguity of the social role of the artist; the withdrawal
of the artist from the social context and the commitment of the artist
to political objectives were positions both marked for failure. In the lecture,
which was later published under the title of "Situation du Surréalisme
entre les deux guerres," he pits the power of the surrealist's frenzy against
the inertia of society which has led to "the desperate situation of man in
the midst of the twentieth century." He rejects with total scorn his own
generation for having learned nothing from the mistakes of the previous
ones; he extols youth and pronounces his faith in the genius of youth. Although reduced to the role of mere observer in a foreign land, his power
of condemnation is not thereby lessened.

Breton attacks the asphyxiating specializations, the indiscriminate verbalizations of the ruling generation, and in situating surrealism historically

between the two world wars, he sees its significance in the context of the two conflagrations as well as in its nonhistorical proliferation beyond the limits of the two disasters: the twenty-year protest against the political myopia that created the twentieth-century nightmare. On the one hand, Breton deplores war not only for the death and destruction that it causes, but because it entails a certain regimentation that reduces the individual's liberty to a state of anonymity: "making an abstraction in each person of what was unique in order to conceive of oneself as an integral and infinitesimal part, more or less negligible, of the whole." On the other hand, later in his speech he sees as one of the principal purposes of surrealism the desire to "return to man the sense of his absolute dependence on the community of all men." If in these two statements there appears to be a conceptual contradiction, it is only so because we may overlook the particular meaning Breton conveys by the words "fraternity" and "association."

"Free union," as he represented in his poem of love, and as he extended it to all human associations, means the free giving of self, which constitutes an enlargement of self, a sense of the inherent unity of all beings and all things, not a submersion of the individual in a nonreciprocal totality where giving is only met by taking as in organized warfare or in demagogical organizations such as Communist cells. Breton's sociology stems as much from his monistic philosophy as from his aesthetics. Not only is there no contradiction in the notion of "free union," but there is a certain intransigence which his enemies were wont to observe and decry. What distinguishes this unflinching, inflexible cast of mind from the usual fanaticism is that as the years went by, the initial anarchy or cruelty of his pen gave way increasingly to expressions of compassion. The speech to the youth of Yale is one of the frankest indictments of society, yet also one of the most compassionate statements on the indelibility of the human heritage. He did not tell the Yale students to burn their draft cards, but to his Ciceronian condemnation of the times he added an affirmation of faith in love; for if in its servitude to government youth is engaged as an agent for destruction, its very essence destroys the greatest of all the antinomies: that of hate and love. Not even the most formidable face of nuclear warfare can obliterate from a young man's consciousness the gaze of a beautiful woman who may cross his path in his most troubled moments. Perhaps, says Breton, if youth is called to serve war in larger measure than any other age group it is because it is sustained against the repulsiveness of war by the power to love; and through love to erase in part the formidable abasement imposed by society:

Surrealism, I repeat, is born of a boundless affirmation of faith in the genius of youth.

On their way back to France, Breton and his new wife, Elisa, were invited by Dr. Pierre Mabille, his old friend, to give a number of lectures in Haiti, where Mabille had become a cultural attaché in Port-au-Prince. No one was in a more sympathetic frame of mind than Mabille to herald all the attractive qualities of Breton as poet, as intellectual leader, and even as social prophet. He had all the luminaries lined up for what was perhaps the most magnificent and official reception given to Breton anywhere in all his life. Before a resplendent and educated, mostly white audience he gave the first of three scheduled addresses. At the second session half the audience was black; by the third session the blacks largely outnumbered the whites. Soon thereafter occurred the Haitian revolution which overthrew the demagogical regime. It has been said, half in jest, that the only political action Breton's revolutionary pronouncements ever produced was the Haitian revolution. Of course, it was rather one of those miraculous coincidences of chance in which Breton believed so profoundly. The overthrow of the government had been long in the planning. Perhaps Breton's fervent tones of sympathy for the Haitian people and his expressed confidence in their autochthonous genius, catalyzed the impending storm, triggered the brewing rebellion, proved to be the *Marseillaise* of the Revolution,—and certainly caused much embarrassment to Breton's host and "deplorable repercussions on his activities as a cultural attaché." [20]

Breton's message to his Creole audience was a continuation of the monologue begun in Mexico and carried on in the United States; it was perhaps most dramatically relevant to the immediate needs of Haiti: that the natural forces of nature, that man's intrinsic manifestations of cult, have as their centrifugal force a high sense of human dignity and liberty, and that the so-called forces of "civilization" intervene not to enhance these innate realities but to obstruct them, and are therefore doomed to self-destruction. Haiti for him was still bearing the marks of French imperialism, and his own visit there, a significant evidence of the unity of intent in surrealism, whose first political protest had been against the war in Morocco in 1925. As Breton remembered the events in Haiti in *Entretiens*: "The newspaper *Ruche*, organ of the young generation . . . declared my words electrifying, and decided to take an insurrectional tone." [21]

In weighing the differences between the ethnic heritage of the Haitians and Western civilization, Breton tips the balance in favor of the former, with his particular flare for finding success where misery exists and misery where success and progress are overtly proclaimed. He contrasts the divisions that exist in European civilization with the monolithic nature of the Haitian. He extols the Haitian's power to amalgamate his African animism with the aboriginal voodoo cult and the best in Christian mysticism, capturing the essential forces of the three in a single potent vision of the unity of the material and the spiritual, of the affective and the rational, and producing a deepening sense of reality. Breton finds the innocent man, as symbolized by the Haitian, closer to the discovery of the Philosopher's Stone, which leads to self-discovery and wisdom, than the civilized man who is bent on discovering only the contradictions and conflicts in himself and in his society. Again, situating surrealism as an extension of eighteenth-century illuminism and the French Revolution, Breton sees it as a tool for the search of knowledge; it is to be an antidote to mere mechanical progress which, "whether man contributes to it by his work or simply enjoys it, tends to isolate him in an abstract world where the meaning of his effort or his pleasure is depreciated, when it does not in addition hurl him into the most cruel disillusionment." [22] Man's effort is ever annihilated by its unnatural direction, his pleasure is obliterated by artificially imposed duties.

Breton was never to lose contact with the French West Indies thereafter, and their major poet, Aimé Césaire, born in Martinique, became one of his dearest friends and disciples, identified in his mind as the symbol of the purity of the savage mind—symbol, not reality, as Aimé Césaire was magnificently trained in the French language and intellectual tradition. The savage state that Rousseau had sought in the heart of the Alps as a region free of the pernicious forces of society, and that Chateaubriand found in the virgin forests of North America, Breton locates clearly outside the boundaries of Europe or even of its North American extension; he situates it in a land where he believes the infections of Europe have been resisted by a vigor and an uncontaminated state of psychic health, amidst physical poverty and an absence of industrial conveniences. It is as if he had found a corollary to the proposition that economic liberation does not necessarily entail spiritual freedom; in Haiti he sensed that the spiritual autonomy of man had survived poverty and political oppression.

It was to Breton a sustaining force as a preamble to his return to Europe to have triggered a revolution against enslavement; it compensated in his mind a little for the inactive role he had had to play in World War II.

XII

THE EPIC POEMS:
FATA MORGANA
LES ETATS GÉNÉRAUX
ODE À CHARLES FOURIER

> "For me no work of art is worth this little patch
> of the multicolored grass in the distant eye
> range of life." —*Fata Morgana*

Despite all the futile waitings, all the disappointments and anguish in his life, as Breton reached the darkest hours of his own existence in exile at home, then in exile abroad, he did not lose his primal confidence in the life adventure. He would not trade the luminous contact between the human eye and nature's demiurgic power for all the "art" creation in the world. Yet in the eyes of the world his own stature will no doubt be measured not according to the life to which he accorded so high a value but according to his art, which he viewed in modest terms. In listing his "accomplishments" in the biographical questionnaire that *Contemporary Authors* submitted to him a few years before his death, he referred to the prose and ideological writings, and to his actions in the field of politics, and in particular to the Moscow trials, but he did not name a single one of his poems. Even the most enthusiastic commentators and witnesses extol Breton the man, praise his majestic prose, and generally stop dead before his verse. Yet he left an enormous body of poetry—enormous in depth, in strata of superimposed rather than juxtaposed meanings—which could keep critics and linguists busy for a long time to come.

Breton's manipulation of language in a poetic context to convey multi-

dimensional meaning and communicate the range of his eye and the turmoil of his mind and heart is the most radical of the provocative features
of his writings. We have seen some of the early manifestations of his
concept of poetry as it illuminated his notion of love, as it sparked his
contacts with nature and with the Parisian landscape through his ambula-
tory, aleatory vision. Most of the poems before 1940 were short, and all
in free verse. With the world-shaking events of 1940, Breton reaches a
new level in his poetic evolution: in the fifth decade of his life he makes
his most marked contribution to the poetic genre, then stops writing poetry
altogether shortly after his fiftieth birthday. Although all the characteristics previously noted in his earlier poetry are carried into the poems of
this period, Breton also developed a new genre, the modern epic, in three
long poems: *Fata Morgana, Les Etats Généraux*, and *Ode à Charles Fourier*. His power as a writer—whether or not he attached any value to the
art of writing—is most conclusively demonstrated with these three poems,
which contain a synthesis of all he believed in, of all he loved, of all he
cherished in this earthly existence. Whereas the earlier poems were short,
these all exceed three hundred lines, and their radically irregular lengths
range from two words to seventy-five per line. With these poems Breton
joins, in fact, Claudel and St.-John Perse in a triptych of France's modern
cosmic poets, in the first half of the twentieth century. But what distinguishes Breton's from the more grandiose manner of the other two
is that he brings himself in collision with world events and searches for
their meaning in the microcosm of his life as well as in the macrocosm
of the natural world.

Before Breton the epic always identified a hero or heroes who tran-
scended cataclysmic events in spirit at least, if not in body; they struggled
against overpowering forces and forgot their personal lives in their participation in the collective phenomena upon which they had an impact.
The tradition of the epic was to be carried on by Breton's erstwhile companions, Eluard and Aragon, in the eloquent exchange between the "I"
and the collective conscience, as virtual heroes of the Resistance. In a
surge of lyricism—except for the more sophisticated *Broceliande* of Aragon—they virtually dissipated all the cryptic character of surrealist communication, as if direct expression heightened the poignancy of the dark
spring of 1940 when "the roses and the lilacs" dripped blood across the
French countryside. From the very beginning, as in *Misère de la poésie*,
Breton had repudiated circumstantial verse and chided Aragon for "Front
Rogue." But if the temptation to write circumstantial poetry could be
avoided in 1930, it was much more difficult to circumvent the immediacy
of events in 1940; and Breton's colleagues yielded to the temptation easily,

unleashing all the obvious clichés which had been repressed in them under the regime of surrealist writing. This suddenly liberated lyricism was
to nourish an anguished population caught unprepared to face the holocaust, and which, in the absence of arms, clung to the hypnotic power
of words for comfort and courage. Beside their unilateral and universal
message so instantaneously understood by the generation participating in
the events of 1940, Breton's poems lack outer vibrance, are indeed *sotto
voce*, and are related dimly to the events that triggered them.

The intransigence of Breton revealed itself once more as he desisted
from the natural and easy path by which he could have given simple expression to the gigantic tragedy. Instead, he created a form of poetry
more hermetic than it had ever been in the days of automatic writing.
The ellipses of language coupled with the enigmas of thought produced
the closed character of these last poems. This is a far cry from automatic
writing. A conscious, architectural pattern structures *Fata Morgana*. But
the closed nature of the meanings, which can be glimpsed spasmodically
as through the portholes of a bark tempestuously moving over an abyss,
is due not to irrational juxtaposition of images, but to the technique by
which various references are combined in relation to the catastrophic
events which are taken out of their historical context and cast in a limitless perspective and measureless time. Part of the mystification is caused
by the cryptogrammic disposition of the words on the page, much like
the last poem of Mallarmé, "Un Coup de dés jamais n'abolira le hasard."
Silences are expressed, simultaneities of thought and perception are recorded in their graphic complexity. The patterns resemble those of a symphony with various recurring themes and variations. Again Breton resorts
to the verbal rebus of the occultists, and it becomes here the basis of his
poetic harmonics: that is, several meanings are contained in one image,
as several sounds produce a musical chord. But whereas in music the
notes that constitute the chord can easily be singled out, the images that
can be extracted from the rebus image appear infinite in number, and
each reading produces a new series, so that one could easily write a whole
book on the single poem, *Fata Morgana*, and generations unborn at the
time of the 1940 disaster can identify their own circumstances of social
and metaphysical exile with the core imagery of the poem.

Fata Morgana was written in Marseilles in the winter of 1940–41, not
in the crucial moment of the fall of France but in its aftermath. The
time for heroism was past; it was a time rather for submergence of personal destiny into the collective exodus. *Fata Morgana* is the poem of
exodus, of stagnant waitings, of exile in one's own land, of the abrupt
transformation of life within the framework of familiar places and cherished faces, a superposition of physical necessity and objective chance

upon personal liberty, of cosmic forces upon daily lives. It must be remembered that Breton, along with a host of friends, had descended to
the unoccupied zone whose capital was Marseilles. To take up the account given by his wife, Jacqueline:

> the state of the world then and the situation of the surrealists [among
> them many Jews in increasing numbers] was such that a climate of
> occultation spread among all without any specific intention on any-
> one's part. But it is quite possible that without the presence of André
> Breton in the Villa "Bel Air" [which Breton refers to as "Air Bel"]
> the climate would have been less directed. No one was more conscious
> than he that there existed somewhere a hidden road to lead out of
> the anguishes, and one of his great powers was to seize each occasion
> to find the one that was needed in each precise instance.

The whole poem is structured on the rebus: it is one thing, and it is
many things. "Fata Morgana" is the Latinized form of Morgan Le Fay,
a Celtic fairy, the creature of Merlin the magician, emblem of salvation.
Characteristically in Breton's works the gods are never vengeful but only
kindly when evoked at all. But *Fata Morgana* is more than an invocation
of a pagan goddess. It is a name given to a natural phenomenon that
occurs principally on the shores of Sicily but doubtless also on other shores
of the Mediterranean. It is the mirage produced by the refraction of the
dawn's light on the Calabrese coast and in the delta of Messina on morn-
ings when the sea is still and the sun rises over the mountains and strikes
the Mediterranean at a forty-five degree angle. It creates a phantasmagoria
wherein objects and gigantic figures of men and horses move as on a
screen, the vapor adorning the colossal shadows with hues and tints of
color. The rebus of optical illusion is created by Breton as he contemplates the mountain range in the background of Marseilles. And on the
mysterious scene of the morning sky he sees the shadows of the forces
of destiny, perhaps in the spirit of the Great Transparents * which in his
scale of creatures ranked above humans. His references to the cosmic
illusion that stimulates his imagination are in terms of a theatrical scene
and large murals. As he grew older, he effected in this manner more and
more intimate links with the great circuit of nature, ever searching an interpretation of human necessity in terms of the cosmic rhythm of fortuitous chance.† His work as a poet consisted, he thought, of seeking indices

---

* See "Les Grands Transparents" at the end of "Prolegomène sur un troisième manifeste ou non" (published in the Pauvert edition of Breton's manifestoes).

† I remember his words to me a few years after the writing of *Fata Morgana* as he
paced the floor of his exile room in New York and said in that sonorous voice:
"There is a chain of events over and above the apparent one, which we are
experiencing."

in natural phenomena that, by establishing contacts with the human imagination, would provide illumination, and confidence in nature's intents. The Fata Morgana illusion was just such an index and triggered this poem, as later in New York the aurora borealis, or northern lights, was to set in motion *Les États Généraux*, as the great wall of the Rock of Percé would frame *Arcane 17*, and the Grand Canyon would exhilarate him in *Ode à Charles Fourier*.

The first image of the poem defines the immediate situation in metaphorical terms that can apply to French refugees in Marseilles or to any other flotsam or outcasts anywhere:

> Le matin la fille de la montagne tient sur ses genoux
> Un accordion de chauves-soun's blanches

(This morning the daughter of the mountain holds on her lap an accordion of white bats)

sounds like a perfect example of automatic writing and could set off the imagination in metaphysical visions. Yet it has very precise, though hidden, references to the Marseilles situation without marring the broader references that could be derived from it. *Chauves-souris blanches* was the term used by which the White Russian refugees of the Communist Revolution had been known in Paris where they flocked in the 1920's, when Breton was a youth. The analogy with the 1940 refugees is obvious. As for the mountain, its primary reference is to the lower Alps which gird like a palisade the coast of Marseilles. In fact Breton mentions the view he had of the mountain from the villa in a letter to his friend, critic, and publisher of *Sagittaire*, Léon Pierre-Quint: "old house, large park, view of the mountains helping to surmount all that would fail to convey a grand air in our situation at the moment." The fairy Morgan * reigns over the mountain in its symphony with the sun and sky as she weaves human destiny. Breton puts the refugees under her benign protection: her like an accordion (the reference is not really musical but visual) opening up larger and larger, as the number of those seeking asylum grows every day, and on the other hand, having also closing movements as from time to time the number also declines when visas are issued and refugees depart. What other image could convey so succinctly and accurately the spiritual and physical moment of Marseilles in the winter of 1940–41, and yet remain completely free of the specifics of the circumstances?

It is a poem of dawn, or predawn: the last line, consisting of the single noun "sun," places before us the image of the rising sun. Character-

---

* Identifiable also perhaps with the statue of Notre Dame de la Garde that dominates Marseilles.

istic of the kind of sturdy optimism ingrained in Breton, entrenched in his incorrigible faith in life, the poem he wrote in the most distraught moment of his life is a poem of dawn, of a new day. The apocalypse has for him its original, etymological meaning of revelation and light, and not the extended usage which makes it so often suggest "end of the world" conditions.

"A new day" is the first theme of the poem, and it recurs at various moments in its course. The poem begins with a *parlerie*, a one-way conversation making us aware of the presence of the woman whose part in the dialogue is silence. The poem then proceeds to a prayer to the god Thoth personified as a mummy of Ibis, the sacred bird of Egypt, and ends in a meditative monologue. Throughout, Breton superposes on the bleeding *moi* of the poet in exile the universal *soi*, confronted and supported by the undaunted forces for survival.

The rebus structure consists of the hotel-room, café-table situation of the homeless poet and his family, which we are made to sense through references introducing a brand new vocabulary: the dresser, the furniture with its medieval decoration, the tablecloth, the baggage of the voyage. Intermingled with this human setting is nature's presence as if negating or compensating for the impoverished accouterments with its own lavish landscape. The third frame of reference is the allegorical one of the labyrinth, man's passage, the thread he follows, the darkness to which his eyes become accustomed, the light he detects, the possibilities of exit he envisions:

> Je commence à voir autour de moi dans la grotte
> Le vent lucide m'apporte le parfum perdu de l'existence
> Quitte enfin de ses limites
>
> (I begin to see around me in the grotto
> The lucid wind brings me the lost perfume of existence
> Released at last from its limitations)

The three levels of comprehension of life's meaning are not correspondences as in Symbolist poetry, but "one in the other" self-contained in the total and single situation, totally integrated one with the other. The word *comme* rarely occurs in Breton's poetry, nothing is like anything else, but one thing is in something else, and, if allowed a natural course, moves toward unity with all else. The problem of the dispersion of human lives by the explosion of war is one with the fragmentation of the soul in its inability to relate to the universe. The disharmony in man's own self-fashioned world is part of the disjunction between man and nature.

Poverty, loss of direction, loss of anchor, if these be the fate of the political refugee, they are at the same time the destiny of Everyman in the world against which Breton had so long protested. To alleviate the anguish of alienation, of estrangement, he has love: "your hand in mine" is the consistent, uninterrupted flow of love "From the brunette to the blond"; "Two hands, it is enough for tomorrow's roof." And there is the dawn, and even the possibility, through love and through intimacy with nature, of escaping one's own destiny whether one reads it in the coffee dregs or in the shadows of the sky.

The complexities of the rebus can be illustrated by a single, dominant image: the bed. It is a hotel bed, on rollers, and it undergoes several metamorphoses in the course of the poem: a bed to signify destitution and transient status, but also love as it enters the tunnel of carnal desire; it is also the way to the dream as it rolls Breton's entire life before him in a series of kaleidoscopic images. It also becomes transformed into a train that alludes to the voyage that brought them to Marseilles and will take them to foreign lands, and movement transforms it still further to a magnetized boat, with uncontrollable direction and unforeseen adventure. From the objective reality (of place) to the subconscious reality (of dream) and the sensual reality (of love) to prophetic reality (of voyage) to sublimated reality (of adventure)!

Another rebus image is the coffee cup in which sugar has created bubbles; it is also a bottomless pit of the unknown destiny which the gypsy has tried to read and toward which the exiled wander gropingly.

The invocation is to *Momie d'Ibis*, the personification of the Egyptian god, Thot, known as a magician possessing the power of resurrection. It was he who helped Isis restore to life Osiris, the dismembered demi-god of civilization. Breton's exorcism is self-evident as a prelude to the uncertainties ahead as he seeks not solutions to circumstantial problems but through tribulations, a sharper comprehension of the meaning of the "great algebra" of existence, even as in the darkness of a grotto after a while, the eye becomes more discerning, more sensitive than in broad daylight:

Il ne sera jamais trop tard pour en finir avec le morcelage de l'âme momie
    d'ibis
Et par toi seule sous toutes ses facettes de momie d'ibis
Avec tout ce qui n'est plus ou attend d'être je retrouve l'unité perdue momie
    d'ibis

(It will never be too late to end the morselling of the soul ibis mummy
And through you alone in all its facets of ibis mummy
With all that is no longer or waits to be I find the lost unity ibis mummy)

Marseilles, a city of vaporous skies, dark grottoes, mystical mountain ranges, bold in their utter bareness, dominated by the Virgin of the Church on the supreme summit, was the predestined emblem of Breton's confrontation with destiny. The physical and metaphysical problem that Breton faced in the winter of 1940–41 is carved in the structure of *Fata Morgana*, the heartbeat of one man cadencing the traumas of the collective conscience of a disrupted society. Marseilles is not a tourist spot, it is generally considered a commercial center where provincial Frenchmen assemble for mercantile purposes or on Ascension Day pay homage to the Virgin. But when you leave the city and its practical reality behind, and scan its coast, its islands, and its overhanging rocks and cliffs, it sheds its menial function and takes the emblematic primeval features so superbly bestowed on it by nature. Elisa once said that André Breton was ever an early riser. The poem of his apocalypse transforms the most unromantic of France's cities into the resplendent setting of a cosmic vision.

The poem was illustrated by Wifredo Lam, a young Chinese-Cuban painter whom Breton had recently discovered. He had caught the sharp eye of Breton as "the one of all the artists I know who appears to have the most to say at the moment." *

If *Fata Morgana* is the poem of Marseilles, *Les Etats Généraux* is the epic of New York. Written in 1943, it is inundated with the "vertical spark" of a natural phenomenon and the optical illusion it creates: it is bathed in the aurora borealis that had visited New York a few months before, equating dawn and twilight, turning the night into a momentary day, shedding starlight "into the fur of the night," as Breton sums it up at the end of the poem.

In fact, the major theme of the poem is illumination in the darkness, an equation he tries to set up between two words and two concepts: *bâtir* and *abattre*, which in rebus fashion seem to lodge one in the other. Can leveling down and building up be historically related as they are in the construction of big cities, where nothing can be added except by the destruction of something old?

Again the poem is designed on several levels. The theme of liberty and struggle against despotism is contained most overtly in the title: Les Etats Généraux was the consultative assembly of ancient France whose meeting in an emergency session had triggered the French Revolution. The other symbols of rebellion evoked in the poem are of Esclarmonde de Foix and Delescluze.

* In a letter to Léon Pierre-Quint, February 4, 1941.

Esclarmonde was a thirteenth-century Joan of Arc of the subjugated kingdom of southern France. She lies buried (so the legend goes) in the flank of Montségur, the mountain fortress of the martyred Albigenses who defended, in a losing battle, their right to interpret the Gospel according to their own comprehension, and who were massacred as heretics by the Crusaders (soldiers of the Catholic Church) for their defiance of orthodox dogma. With the Albigenses went a way of life, swallowed up in the culture of the northern kings of France; this is one of the reasons why Breton, ever the champion of heresies, was to believe that written histories, one-sided as they are, never tell the truth. Esclarmonde, whom he invokes in this poem of rebellion against all the downtrodden of the world, is a symbol of the pure and selfless rebel. Breton's choice of her as his symbol is characteristic of his general inclination toward heroes of lost causes, of physical defeats and moral victories, rather than toward those who accomplish their missions. Esclarmonde de Foix was just such an undaunted figure. Though she was defeated, her soul wanders over the world, as Breton envisions; she is the power of protest that combats tyranny millennium after millennium. Even if the power of rebirth of such a heroine is ephemeral, it is a recurring phenomenon. The spirit of Esclarmonde is identified for Breton with the power of metempsychosis that makes mankind spring back from successive tyrannies even as the phoenix rises from its ashes, though it may be true that "the phoenix is made of ephemerids."

The third figure of rebellion, Delescluze, was a journalist during the socialist revolution of the Commune of 1871; he fought the Emperor's army and paid with his life on the barricades of Paris. He too is the incarnation of the unsuccessful but unrelenting rebel.

The Etats-Généraux, Esclarmonde, Delescluze! They sustain Breton's faith in the powers that can transform the world. The basic structure of *Fata Morgana* was a vast interrogation of destiny; the question continues in *Les Etats Généraux* under the verbal device as repetitive as it is urgent *"dis," "polis mes yeux"*: tell, polish my eyes that I may see more clearly in the crystal bowl. But there are more answers here than in *Fata Morgana*; the poet gives social and ethical context to his visions of the future. The social message has the color of the times, as does the next poem, *Ode à Charles Fourier*. The dream, so totally scuttled by subsequent events, was that of "one world": not a paranoic confrontation of nations but the spirit of unity which Breton so majestically expressed as he called upon people, under the fertile sign of the shovel that digs and erects, "to conceive of itself as a whole and become that whole."

Pour qu'il s'élève au sens de la dépendance universelle dans l'harmonie
Et que la variation par toute la terre des couleurs de peau et des traits
L'avertisse que le secret de son pouvoir
Est dans le libre appel au génie autochtone de chacune des races
En se tournant d'abord vers la race noire la race rouge
Parce qu'elles ont été longtemps les plus offensées

(That it may rise to the sense of the universal dependence in harmony
And that the world-wide variation of colors of skin and features
Be its revelation that the secret of its power
Is the free appeal to the autochthonous genius of each race
Turning first of all to the black race and the red race
Because they have been for so long abused)

He sees the workers hand in hand and he sees a more intense polarization of man and woman, and the freedom of woman from man's domination; for Breton puts woman in a class with the downtrodden, the enslaved, even as Rimbaud had before him suggested that woman would not be able to realize her potential until she was liberated from the servitude of menial chores to which a man-structured society had assigned her. "So that man and woman more closely eye to eye/She accepts not the yoke/He pronounces not her doom." This part of the poem presages the last major work of Breton, *Arcane 17*, in which the notion that woman must be liberated and in turn must become a force for liberation of the world, will reach its full poetic image.

The end of this sequence, which was cast under the symbol of the shovel, ends with the image of the scaffolding, ambiguous in that it could be the ghostlike remnant of a crumbled society or the foundation of a new edifice. The uncertainty of the future course of man is further symbolized in the tossing of a coin as in gambling; and when the coin turns up tail, Breton interprets the sign to mean "The inclination unwitting but irresistible toward the better." If in *Fata Morgana* a series of hypotheses, unrealistic and physically impossible, had suggested Breton's desire—against terrible odds—to escape his dark destiny of personal exile and the anguish of the collective defeat of Europe, here he appears to put destiny in the service of humanity, a star shines deep in the darkness as Breton contemplates a better future. The theme of "a new day," which had a poignant personal tone in *Fata Morgana*, carries a more universal import in *Les Etats Généraux*.

But Breton's multidimensional frescoes of a world torn apart by war do not omit the thread of his personal wanderings. He is the dominant figure in the image of the nomadic tribes that pass in the sand. Like a man drowning in a cataclysm he has flashbacks of involuntary memory, reminiscent of *Poisson soluble*, taking him to his early youth: a whiff of mint, and he is twenty in a section of Lyon with a woman in all the hypnotism of love, or the lights of the Seine River emerge and with them the power to forget; a grain of oblivion as delivering from reality as the recurrence of a patch of image from one's youth. The final personal image is that of the immediate self, at the end of the poem; the pleasure of smoking, the wound that heals as he speaks and finds once more the silent but beloved listener facing him.

As in *Fata Morgana*, there is the analogical pattern, steeped as ever in occult references: here there are the images of the Hebrew alphabet, of the Cabala, the Egyptian tarot cards, the key, the Quadrilateral figure in the sand and the dark oval, all part of the universal hieroglyphics, the mysterious relation and affinities of things and beings. Breton refers to Jersey and Guernsey, seat of the spiritualist séances of the nineteenth century and seat of the illuminists. He evokes Fabre d'Olivet, who dreamed of a universal language. All the emblems of mystery are rallied to create an atmosphere of hidden meaning as a backdrop to man's innate desire to "lift the forbidden barrier."

Finally, again following the pattern established in *Fata Morgana*, an item in the personal reality of the poet is transfigured into a vehicle for the visionary image. It is the coffee dregs that foretold destiny in the previous poem; in *Les Etats Généraux* it is the tobacco leaf—or rather, as he calls it, the flower, as the filter of his pipe is transposed to the open field and the surface of the large tobacco flower is turned into a fresco, in which Breton sees humanity marching as on a battlefield, as he ponders the riddle of "man and his problems." The whole series of associations is under the aura of a world transformed according to the poet's desire.

Just as *Fata Morgana* ends with a dream tableau, incongruous in the light of the sun but rich in historical and legendary references to the phenomenal annals of humanity, so in *Les Etats Généraux* the phantasmagoria that surges out of the tobacco flower like a "paradise" of Rimbaud's, fades into the light of awakening from the sands of the dream; the arena is emptied except for one little bird who, as it disappears, leaves behind a stalk of hay; the images of "swarm" and "arrow" intensify the departure of the mirage, but the power of metamorphosis is in action: the image of the arrow becomes an image of light. As *Fata Morgana* evolved the predawn into sunlight, this time the twilight is resplendent in a single bright star, for whether in life or death, as he inscribed into the poem his own last will and testament, Breton gravitates under the sign of the North Star. It is bright with its mystical folklore as it is practical in its power to provide direction for the lost and the adventurous.

The final poem of the trilogy is the *Ode à Charles Fourier;* except for fragmental, apocryphal pieces, it was to be the final poem of Breton's literary career. Unlike the two preceding poems, which were lost to literary criticism in the scuffle of Breton's peregrinations, the *Ode* was given a handsome publication and in fact announced Breton's return to the Parisian literary scene after World War II. As a result, it is much better known than the other two and has been the subject of a number of interpretations, including two expert efforts: one by Gérard Schaeffer and the other as a doctoral dissertation by Jean Gaulnier at the University of Strasbourg. The basic difference of attitude between the authors of these two exegeses of this, the longest poem Breton ever wrote, is that Schaeffer considers the poem to be still partially under the effect of the technique of automatic writing, whereas in Gaulnier's opinion Breton has in this poem totally abandoned the forces of psychic automatism and, in conveying the utopian philosophy of Charles Fourier, has bowed to rational communication. Schaeffer quotes an answer of Breton on this subject to Aimé Pétri, in which he said in effect: that the *Ode* "takes its place on the curve . . . which admits automatism as a point of departure but does not along the road deprive me of certain contingent obligations." In other words, automatic writing can no longer be the primary characteristic of the poetic composition. But we had already noted Breton's departure from spontaneous structure to architectural composition in the two previous instances. In the *Ode* automatism of detail persists, but the major relief is even more ideological than in the previous poems. The automatism of certain images only serves to dramatize the labyrinthine analogies between Breton's conceptual communication and the images arising out of immediate reality.

One could say that the *Ode* is for Breton what the *Multiplication of the Arcs* was for his artist friend Yves Tanguy: a summation of all his beliefs, of all his visions.

Why Charles Fourier? In a letter to Gaulnier, Breton explains the interest in Fourier on the basis of one of those coincidences that determined so many of the turning points of his life. It was in New York that he found the full edition of Fourier's works, and the time of the discovery coincided with the moment of his life when he would have free time on his hands. He apparently read Fourier on the long train ride across the United States to Reno; and while he was waiting for the divorce, he took a side trip to Arizona and Colorado where he visited Indian reservations, which had always fascinated him in the naive but powerful premises of their spiritualism. A definite break in the middle of the poem marks the side trip and return to the *Ode* with the enrichment of faith produced by the contact with the American Indian.

Breton, the leader of surrealism, who bears much resemblance to Chateaubriand, the first romantic writer, experienced the same refurbishing of the imagination through the American landscape as had his antecedent. For both poets the Indian became a symbol of purity of creed; both marveled at the Indian's intimacy with nature and of his canalization of the supernatural into the web of his daily reality. Both poets, endowed with an immense sensitivity to the animism of physical nature, saw in the still virgin American landscape a magnification of the dynamism of the physical universe and the role of the Indian as the most faithful and authentic of nature's children, educated to accept the mystery of incomprehensible forces as a continuum of those things we understand, rather than as their antithesis. Reno was to Breton a symbol not of liberation from conjugal shackles but of the resumption of marital bonds and of the reaffirmation of his faith in the "one and only love," with the entrance of Elisa in his life. It turned out to be at the same time an opening to an anthropolgical adventure that reinforced his belief in the natural forms of religion, conceived as an extension of the frontiers of reality. It would seem as if only at the two limits of mental development, the primitive and the highly sophisticated, did this comprehension of the real manifest itself.

But finding a complete edition of the works of Fourier does not alone justify writing a major poem. The question remains: "Why Fourier?" We have already noted Breton's debt to the alchemists from Zoar to the cabala, to the illuminists of the eighteenth century. When in *Les Etats Généraux* he mentioned Fabre d'Olivet, he did not know that he would devote his last major poem to the philosopher of the nineteenth century who owed most to Fabre d'Olivet.

Without entering into the intricacies of the Fourier system of philosophy and sociology, we can note that there is a distinct parallel between what Eliphas Lévi did to Swedenborgian philosophy and what Fourier did to utopian socialism. As we have seen, Lévi departed from the dualistic notion of correspondences between the spiritual and the material in the universe. He transformed the system of analogies into a monistic and materialistic relationship regulated by the natural powers of magnetism. Fourier applied the analogies to the social structure and devised a complicated but concise mathematical system whereby the polarization of human creatures could be explored as the basis of the social pattern; each man's function in society would be determined not by objective economic necessities of the group, but by personal inclination, his pleasures and his erotic as well as economic needs. Fourier was a social visionary, but in opting for the transformation of the world he had based group dynamics on individual dynamics and made collective progress dependent on a more subjective differentiation of individual functions in society. By replacing material motivation with spiritual stimuli, he had aspired to exploit for practical purposes the grain of mystery imbedded in human nature. His essential premises were that it is not so significant what you do as *with whom you do it*, and that an ambiance charged with love is more apt to prove fruitful than an arbitrary association of humans. His will to obliterate the incoherences in human relationships, whether it led to metaphysical serenity or economic security, was symptomatic of the attitude of conciliation between the political and the personal basis of any future transformation of the world.

As Breton's basic concept was that social progress could not be achieved without the liberation and the exploration of human imagination, and without the resources of sensibility, Fourierism proved to reinforce his own philosophy; for it contained the principles of occult analogies, physical attraction, and faith in the probity of the sexual instinct and in the possibility of putting natural personal appetites to the human good. The marriage between Venus and Mammon that Fourier had suggested had been derided by sociologists; but Baudelaire's poetic imagination had been drawn to Fourier before Breton's; and many references to Fourier appear in Baudelaire's treatment of romanticism.

In the beginning of his poem Breton takes us back to 1937 as the date when he first discovered the mystic-sociologist. Fourier's statue was not far from the Place Blanche, near his own rue Fontaine. He had noticed a bouquet of flowers deposited at the base of the statue on the centenary of the death of Fourier.

The *Ode* is structured more obviously than the other two long poems. In the first part he sees Fourier as a reserve saint, one of those to be conjured up in times of extreme danger as when a boat is battered by heavy storms. He is for times of extreme inner and outer turmoil, "when in the forest birds are made of pure flame," a time of hurricanes and eruptions. In the next section he describes the world of the mid-1940's, which went from active to latent war, as just such a time. In an address to Fourier he declares that nothing has changed, that the world over "it is still the same furnishings," a world over which stretches a net of blood and which is drowning in deluge upon deluge. He weaves into his critique of society as it exists the bonds that all his life he had considered retrograde: those of family and "the anesthesia" of flag-waving patriotism. The allusions to the war are not military but show how it warps man's ethics— for instance, the abuses of the black market: "the monkeys of the grocery store." Nothing announces "the reign of harmony."

The next section of the poem is heavy with allusions to Fourier's system and terminology. Although most explication has been done on this part of the poem, it is actually the weakest since it is composed in a strictly rational manner, with the least reliance on the sequence of imagery to direct the stream of thought. Acrimonious in his progress report of the ethical evolution of man in terms of the values Fourier has signalized, Breton reveals through the maze of his criticism his own values and disappointments; the highest place belongs to friendship and love. The power of projection of love is identified here, as many times previously, with the image of *le grand brillant* in its illuminating progression from personal love to love of humanity.

The next section is poetically more potent, as it transfers Fourier's scale of values to a cosmic level: the search for unity and concordance in nature from the most distant stars to the smallest boat tossed upon the seas. And the reaction of modern man to the universal harmony has been to perfect the forces of disintegration: the atomic bomb.

The scene shifts to the Far West and its Hopi civilization, which symbolizes the love of life and man's natural inclination toward good. The Hopi derive their significances from the sun and the earth, and the female spider: the sun which implies life and magic; the spiderweb which represents the arts of life; and the earth which in death becomes the repository of life. The union of the three forces is the representation of the continuum of these forces. "There is no separation or heterogeneity between the supernatural and the natural (the real and the surreal). No hiatus. It is a continuum. You think it is André Breton, but it is an ethnographer who is speaking on behalf of the Soulteaux Indians."

Finally, despite our poor historical record and the present social and moral chaos, Breton ends on a note of optimism, as he did in *Les Etats Généraux*: "the unreasonable faith in the march toward an edemic future" and his faith in youth, as he had previously declared to the students of Yale University. The last word of the poem is "liberty," the key word of Breton's vocabulary, as with the sun and the star it closes the orbit of his modern epic which sums up the essence of his creed.

But on the basis of the thoughts expressed in the *Ode* it would not stand up better as a poem than one of the philosophical meditations of Voltaire in verse form. As T. S. Eliot has aptly discussed in his essay on Dante, philosophy can be justifiable in poetry only as a scaffolding and must submit to modifications to be deemed poetic. Indeed, so many "poems" have fallen on the reefs of philosophical abysses to survive only as the driftwood of philosophical concepts. If all Breton had to communicate was that in this era of chaos and disintegration we need the visionary if somewhat lunatic utopianism of Fourier, and that as the personification of the noble savage only the red Indian is left to demonstrate the wisdom of living according to the basic laws of nature, he would have left a somewhat lyrical essay, documented by his reading of Fourier and his journey in America.

The explication above of the form and ideological content of the poem does not suggest the power of the piece as a poem, its power to give vision, to produce impact on the imagination, to kindle the senses—which are indeed the only conditions under which, according to Breton, there is any reason to call any piece of writing a poem. It is only in terms of rhythms, images, analogies that the poetic value of the work can be defined.

In using the interrogation and the apostrophe as his structures, the long breath sentences of Breton seem like calls from one summit to another, with deep and prolonged echoes and open, out-of-door vistas:

"Fourier es-tu toujours là?"
("Fourier are-you still there?")

It is like a long distance telephone call. But the sense of distance he creates is not one merely of space but also of time. From the new world to the old, from one century to a past one, he creates a sense of abyss which he seems to want to bridge with his chain of words, heavy with facts and words of chastisement. But at the same time the poem is possessed of the lilt of biological and botanical images teeming with the life surge, almost belying the complaints. How close indeed he comes thus to the most intimate character of the human condition, which in terms of the sensitive so often rejects the cogitative; or to put it another way, a poet in his knowledge of evil never quite obliterates the beauty that his senses absorb almost in spite of himself, and that his tongue communicates in syncopation with the rebellion.

While Breton's thoughts are speaking to us of the evil that has not been erased from the world but which goes on snowballing from age to age, the images to which he anchors his ideas encompass the convulsive character of the beauty of the world, his wonder at its dynamics, his sensitivity to its mysteries, his persistent search for openings in the labyrinth.

Vision, Breton had said, is the highest mark of the greatness of the human condition. In this most grandiose of his poems, the power of observation is extraordinary and has been rarely matched by any of his contemporaries; it combines the geological perception of St.-John Perse and the intimacy of animal relationships one catches sometimes in Jules Supervielle's imagery. Each image opens up a vista, and analogies are never closed but suggest levels of rapid and successive relationships. In fact he calls them "planes," as he proceeds from one sphere to the next in an upward movement precipitated eventually into the cosmos.

Among the analogies, too profuse to enumerate here, there are major ones that attract others to form clusters or set the tone of an entire passage of the poem. The forest of firebirds creates the electrifying atmosphere from the outset, leading up to the "incandescent" statue of Fourier (and its illuminating message). As Breton contrasts the hope for union with the force for decay and disruption, he suddenly populates the poem with rats and reptiles, toads and vermin that invade the earth.

The lack of progression on the part of man finds its image in the prehistoric fauna, and his apathetic bondage is represented by the figure of the dolphin in a zoo in tepid waters of effortless stagnation. To suggest black market manipulations he shows us some of the ugliest images in all his poetry—they are a strain on his normal beauty-seeking vocabulary; they converge in a blood-drenched handprint on the butcher's apron at the spot where his heart should be. Then there are the "gutter" images of history—its labyrinth, cyclones, and ashes.

Breton alludes to mythological symbols such as Orpheus and the Golden Fleece only to deplore their absence or mutilation. There is the magic ram whose horns spell violence, but in the depth of whose eyes is reflected the nostalgia of springtime: in other words, the ambivalence of the alchemic animal symbol, emblem of death and of life.

The most striking of the analogies are those referring to the Far West: the petrified forest of human culture:

> Je te salue de la Forêt Pétrifiée de la culture humaine
> Où plus rien n'est debout
> Mais où rôdent de grandes lueurs tournoyantes
> Qui appellent la délivrance du feuillage et de l'oiseau
> De tes doigts part la sève des arbres en fleurs
>
> (I salute you from the Petrified Forest of human culture
> Where nothing remains standing
> But where prowl the great turning lights
> Which call for the deliverance of leaf and bird
> From your fingers rise the sap of trees and flowers)

In other words, the petrified character of the world has preserved in its congealed condition the tremor of life and the benediction of light. Nevada as the site of the old gold rush is equated with the Golden Fleece, and the chain of concepts it releases are all centered around man's quest for knowledge and wisdom:

> Je te salue du Névada des chercheurs d'or
> De la terre promise et tenue
> A la terre en veine de promesses plus hautes qu'elle doit tenir encore

> (I salute you from the Nevada of the gold seekers
> From the land promised and held
> To the land containing veins of higher promises that it has yet to hold)

The labyrinth image we have met so often is here a cryptogram that man has to decipher. It turns starkly concrete as it becomes identified with a grotto at the bottom of the great schism of the Colorado River. The Grand Canyon sums it up with its marvelous subterranean phantasmagoria which Breton commemorates by putting into the poem the only circumstantial data: his name and the date of the cosmic experience, sealed in faith. So powerful is the next long, majestic line of the poem that one is left to believe that the supreme summit toward which Breton aspired came within sight not on a mountaintop but in abysses of crystal.

> Du fond du pacte millénaire qui dans l'angoisse
>   a pour objet de maintenir l'intégrité du verbe
> Des plus lointaines ondes de l'écho qu'éveille le
>   pied frappant impérieusement le sol pour sceller
>   l'alliance avec les puissances qui font lever la graine

> (From the pith of the millenary pact which in anguish
>   has as its object to maintain the integrity of the Word
> From the most distant ways of the echo awakened by the
>   foot striking imperiously the ground to seal the
>   alliance with the powers which foment the grain.)

As he talks to Fourier, he talks as well to his friends, those of his past and those "who do not yet have a face."

From *Fata Morgana* to the *Ode à Charles Fourier* Breton comes to grips with the cosmos as he never does in his earlier poems; he faces world-shaking events as he faces the natural perils of the cosmos, trying to relate to them instead of fighting them singlehanded. If he harbors the romantic notion that nature is on our side, and that we are our worst enemies in our fratricidal struggles, he is very modern in that he does not make himself the center of his universe as a romantic would have done. Whereas in his early works his interrogation of the mysteries is strictly related to his own personal identity, in the wiser, more adept human that he has become the questions are: "What are we?" "When will we learn?" Personal salvation is not possible without group liberation; his destiny is intimately linked with that of all others, and the macrocosm of the human condition as a totality finds its correspondence in the vistas of enormous mountain chains, deep schisms, and unmeasureable vaults. Man no longer triumphs singlehanded over anything; that is why there are no more heroes. Theseus does not go through the labyrinth alone; he leads generations in march, and his epic struggle is not deliverance from the human condition but a weighing of its imponderables, so that out of wisdom may come liberty. The word "liberty" shines like a star as it becomes the last period to the last and most statuesque poem of André Breton.

XIII

ARCANE 17

When André Breton wrote *Arcane 17* in the summer of 1944, he must have thought of it as the Work in the alchemic sense of the word, the summit and supreme point of all that preceded, as close to the top of the mountain as he could expect to come, and that everything after that would be anticlimactic. As a matter of fact, except for the *Ode à Charles Fourier* and a few fragmental verses, the poet in him remained thereafter silent, though the polemicist and essayist continued to communicate to the end of his life. The title *Arcane 17* indicates that he thought of the work as the Great Book, the synthesis of all that went before; and in truth it amalgamates all the elements that we have seen to characterize the writings of Breton as a poet.[1]

Arcane 17 in the lore of the Hebraic-Bohemian-Egyptian tarot is also known as the "great secret." In the cards of the tarot it is the seventeenth of the twenty-two, all of which are hieroglyphic in their emblematic representation; it comes after 15 and 16, which are assigned to the work of the devil: war and darkness. But after the fall of Lucifer suddenly the skies become luminous, and love and peace triumph, through the intervention of the beautiful young woman who pours the contents of two urns upon the earth; the urns are endowed with the power of fire and water, fermenting and procreating, as hope of resurrection surges again in men's hearts. Thus the seventeenth sign of the tarot is under the aegis of love and intelligence. *Arcane 17* is Breton's Mystic Book, written in the darkest year of the war and of his life, which the power of love was able to transfigure for him.

It was a time of *De profundis clamavi*. It was a time of the most somber of Jean-Paul Sartre's dramas, of Camus' stolid *Stranger* and the grim stoicism of the *Myth of Sisyphus*; it marked Anouilh's tragic play about the putrefaction of Antigone's brothers and of her immolation, and Vercors' *Les Silences de la mer* with its ambivalent message of patience and endurance.

Breton put to the most difficult test the notion of the conciliation of opposites, turning darkness into light under the symbol of the brightest star of the religious allegories of the past: the Pentagram, the morning star.

He had met Elisa a few months before by magical chance. She had come back as Eurydice from Hades, having twice gone into the valley of the shadow of death, first in the pain of the loss, in the accidental death, of her seventeen-year-old daughter, then with her desire for her own death. The darkness in Breton's life had been well-nigh equal to hers, as we have already seen. Paris was silent in its hour of occupation and ignominy, his friends were dispersed, he was a wandering shadow of his formerly vibrant, secure self. Although all his life Breton had insisted on the importance of destroying in oneself the notion of nationality and of ridding the mind of this parochialism, he was unable to adjust to exile. He was in truth Nerval's *El Desdichado: "Le veuf inconsolé."*

It is under these tragic circumstances that he and Elisa set off on a *fugue* to one of the most northern confines of the American continent, as close to the North Star and the North Pole as one could hope to reach. In fact, Elisa described it as a long and painful journey lasting three days and three nights. They found a small cabin in Ste Agathe at the tip of Gaspé near Le Rocher Percé.[2] According to Elisa, he did his writing every morning for three months from August to October, waking at five and writing until noon. In the afternoons they would take walks, gather agate stones, visit the bird sanctuary of the island of Bonaventure where the resplendent array of birds seemed to Breton like a moving rainbow. They would watch the fishermen with their nets on the rugged coast of the Canadian peninsula, and the strata of sediments and erosions that spelled the history of the struggle of the soil against water, wind, and sun. It was still the season of light; at five in the morning the air was luminous, and the sea had shed its night. The earth was in a constant state of metamorphosis as it now wrapped itself in mist, then shed it in triumph. To Breton this fluctuation, dramatic in its suddenness, was to seem like a curtain going up and coming down.

It is in this environment that Breton undertook the writing of his last meditation, in which he combined the themes of love, war, and resurrection, using the same analogical form of expression that he had previously used in *Poisson soluble, Nadja, Les Vases communicants,* and *L'Amour fou;* here it is a series of analogies of curtain, darkness, trans-

ARCANE 17 203

figuration, light, purifying the circumstantial elements into images of universal radiation.*

He drew his analogies from three sources: hermeticism, legend, and the terminology of physical, botanical, and biological nature. We have already noted how close he was to occultism. By coincidence it was while he was in America that he came across Auguste Viatte's richly documented and inspirational book on the influences of illuminism on the romantics and particularly on Victor Hugo.[3] It renewed for him the impact of Eliphas Lévi and made him cast his prose in the basic framework of the sign of the tarot. As he says toward the end of *Arcane 17*, what attracts him most incessantly to hermeticism is the power of analogy ingrained in the doctrine. In turn it keeps one incessantly aware of the analogies discernible in the universe, making communication with the so-called inert environment around us a lively and two-way exchange:

> Esoterism, despite all reservations one may have about its principle, offers at least this immense interest, that it keeps in a state of dynamism the system of comparisons, in an unlimited field, available to man, and it makes it possible for him to recover relationships capable of linking objects which in appearance seem most distant from each other, and to discover partially the mechanism of universal symbolism.

The hermetic element is closely translated in the illustrations that Matta was to conceive for his friend's book.

The legendary source here is—as in *Les Etats Généraux*—very French, rather than the Hellenic myths that have so often been the principal frame of reference in French writings. Mélusine,† the most French of French fays, was immortalized in Jean d'Arras, account of the fifteenth century. She belongs to the heart of France, the Poitou region; she is the guardian of the fortress of Lusignan, the powerful lords of the Middle Ages. According to legend, Mélusine was one of the triplet daughters of Presine, the mysterious fay who married the widower King Elinas of Albania. The queen transmitted to her daughters the malediction of not being totally human; in the case of Mélusine, she doomed her to return every Saturday to the state of *ondine*—half woman, half water serpent. If Mélusine married a mortal who had the endurance and will power to abstain from

---

* Among the tokens of *Arcane 17* preserved in Elisa Breton's copy of the first edition are their railway tickets, the tarot cards, matches with the French-Canadian *coq gaulois*, and, most interesting of all, the caption, torn out of *Petit Larousse*, identifying Breton's basic mythical heroine: "Mélusine, fairy whom the novels of chivalry and legends of Poitou represent as the ancestor and protector of the House of Lusignan."

† The legend of Mélusine bears explanation since it is one with which most of Breton's readers are not likely to be familiar.

seeing her on Saturdays, she would bring him only happiness and, with great conquests, would help him to build the most powerful of empires. But if he succumbed to human weakness and curiosity and revealed a lack of confidence in her integrity, she would fall out of the human context and become a creature of the waters and the air, and would only hover over her loved ones to warn them of impending dangers. It comes to pass that Mélusine marries Raimundin, nephew of the Count of Poitiers; she meets him in the same fashion that her mother had met King Elinas: in an enchanting forest, at a magic fountain. She tells Raimundin how to extricate himself from the highly compromising situation he finds himself in after having killed his uncle accidentally while helping him to fell a dragonlike boar; this happened just as the count had seen in the prophetic skies that Raimundin would succeed him in power after killing him. When Mélusine's advice turns out to be highly useful and actually saves his life, Raimundin comes back to her with a deed from the new ruler of Poitiers for a small strip of land, on which Mélusine, after marrying Raimundin, builds him the powerful castle of Lusignan, named thus because, as he says, it is the Greek form of her name, meaning "marvelous." Thereafter, as predicted, with Mélusine's magical powers Raimundin becomes the most powerful lord, and his descendants become the rulers of the Mediterranean world, extending their powers to Cyprus and even to Armenia. But meanwhile Raimundin, like Orpheus, proves unequal to his promise to abstain from looking at Mélusine during the day of her metamorphosis. In consequence Mélusine has to relinquish her human form and re-enter the realm of animal and divine existence. She utters a heart-rending cry as she departs, and hovers ever after longingly over her dear husband and children and their descendants. Each time they are in mortal danger, her cry can be heard in the atmosphere.

What makes the legend of Mélusine particularly appropriate is that she is the unjustly cursed mortal, the uprooted, homeless, anguished protector of her breed.[4] The identification Breton makes of her is twofold: she is both Elisa and himself. She is the symbol of the dispossessed like Breton, watching from afar the misfortunes of his country, and at the same time she is the mediatrice in her half-human, half-divine state, coming to the aid of the man she loves. "The woman deprived of her human dish" is taken by Breton in a double sense: it is Mélusine, dislodged from her home, even as he and Elisa have been uprooted; but beyond that, it is woman herself who has been banished in modern civilization from a position of power for good. What Elisa has meant to him, Breton thinks that woman in her total sense can mean to a world distraught. He sees as the only possible salvation the restoration of woman to a position similar to the one Mélusine occupies in the legend, with her almost magical resources put to the service of humanity because intuitively, like Mélusine, she is closer to nature, and thereby divine as only those beings who are wise in the intentions and mysteries of natural forces can be said to possess magical powers and, therefore, foresight and divinity. For to devine (to foresee) and to be divine are parts of the same rebus.

Within the context of the Mélusine myth and its analogies, Breton's previous pleas for woman-power reach an apotheosis as he looks upon the savage state of the world which has been denied woman's spiritual intervention. His attraction to the Mélusine symbol lies not only in her power for salvation but in the fact that she also embodies the power of metamorphosis since she turns from woman to serpent, even as night into day, and the worm into a butterfly, all representing the unifying element in Breton's book as they seem to represent to him the basically dynamic character of the universe.

The third set of analogies are gleaned from nature's emblems; we have already seen the presence of the Fata Morgana phenomenon, and the Northern lights; now it is the Rock of Percé, erected by nature at this septentrional limit of the continent, making the barrier that protects and shuts Breton from "the insanity of the hour": "*Sepentrone pandetur omne malum*" ("All misfortunes of the world are written in the northern sky"). The Rock of Percé, shutting out the agony of war-torn Europe, gives Breton a poignant symbol of his isolation, an anguishing stigma of nonparticipation for one whose philosophy was anchored on the premise that the artist had to be a major participant in the life of society. He who had bitterly criticized the Mallarméan ivory-tower dissociation of the artist from the social and moral rhythm of society, found himself behind this formidable curtain of rock. Significantly he saw in the rock his barrier and at the same time the barrier of the French-Canadian whose whole ethnological fortune was that of the alienation of the group from the mainstream of French culture, preserving a dead way of life, arrested by migration and geographic distance. There is the tremor of apprehensiveness, weighing on him like a foreboding of doom: is he to share the remoteness of the French-Canadian in his condition of exile?

But the Rock of Percé has other more fascinating qualities. It disappears in the twilight and morning mist, as if melting into the sea. It has multitudinous evidences of erosion, grim reminders of the passage of the ages and of the possibility of future annihilation. It puts Breton in a state of wonder and awe, reminiscent of Pascal's moment of humility between the microcosm of his own being and the macrocosm of the universe. That Breton considered this to be his ultimate work is not only indicated by the title but by the internal structure of the work. What **Breton seems to** have discovered in this evolved form of his writing is that if automatic writing was the psychic association of words into illuminating images, in its highest form it synthesized the letters into code and resulted in an automatic metaphor, for *Arcane 17* depends *not* on the juxtaposition of images, created by the spontaneous marriage of words, but on the psychic progression of metaphors, objectivizing the analogical patterns of Breton's thought process. The hermeticism is no longer verbal—indeed, his language is very clear—but arachnoid as his thought is multidimensional, like the strata he discerns in the Rock of Percé, and as profound as the reflection of the eye of the magical bird of his dream in a bottomless pool.*

The Rock of Percé becomes an emblem by means of which Breton can build analogies between cosmic and human modifications. The rock is composed of geological strata, as civilization has its historical epochs superimposed one on the other. Breton's analogical eye, with its habit of seeing one thing in another, equates or merges the hues of the rock, rose to deep hues, with the soldering of human cultures in human blood; he sees in the tempests and rain that batter the rock and leave in it their everlasting marks and the foreboding of eventual dissolution, the bloodbaths of European wars and Europe's much more rapid effacement. But the analogy of disintegration and division that the rock spells out on the one hand is compensated by the image of unity and cohesion that the

---

* The *épervier*, the rapacious hawk, has its hermetic meaning in the work of Breton; he often identifies it with the legendary ibis as well. Here its simple food-getting activity is turned into mystical illumination, creating one of the most poetical descriptions in *Arcane 17*:

> The hawk scrutinizes the pond while in his heart a lamp is lighted which permits him to see all that passes into him. In this heart there transpires with pomp the mystery of remembering and seeing the future, and I who, at this moment, am contemplating him, I am the first to fear to be blinded by that light. Now we have the whole pond emptied into the eye of the bird, and the bird tortures himself for the depths of the pond are within him, and these depths are revealed in their turn. In its aerial reflection the pyramid is restored to the totality it produces with its base immersed and this totality is a long coffer; the bird's cry reveals that it is hermetically sealed over a desired prey. . . . There at the very moment of greatest crisis when he has discovered the coffer and has greeted with a cry of distress the irremediable [the prey that he cannot obtain] that turning his famished beak against his own heart, in his supreme agitation he only succeeds in enlarging it. In a spasm which of itself bespeaks of the glory of the world, this heart bent on strangling itself is briskly dilated to receive at the height of the paroxysm what the future holds. And in this heart full of shadow is opened at that moment a young heart full of light, still totally dependent on the first and which claims its sustenance from it. Nothing more was needed than the vertigo caused by that abyss for the tide to turn and the blood to flow back through the canals of life. Old Egypt was not able to find better symbols to represent the circumstances which surrounded the conception of a god.

strata's solid appearance embodies, even as in the face of Europe's fragmentation he affirms his faith in her unity and in the oneness of human-
kind. "Substratum, complex and indivisible" qualifies the double image
that presents itself to Breton. "Civilization is one even as this Rock," and
to think of it any other way is to strip one's own identity, Breton tells
us as he adheres to the notion of unity and cohesion at a time when
the world seemed to be cracking into a million fragments. Thus the Rock
of Percé becomes for him the final manifestation of the supreme point:
"That luminous point concentrating all that can be common to life."

What is the basic message of *Arcane 17*? That in such times of darkness as Breton was experiencing, all the myths of the world concur to
spell out in their hieroglyphic emblems a basic, hope-giving hypothesis.
From darkness comes light, the only enemy of man is despair and resig-
nation, the source of light is rebellion, and resurrection is a physical, material fact of life that is as undestructible as the emergence of the morning
star after the night; the impelling forces of human life are love, liberty,
and poetry.

The power of liberty is embodied in Lucifer and Osiris. For Breton
as in occultist lores, Lucifer is not an evil genius, expelled from heaven,
but the rebellious Satan, whose seeming power of destruction and temptation is in truth the power of knowledge, through which occurs regeneration, even as it is written in the great Arcanum. "The black intelligence
is the divination of the Mysteries of the Night, the attribution of reality
to the forms of the invisible," said Eliphas Lévi.

The haunting search for purity, which dominated the entire life of
Breton, reaches its apotheosis here. Opacity is darkness of mind as of the
elements. That opacity which Mallarmé thought to be surmountable
only in death, Breton tries to overcome in life as he searches for transparence here and now, in the gaze of a woman's eye as in the polished
agates rolled onto the shore. The power of light in the material world is
synchronized with the distillation of love, to reach in its triumph over
material ills a state of mental serenity and sympathy. To find "the poetic
intelligence of the universe" corresponds with the harmonious reciprocal
relationship of two beings, which the diamond and the star emblematize
in material existence. Breton senses the same iridescence as in his earliest
writing in *Les Champs magnétiques* as he observes with tenderness "the
radiation of the spiritual life" on a human face. The anger has subsided at
the very moment you would expect it to be at its height. The angry young
man of the pamphlets and the manifestoes learns to tolerate life—"You
end up by tolerating life again"—and once more to turn defeat into
triumph over the most flagrant personal and global disaster.

The allegory of Osiris is identified with that of Satan as a force for resurrection. According to the legend, after Osiris has been dismembered, he is put together again by his wife-sister, Isis, and comes back to life. But the element of the legend that Breton presses on his reader's consciousness is the hypnotic sentence "Osiris is a black God." The power of blackness is taken to mean despair and anguish, but also rebellion and triumph. "One must have gone to the bottom of human sorrow, to have discovered the strange capacities, in order to be able to salute with the same limitless gift of self whatever is worth living for." Each time Breton sees a cloud cross Elisa's beautiful, limpid eyes, he whispers in her ear: "Osiris is a black God." Association is made at the same time with Elisa's loss and Breton's dejection, and the world chaos; and, just as in the tarot cards Arcane 17, with the luminous maiden, appears after emblems of destruction, so in the depths of the darkness of the soul resides the power to reject despair and renew hope.

The images are part of the matrix image that Breton carries in the depth of his being: the conciliation of opposites, which at one time was crystallized in the Alpine peak of Moustiers-Sainte-Marie and is now one with the Rock of Percé, a physical elevation supporting the spiritual one from which the contradictions of life disappear, and our sorrows become exaltation, as defeat turns into victory. As Satan falls from grace, he rises to the peak of his rebellion.

Here is the ultimate crystallization of what rebellion meant to Breton. From his First Manifesto, it meant an attack of the conventional limits of freedom, not against the essential capacity of the human condition. Thus Breton could never believe that rebellion limited purely to its social targets could achieve real liberty for man. That was his basic argument with Soviet communism of the 1930's. It is also why, at a time when rebellion could not possibly find pragmatic objectives, in the isolated confines of Gaspé, with ostensibly no targets for revolt, he champions more passionately than ever the Satan emblem of rebellion: "Rebellion bears its own fortification" he says, whether it has any chance of changing things or not. That is also why he does not wholeheartedly accept the notion of "liberation" around which so many of his literary colleagues built their aspirations at a time when Western Europe was muzzled and besieged. For Breton liberation could not be equated with liberty. Liberation was a temporary remission from a great illness, with no assurance of its elimination, but only hope for its temporary arrest. For him liberty is a constant state of mental rebellion against all that prevents the full exercise of the human potential for knowledge, for comprehension, for enjoyment of the human habitat: a state of *erethism* he calls it. If his concept of political rebellion does not correspond to the attitude of the time, the metaphysical rebellion revealed in *Arcane 17* is distinct from Camus' notions in *The Rebel*, a work of approximately the same era. For Camus, man's metaphysical rebellion is his expression of frustration against the human condition; it is a hostile confrontation with the jealous gods and a competition between Olympus and man for power over the human domain. None of this hostility exists in Breton's concept of the universe. The rebellion of Breton is against human myopia, and the element of risk (as the emblematic fall of Satan into darkness) is a catharsis that eventually can lead to light—that is, to elucidation of the role of the human in a well-integrated universe. "It is revolt itself, revolt alone which is a creator of light." The fall rebounds in all Breton's imagery, and the entanglements of man in the labyrinth are never viewed as fatal. "Passion must be put back into life," says Breton and he means it not only in the erotic sense but in the total extension of its meaning. Camus, who understood the distinction, called it "an impossible wisdom" but sympathized with Breton's isolated position in a world where rationalism led to insanity in the unleashing of destructive forces. It is always the most rational of men who lead us into war; and it is in the poet's dreams, which seem to us fantastic, that we find ultimately the only hope for a new dawn. Camus expressed this tribute to Breton admirably: "The splendid night in which he confronts himself while reason, passed to the field of action, makes armies roll over the world, announces perhaps in truth those auroras that have not yet shone." [5]

As the dispossessed Breton and Elisa forge a new union out of the disjunction of their lives, love in *Arcane 17* takes on a more mystical proportion than in the previous books. We have seen Breton's faith in love, with its sexual-spiritual intertwining, becoming the guiding motivation of his life. Woman was medium with Nadja, then a source of integration with Jacqueline; in *Arcane 17* she is the new Eve; not only is the notion of sin separated from love, but the power of redemption is associated with it. Elisa, Mélusine, and Esclarmonde, as in *Les Etats Généraux*, are man's sole remaining source of spiritual guidance as they are his source of redemption and self-realization. The extraordinary image of purity that Breton weaves around woman crystallizes into woman-child, which in the tenderness of the image is closer to Aube and to the nine-month-old girl-child of his friends, the Archile Gorkys, to whom he alludes, but is also identifiable with Elisa and Mélusine. When one considers that Elisa was a widow and mother, and Mélusine a contriving sorceress and mother of eleven children, the notion of the child-woman is disturbing until one considers the sense in which Breton uses the image of purity: it is because, as he says of Mélusine, "time has no hold on her." The moment of love for Breton is reflected fathoms deep in the eyes of the woman he loves, so as to banish time and its powers of alteration. The symbol of the woman-child is this affirmation of faith in the purity of the union of man and woman. Love in the amalgamation of its parts spells unity, even as the Rock of Percé, in the sealing of its strata, presents a single, undaunted appearance.

Breton has never been more the poet than in this hymn to life, in expressing the solidarity of all living creatures and the cohesion of the universe that refuses to be disintegrated by the forces of military evil, even as Osiris refused to stay dismembered. If, as Breton thought, to be a poet is to observe the relationships of the supreme allegory of the universe, nowhere else has his pen been able to unite in a single, vibrant block all the threads of his poetic labyrinth; all the ingredients previously noted consolidate into an intricate but luminous whole. The technique of the rebus is used to its fullest extent: the tarot girl, Mélusine, Elisa, the power of blackness in Satan, Osiris, and the allegorical night that is at the same time the polar night, reminding us of Baudelaire's *gouffre* and evoking Novalis' *Hymns to Night*. Here is the Rock of Percé, with the curtain of fog falling on the isle of the birds but making way for the stars; it becomes at the same time the magnetic pole, which previously we found in the rue Lafayette, in the Café de Babylone, in the Tour St. Jacques, and which is now a more natural monument. The play of divine chance here is manifested in the encounter of Breton with Elisa; the various images of natural and mythical resurrection culminate in the Egyptian legend of Osiris; the emblems of the acacia plant and the butterfly, which alighted on his table in the little cabin where he was working, are interlinked. The power of metamorphosis in his images, which made it possible for one image to fall into another, is displayed in the butterfly, in the rock that appears and disappears, in the character of Mélusine now woman, now goddess.

The imagery here is in a constant state of flux. In the more frightening movements of nature Breton sees the analogy with human peril. As after the terror of a storm the fisherman comes in from the sea bringing a pearl, so Breton realizes the disparity between the controllable social condition of man (with no pearl in sight) and the precarious condition of human adventure (where the prize is at such great stake). The sense, therefore, of the immediacy of the human experience, its evanescent character, is something terribly precious to Breton; he makes it the basic impulse of poetry. The psychic nourishment and sustenance of man, which religion no longer seems to be able to provide in evolved stages of civilization, becomes the major concern of the poet. So *Arcane 17* becomes the Mystic

Book, embodying all the qualities normally associated with religious inspiration: love, hope, the broad sense of charity toward suffering mankind; but it differs from most religion in that Breton puts what possibility of salvation there is in the frail hands of man and within the confines of his battered, wounded, multiscarred world. The "great secret" of life that ancient mystics sought in imponderable symbols of labyrinth, and oracles, and the manna, Breton translates into Everyman's adventure and restores it to the daily lifestream. Where Symbolist poets had so often represented the "daily tragic of existence," Breton transforms the tragic into the daily battle of man rising from darkness into light even as the universe increasingly delivers the earth from night to dawn, with the star as its emblem of transition, ever reminding the earth in darkness of the existence of light. The morning star's glory is that it bridges the sky from dark to light and becomes the emblem of survival. Breton's last prose is, as he says himself, "a hymn to the unique glory of nature and of love."

But putting the power of self-salvation into the hands of man does not produce his deification. In fact, Breton restates in *Arcane 17* what he has often intimated before, that man is far from being the *élu*, the chosen being of creation. One of the things that surprises Breton most about modern man is the fact that his increased knowledge of anthropology, which should have taught him about biological necessity, has not curtailed his vanity. No new notion of humanism will be born as long as man maintains this false notion of superiority and refuses to enter within the physical context of life to seek a fusion between essence and substance, "to hold sacred to the same degree the flesh and the soul, by thinking of them as undistinguishable." Again the seal of the thought is the image of the Rock of Percé as it represents earth, and like a chameleon is transfigured from rock to nave, from nave to rose window, to an organ playing Bach in a place of worship; there is a clear similarity with Baudelaire's "Harmonie du soir" in the ambivalent imagery that links physical phenomena with spiritual states, except that Baudelaire's key image is a twilight zone whereas Breton's is the aurora.

Can Breton in 1944 still be viewed as a surrealist, or has he changed in mood and technique as drastically as his early companions such as Eluard and Aragon, whose wartime poetry can at most be characterized as "post-surrealist"? Even as in the long poems of the last period, the final prose has a greater clarity of language than the earlier works. This may be considered a flaw if we think of surrealism primarily as a mutation of form and a revolution epitomized in violence. Indubitably Breton is not violent in *Arcane 17*, and he is not unintelligible in his language or references. It is often thought that while others left surrealism, Breton maintained his initial position and original commitment; but the works themselves give internal evidence of change and evolution. Surrealism itself as it is identified with Breton changes in its manifestations, so that the surrealism of *Arcane 17*, of an older Breton, is quite different from his early *coup de revolver* attitude. While others of the original surrealist group, and principally Antonin Artaud, maintained the severity of youthful subversion in their later years, Breton's own nature developed away from that of the perennial adolescent. Rebellion assumed a far-range target, and the freedom of imagination found broader vistas than attack on the habits of verbal reference.

If the imagery is rationally more tangible in *Arcane 17*—and its language more understandable—its ramifications are just as complicated and more taxing to the reader, because of the very fact that they appear decipherable. Each object Breton names is in constant process of metamorphosis, from the Rock of Percé (whose metamorphosis we have traced to a certain extent) to others that are more intricate: the flower, the bird, the butterfly, the allegorical night.

The most fecund of the metaphoric chameleons is the stone of the Apocalypse. From the fall of Babylon there is created a deep abyss, juxtaposed with a stone tossed by the dark waters; the stone is also associated with the Rock of Percé, which in turn becomes Montségur, the undaunted fortress of the Albigenses, which in turn makes Breton think of the fire, fire of destruction and of love, of the tower of Mélisande and of Juliet. It is the "marvelous iceberg of moonstone," it has the power of flight, of elevation.

The butterfly is a powerful emblem of metamorphosis: "The heart of a human being can be broken and the books can get old, and everything must, outwardly, die, but a power which is in no way supernatural makes of this very death the condition of renewal. It assures all exchanges ahead of time, that nothing precious may be lost within and that through the obscure metamorphoses, from season to season, the butterfly regains its exalting colors." Breton shows the physical, fertile link between the butterfly and the plant as indicative of the many communicating vessels in the universe.

At the same time he sees in the invisible but undeniable link between the plant and the butterfly, the nonsupernatural evidence of resurrection, of renewal of life, which makes winter, death, and destruction a passing thing:

> before flying away to work at the dissemination of the fertilizing substance, to regain the dotted and sinuous line which directs its flight, it

seems to exist only to display the sumptuosity of its wing. And in turn it speaks in order to tell us what a consoling mystery there is in the rise of successive generations, what new blood incessantly circulates, and, so that the species may not suffer because of the wasting away of the individual, what selection occurs just in time, succeeds in imposing its law in spite of everything. Man sees the trembling of the wing, which is, in all languages, the first great letter of the word Resurrection.

Thus even as darkness is luminous, winter is fertile, life is a subterranean torrent that penetrates everything, and destruction gives promise of new life.

Arcane 17 is extremely ethical. There are of course passing attacks on institutions, which we have come to expect from Breton: on school, family, church, barracks, bank, factory. But his approach to the future is benign and personal; love, recaptured, overflows into a tremendous compassion for mankind: "It is in human love that resides all the power of regeneration of the world."

In the midst of death and war Breton's hymn to life sounds like the work of a secular messiah. In the eyes of a woman, in the austerity of a rock, in the grace of a butterfly he reads the eternal values that cannot vanish, when all else vanishes, because they are the surest signs that death is passing, and that despite all the efforts of the human race toward self-annihilation, life is indestructible.

XIV

THE EXILE'S
RETURN

"Those who came back are exiled among us"
—Sartre

The return of André Breton to Paris in the spring of 1946 was an awkward one. As he reminisced six years later,* the difficulties of re-entering the intellectual life of Paris were still vividly implanted in his mind. With total candor he admitted the major fact: after all, he had left France in the period of its agony and had not returned until the liberation. Although every rational evidence supported the fact that it would have been impossible for him to stay in Paris during the occupation, still in retrospect absence had a psychological reality that could not be erased from the minds of Parisians who had stayed. He had not suffered the physical privations, and the scars that mental anguish and worry leave on a man are not as ostensible as those of physical involvement in danger, fear, battle, famine. There was a general feeling that he had sat out the war, he who had professed to be so militant, so libertarian, so courageous in the use of words. A poignant portrait of what it is to return after the holocaust is presented by the companion of his youth, Philippe Soupault, in a 1945 book called *Journal d'un Fantôme*. Indeed Breton was also a phantom, a stranger in his own country. He was the first to admit it with that open mind and disarming innocence from subterfuge that was so characteristic of his demeanor. He tried neither to defend nor to rationalize his ambivalent situation in the mêlée of the Parisian scene. He was fifty, and Paris was full of new philosophies, new forms of literature, new alignments, new directors in both the field of politics and in the arts. There was a sense of loneliness in the fact that the head of a major literary and art movement had lost most of his

* When I saw him in the fall of 1952 in his Paris apartment.

214

supporters. Those of his former friends who were still in Paris were surrealist no longer; those who had stood closest to him in the war years had not come back to France. Tanguy and Ernst had married Americans and taken up permanent residence in the United States. Duchamp, who had given him most companionship in his years in New York, and who most vividly embodied the vigilant days of his youth, had permanently settled in New York long before the war. Mabille was in Haiti; Péret, in Mexico.

It was not hostility that Breton met in Paris but an impression of estrangement. There was the ghost of an experience unshared—life in occupied Paris, magnificently described by Sartre in *Situation III*. The isolation of Paris from the rest of the world during those four years, the sense of a fictitious existence created a solidarity among the isolated, which the most humanistic, the warmest personality in the world could not penetrate. "How can one convey what the occupation was to the inhabitants of countries which have remained free? There is an abyss between us that is not easy to fill with words," said Sartre.[1]

Sartre and Camus, the reigning counselors of the human spirit in the aftermath of the war, saw no place for returning surrealists in the austere literature and philosophy of the postwar world. Indeed they made it very clear to returning exiles that this postwar period was to be quite different from the last one. This was not a time for happy revolution of words and clownings. The aftermath of defeat is not the same as the aftermath of victory. After a glorious war a strong nation can afford the verbal attacks of youth, against which it is fortified by reason of its obvious successes. But after World War II, France never shared any of the elation of victory of its "liberator nations." The French had a sense of humiliation in confronting both their former enemy and their so-called allies. France was defeated no less in 1945 than in 1940, and a vulnerable nation was more ready for a philosophy of grim resolution, of togetherness in mortification than it was attracted to propositions of individualistic liberty. Involvement was the byword, although it was never quite made clear by Sartre whether the only possible involvement was in effect in the Communist Party. Most writers of the Resistance had indeed joined the Party. To them returning surrealists presented an incongruous sight: as one remembered the old manifestoes frothing with promises to change the world, they now seemed tamed, chastised, and inarticulate, painfully out of step with the times. In the darkest hour of the war Breton had met Sartre in New York, and the two had conversed about France's agony; there had been a tone of sympathy and commiseration between the long-term visitor and the short-term one. But by 1947 there was a gulf, created by the large effort in which Sartre and Camus had participated to bring about the Liberation. They had been the voices of that Resistance, while Breton's role had been confined to that of reading other people's messages on the Voice of America. They had a faithful public, tightly, fanatically attached to them. So did Eluard and Aragon, now as nonsurrealists, poets of the Resistance. Where Camus and Sartre taught their readers stoical acceptance of the human condition and dignified tolerance of its indignities, Aragon and Eluard had been restored through their own lyricism to a sense of patriotic responsibility, which they were at least verbally able to reconcile with Communist solidarity.

Surrealism seemed like a thing of the past, like the Front Populaire, like old franc notes, now horribly devaluated, and like everything else that was associated with the prewar world. You could have bought a Max Ernst painting for $75.00, a Victor Brauner for less. It was not a belligerent Breton who was returning, nor a revolutionary one. He expected fully to be on the sidelines, in the shadow of the luminaries of the current literary scene. It was they, not he, who opened the attack.

First came Sartre's derogatory remarks about the surrealists in "Situation de l'écrivain en 1947," an article in his Les Temps Modernes, the most widely read and the most prestigious periodical of the epoch. The article was included later in his Situations; the somber Sartre took the surrealists to task, accusing them not of mistakes but of insincerities in their own time and of silence now. Actually Sartre was berating them for having aspired to what they must have realized from the start was impossible: "The originality of the surrealist movement resides in its attempt to appropriate everything: the déclassement from the top, parasitism, aristocracy, metaphysics, consummation of an alliance with revolutionary forces. The history of this attempt has shown that it was doomed to failure." [2] Although the condemnation is in the plural, it was obviously aimed mainly at Breton, for by 1947, except for him, and a few artists, no one remained from the first coterie who could still be labeled surrealist. Artaud was in a mental asylum, Crevel had committed suicide, Desnos had died of illness caught in a concentration camp, and of course, Aragon, Eluard, and Tzara now sang in a different key. In fact that same year Tristan Tzara, who had for twenty years been as mobile as a weathercock, proclaimed in a lecture at the Sorbonne that surrealism had been anti-revolutionary.[3] Péret was to join Breton in Paris and remain faithful to him to his own last day; but for the moment Breton had to resist the attack almost singlehanded. This is what Sartre said:

> They condemned their country because it still was in the insolence of victory; they denounced the war because they believed that the state

of peace would be of long duration. They were all victims of the disaster of 1940: the fact is that the moment of action had come, and
none of them was armed for it. Some of them killed themselves, others
are in exile; those who came back are exiled among us. They were the
announcers of the catastrophe at the time of the fatted cow; at the time
of the lean cows they have nothing more to say.[4]

In his "Situation de l'écrivain en 1947" Sartre had securely closed the
surrealist era as a "determined epoch"[5] now passed, as if in what he
called "its pretty stupid optimism." He was equating it with the irresponsible age of innocence of the twentieth century. He complained that the
surrealists' legacy had not been tangible: "not a single revelation, no intuition of a new object,"[6] although he begrudgingly admitted that they
represented the effort of the mind to surmount its own barriers; but he
labeled the effort "empty." He also conceded that "surrealism was the only
poetic movement of the first half of the twentieth century."[7] But the
truth of the matter is that, judging by the tone of the writing, poetry was
not worth much according to Sartre's literary values for the age; and this
poetry that he acknowledged as a fact but to which he could not relate
effectively, was perhaps the thing that irritated him most about surrealism,
because, as he says in a long footnote that is an article in itself, every time
one proved the dialectical inconsistencies of the surrealists, they hid themselves under the mantle of a protean and intangible "poetry."

Sartre brought upon himself a deluge of criticism for attacking the under-
dog; if he was so strong, why did he have to cast the first stone upon someone who was silent and inoffensive? The answer is simply that Sartre was
at the moment in the thick of his philosophy of political commitment and
engagé literature and could not resist using the most perfect example
available of what happens to a literary movement when it claims to be
revolutionary yet shies clear of political involvement. All the reasons of
conscience that made Breton steer his ideological revolution clear of political compromises were evidences of failure in Sartre's eyes: failure on the part
of the surrealists to gain a reading public, failure to detach themselves from
the bourgeoisie, although Sartre never made it clear how he or comrades
Aragon and Eluard were any closer than Breton to being understood by
anyone other than the members of that much-abused bougeoisie. At least it
was to Breton's credit that he had awakened the response for freedom in the
soul of Aimé Césaire and touched the indigenous population of
Haiti, even probably sparked their revolution. Sartre had asked pity for
native colonial populations; Breton had treated them as equals and
brothers and encouraged them to lift their voices in the freshness of their
own genius.

Sartre accused "the surrealists"—that is, Breton—of being intellectual and theorist, of having had an impossible dream, of having wanted to be something more than human. Sartre's attitude was one of irritation and incomprehension rather than of outright hostility; he was perhaps exasperated to see the return of even a glimmer of surrealist activity in the International Exposition of Surrealist Art then being held in Paris. He asked quite pointedly: was not the bourgeoisie that surrealism had attacked the very one that was attending the exposition? Was it not this bourgeoisie that could be counted on to buy the paintings and the books? While others protested in defense of Breton, he himself made no frontal attack on Sartre. He maintained that despite differences in ideology and intellectual training he held for Sartre "a keen intellectual esteem." [8]

Actually there were not many of the books around. For nearly ten years thereafter surrealist literature was to remain out of print. It is extraordinary that Breton made no obvious effort to get his works back in circulalation. He seemed to have no more desire to write. Although he brought out *Entretiens* (a series of interviews) in 1952 and *La Clé des champs* (a series of articles) in 1953, it appears from his letters to his old and faithful friend Léon-Pierre Quint that the motivation may have been primarily economic. He was in embarrassing financial circumstances. At one point he was so devoid of any kind of "budget" that he had to wait an advance on *La Clé des champs* to be able to come back to Paris from a provincial summer place where the cost of living was much lower and survival more possible.

The other frontal attack was to come from Camus in 1951 with *L'Homme révolté*, in which he examined surrealism as one of the examples in his study of the manifestations of rebellion. Camus calls Breton to task for his "revolver shot" in the Second Manifesto. He could not conciliate so much love and so much hatred as are mingled in surrealist philosophy. "André Breton wanted at the same time revolution and love, which are incompatible." [9] Again, before the existentialist tribunal Breton appears irresponsible in statement, ineffective in action. Ironically, even though on the one hand Sartre and Camus tend to place Breton in a historically closed circuit, they fail to situate the revolt in the context of the circumstances that triggered it. They fail above all to understand what Aimé Césaire expresses so beautifully to Breton in speaking about Lautréamont: "poetry begins with excess, with immeasure, it is a search fascinated with what is forbidden." [10]

Breton answered back to defend not himself but Lautréamont whom in the same book Camus had chided for having acted like an excessive adolescent. Breton deplored that in line with Sartre's moralistic interpretation of the destiny of Baudelaire,* Camus contributed to building up an irresponsible picture of successful men of letters, sitting so comfortably on their pedestals and demonstrating less than wisdom and humanity toward their anguished brothers.

But despite the attacks, and a position less than central in the literary scene, Breton was entering a more peaceful phase of his life. With a devoted wife, he re-entered his old apartment and made only one slight move in the rest of his life: when his daughter came to live with them in 1947, he moved a half-flight down to have a room for her. For to have her back, to give her a home, was to be one of the purest gratifications of this later part of his life. Indeed, Breton had returned to the semblance of the bourgeois way of life, to live in domesticity with his wife and daughter. Providing for them was an extreme embarrassment, for he had virtually no means, except the old one of being able to part with a painting he may have loved very much. His heavily laden walls were to become gradually lightened of their treasures, but new ones always came. There were changes in the furnishings of the apartment. To the many paintings had been added objects that had stimulating, evocatory meanings for Breton: Eskimo masks, Indian heads, emblems from the South Seas, dolls from the Hopi Indians of Arizona, all "justifications" of the ageless surrealist vision which was so relevant to the primitive, innocent vision.

He furnished what he thought was an exquisite room for his daughter. just fresh from a boarding school in Vermont. He waited with almost childish anticipation for her reaction. Aube was astounded—as she told me many years later. It was simply not a little girl's room; it was an antique shop or a museum; it was full of all the things that her father cherished, but hardly an environment to make her feel at ease. But of course she had her father's delicacy; she could not possibly hurt his feelings; but he understood. And they agreed that she was to put outside the door whatever she thought inappropriate. So little by little, oddities. fetishes, Indian heads, and sundry phantom objects discreetly found their way outside the door and were quietly taken away by the father, who did understand, though somewhat wistfully. Upon his death Aube was to pay him this tribute: "Everything I love of life I have discovered through his eyes." [11] When it came to her education, it is significant that he chose the human sciences rather than literature as a proper field of specialization. He knew how poorly one lives off literature if one is rigorous in one's thinking and not a popularizer. He saw in the social sciences a surer means of

---

* In a small book that Sartre had published on Baudelaire he demonstrated what a failure Baudelaire had been as a mortal even if his poetry had made him a successful immortal.

sustenance and also the possibility of doing good in more tangible terms than through words that no one took seriously. His daughter took his advice and in due time held a job helping in the rehabilitation of children from broken homes, of which she had some personal experience.*

Breton did not long remain a solitary figure in postwar Paris. Although his old friends were gone physically or spiritually, soon a new generation came to seek him out. The position had changed. In the 1920's Breton had been a master among his peers. Now he was the leader, the idol, almost legendary while still alive, to those much younger than himself. Characteristically his love of companionship prevailed, the utterly simple fraternity that made the young call him "André" as if he were their contemporary, and communicate with him as equals linked in closest friendship. His door was open to the young, sometimes at great risk to his safety. His wife Elisa remembers a story, typical and profoundly characteristic. One day they arrived home from a gathering to find a foreign-looking young man standing at the door. He insisted on seeing Breton, although Breton recognized neither his name nor his sponsor. Breton let him in, however, and listened to what appeared to be a young Hindu's recital of his aspirations, the conditions in his country, and other sundry details. Finally the young man asked Breton, who had spoken with his usual, unguarded candor, for an autographed picture of himself. When Breton replied that he was not in the habit of giving photos and in fact was not sure he had one around, the young man burst into tears and begged him for the token. Breton, touched by such fervor and devotion, asked his wife to find a photo; he autographed it, and with many expressions of gratitude the young man left. A few days later Breton suffered the painful results of his indiscretion. The man was a Soviet reporter in disguise; and he had gone back to Russia to write a scathing interview, displaying the photograph as evidence of Breton's vanity. One would expect Breton to have raged and roared in indignation like the lion to whom he was so often compared in the press. Instead, he said to Elisa that he would rather take the chance of having his confidence betrayed than close his door to so

* As beautiful Aube told me her story of the days with her father and stepmother, they were happy ones, always full of unexpected visitors. One day a young man walked up the long flight of stairs and asked for her father. Yves Elléouët, also of Breton stock, a poet and a painter, had come to call on André Breton whom he admired. Breton happened to be at a café where he had resumed his role of mentor to a daily and ever-growing new coterie of younger writers and painters. Aube offered to take Yves to her father. Eventually, Yves found it even more interesting to be in the company of Aube than of André. They were married. They now live in the Loire Valley, in Balzac country, not far from where Alexander Calder, one of Breton's most faithful American friends, has taken up residence; he loves Aube like his own daughter Sandra, who was once Aube's classmate in America.

many other genuine young people who sought him out and to whom he might be helpful.*

The pattern of the last twenty years of Breton's life was not sensational or creatively exciting, but it was rewarding to his spiritual needs. It was one of total commitment to art and love and friendship, rich in human contacts and the pursuit of knowledge. He seemed to have as many friends as he had books, and he kept abreast of every form of protest against static society, every new surge of intellectual movement in the world. His rivals complained that Breton jumped on every bandwagon to show how young he could remain. But the truth was rather that every new tremor came to shake his abode. Every wave of imagination, every new poet, new concept of human brotherhood, new courage, new defiance against the slavery of life sought his approbation. He had long ago learned not to accept a "public" but to be delighted by readers who appreciated vigorous writing. His tremendous compassion for an illiterate, stolid humanity did not imply that one had to write in the simple language that they might understand. He accepted the paradox of not being understood by those toward whom his heart went out in compassion and confidence. He felt that for a while there could really be no proletarian literature, that even when in Communist countries the so-called proletariat came to write, they would do so with the borrowed devices of bourgeois language, and with structures betraying bourgeois prejudices. He was too keen a student of linguistics and sociology to be carried away by the thought of a spontaneous proletarian art, integrally different from the bourgeois one. All he hoped for his own writing was that it might awaken and alert those of the working classes who could read his words and understand that he sought not emulation on their part but, quite to the contrary, the discovery of their own individual identity. "Twenty years ago, I was already asking how one could think of participating in the surrealist spirit and care at the same time about one's position in the world." [12]

In writing as in painting he envisaged his role clearly as that of provoker: all that he would want to convey to others was the legacy of free adventure and mastery of one's universe, which artists have striven for in the Western world; but he did not want to impose on anyone any particular image of what that might be. "To my eyes that was where my chances lay of not being unworthy of the human adventure." [13] He expressed this attitude more explicitly in his article "Why Are They Hiding Contemporary

* But the last time I visited Breton in 1964, I noticed that the simple inscription "André Breton" was gone from his door. He explained that just a few months earlier some heavily drugged young people had found his apartment and set fire at his door in the middle of the night. He had to bow to reason, and make his availability less ostentatious.

Russian Art from Us?" where he worries about the lack of understanding of this principle among those who govern the artistic conscience in Communist states:

> It is already quite evident that we are dealing here with an enterprise of systematic destruction, of extirpation by all the means of what in the course of centuries we have learned to hold as an art worthy of the name and very particularly of all that can relate to the concept of a living art, in the sense of a passionate quest of a new vital rapport between man and things, in what way this man and these things find their common ground and highest expression. All who have some sense of this art understand that it entails a spiritual adventure which cannot at any cost be permitted to be interrupted. They know that on this royal road are inscribed in the modern period names of Blake, Delacroix, Géricault, Füssli, Courbet, Manet, Cézanne, Gauguin, Van Gogh, Seurat, and that it is magnificently prolonged to our time. Those were free and fully the *masters of their universe*. It is too evident that not a single artist of their stature could today find grace in the improvised tribunals which sit in judgment in Russia, supplied as their only code with some academic rudiments and armed with an ever-growing list of prohibitions (the naked is banished, *nature morte* less and less tolerated, and so forth).[14]

In another of his last articles he tackled the question of social realism head on and declared it an "imposture" of the highest magnitude, which the Soviet regime had imposed on its writers. Basically on this score Breton's position had not changed in twenty years. As he had so unequivocally explained in "Position politique du surréalisme," the two fundamental attributes of the artist were, in his opinion, emotional depth and ability to communicate, but the one was not to be made directly to feed the other. A great loss, a great admiration, when channeled directly into writing becomes either eloquence or propaganda and provides a field day for biographers who will later situate the circumstances that provoked the writing. Breton opted then, and until the end of his days, for the subterranean penetration of the event into the sinews and bloodstream of the writer, there to become part of his essential being and not recorded directly into the writing. The implication for the new class of intellectuals is that only when their human endeavor has found an adequate means of expression, can it be expected to communicate in a manner commensurate with its needs; only then will there be a truly new art representative and at the same time directive of the new society. Aragon's position in this respect—what Breton deemed either myopia or aspiration for worldly power or gain—afflicted Breton more than Sartre's or Camus' misunderstandings of or lack of empathy with surrealism. He addressed his old spiritual brothers, Eluard and Aragon, time and again in open letters or articles, inviting them to pronounce themselves more sincerely on the misalliance between art and politics. He considered it a form of betrayal on the part of his old friends, which remained a bleeding wound in him to his last day.

On the other hand, it did not prove too hard for Breton to recover his spirits and to keep his morale in a buoyant state. He had resumed his surrealist activities. The first literary magazine to which he contributed was *Les Quatre Vents* in 1946–7, which ran special numbers devoted to surrealism. It is here that the French were able to find easily accessible for the first time his 1940 poem, *Fata Morgana*. Breton's adherents began to multiply, although some of them did not remain permanently in his entourage—just as many of his collaborators at the time of the First Manifesto had defected by the time he wrote the Second. But time had mellowed Breton; he did not become indignant at the fluid character of the postwar surrealist coterie. They still met in cafés regularly to explore psychic games and to question themselves and each other on spiritual and social problems. Of course group activity was intimately linked with a collective publication. A series of these followed each other sporadically. Characteristic of the surrealist rejection of routine activity and subject to its ever-present financial insecurity, the reviews *Néon, Medium, Le Sur-réalisme même, Bief,* and *La Brèche* succeeded each other irregularly from 1948 to 1965. The last surrealist magazine, *L'Archibras,* was conceived just before the death of Breton; and its first issue, in 1967, was to become a testimonial to him. The signatures and the distribution of editorial responsibility in these magazines indicate who were the new and the most active affiliates of surrealism. Most in the foreground appear to be Jean Schuster, Gérard Legrand, Jean-Louis Bédouin, José Pierre, and Robert Benayoun; of these, Jean Schuster was to become the most fervent surrealist and the one closest to Breton at his death, entrusted with his last wishes and testament.[15]

Other poets like Jean-Pierre Duprey, Yves Bonnefoy, Malcolm de Chazal, and André Pieyre de Mandiargues found it possible to relate to surrealism's concern for rebellion and sensuality, for erotic literature and the liberating power of poetry, but resisted total submission to the surrealist label. And like the prewar periodicals the postwar ones covered developments in art as well as in poetry. Among those highlighted were the Swedish painter Max Walter Svanberg, of whom Breton wrote high praise, and Wifredo Lam, Toyen, and Leonora Carrington.

Breton was fully aware, as he had suggested in his *Prolégomènes à un troisième manifeste du surréalisme ou non* (1942), that when an idea is proliferated, it is apt to lose it pristine character. Although in 1942 the possibility of a neosurrealism disturbed him, in the 1950's and 1960's he was much more receptive to the larger orbit of surrealistic expressions. On the other hand, he had from the first felt that the evolution of human thought must relate to explorations in the field of physics, mathematics, and biology, and that the barriers between art, psychology, and anthropology must be lifted. It is in line with this attitude that the surrealist magazines included articles on the law of mathematical probability, essays by psychologist Roger Elleau, references to the Dutch philosopher Johan Huizinga and his book, *Homo Ludens*, and to physicist Werner Heisenberg. And in keeping with Breton's faith in the future, the last of the surrealist periodicals is given priority over the old for its relevance and power of direction: "Surrealism is a form of dynamics whose vector today is not to be searched in *Révolution Surréaliste* but in *La Brèche.*" [16]

In 1952 Breton told the interviewer for *Entretiens* that he had no regrets and was content to have lived his life exactly as he had lived it. There is no reason to doubt his sincerity. "My life will have been devoted to what I held to be beautiful and just. All in all, I have lived to this day as I had dreamed of living. In the battle which I led, I never lacked companions as firm as I; thanks to them I have never been deprived of human warmth.[17] The evidence is in the broken pieces of the prewar pattern which he put back together again: the role of mentor, of critic at large.

Books of all kinds found their way to his mailbox. The life of the café was resumed, as were the long stream of visitors to 42 rue Fontaine; the art exhibits, which he assembled or which, if assembled by others in a way distasteful to him, he demolished with his abundant resources of verbal acrimony; the walks through Paris, the discovery of a statue, the excitement of finding a new form of the *insolite*; the polemics, the championship of a new cause in the fight for freedom; the tremendous correspondence with major writers around the world, as well as a modest letter from a little French girl in Washington, D. C., asking his advice on art education in the elementary school, on free drawing versus formalistic training.[18] The badges of his own pure subversiveness to conformism or to dictates other than his free conscience were the black shirt he wore under an otherwise traditional appearance, and the pipe he smoked jerkily so that uneven puffs of smoke matched the intensity of the flow of words whose fervor had never marred the perfect syntax. He became a poet's poet, a writer's writer, an elder statesman; the deep and compassionate heart, the luminous mind brought the world that counted for Breton to his door, and he no longer felt the need to travel. His appearance had considerably changed. Although one could never say that he was "tamed," he presented the appearance of a sage, of a philosopher, of an extremely moral man, deeply pained by the slightest flaw in ethics on the part of anyone whom he had at some time or other loved. He was particularly troubled by the lack of purity in current revolutionary tactics.

The case of Garry Davis was a good example. When Breton heard of Davis' denunciation of nationalism on the floor of the United Nations, he was one of the first to applaud him. His own utopian dream had been that no potential harmony and pacifism can become a reality in this world until the notion of nationality is eradicated from human consciousness. This "citizen of the world," then, was welcomed. Breton supported his daring, his visions, walked with him along the "world highway" to that small town in the heart of France, Cahors, which had declared itself an international town (ten departments in all had made the same declaration). But soon he was accusing Garry Davis of having used a beautiful idea for personal publicity. The enchantment vanished into one more disappointment for Breton.

The Garry Davis incident had one personal advantage for Breton. The Valley of the Lot in that southwestern region of France was full of medieval lore particularly attractive to Breton for its heretical character steeped in the Albigensian legend; there, in the village of Saint-Cirq La Popie, he found a rustic house with which he fell in love. He who had never felt the need to own property had a sudden longing to be the proprietor of that old and modest residence on top of a high hill, overlooking the enchanted medieval valley, a sort of unbelievable Camelot, untouched by industry or tourism, dominating the lazy Lot River, and populated by a truly peasant population. His father, still alive, fulfilled the wish through one of those small bourgeois qualities of parsimonious economy. He bought it for his son, and thereafter until his death Breton spent every summer but one in those ancient stone rooms, where modern facilities were not even dreamed of. The darkness of the interior made sparkles of the bright and hot sunshine outside tremendously theatrical in their communicative effect. The contrast was in keeping with Breton's vision of *Arcane 17*. Upon seeing his little castle of Saint-Cirq La Popie, one thought: *"brèche"* and *"étincelle,"* cracks in the darkness, inundated with sparks of light—that is how life had been for André Breton.

The sixth decade of Breton's life was relatively tranquil, subject only to economic difficulties, which he kept as discreetly to himself as possible. His greatest source of happiness, as he indicated in *Entretiens,* was the fact that despite the lack of literary publicity he was indeed reaching the very sectors of the reading public that he cared most about: "the attraction, which the surrealist temptation for youth is more amply than ever exercising itself." [19]

He had never striven to be one of the "public writers." In fact part of his preoccupation had been to guard surrealism from the *salon* world and from circles that would be attracted to its surface sensationalism. In an era profoundly marked by existentialism it was indeed not likely that surrealism would fall prey to group acceptance. But another phenomenon was burgeoning. Studies were beginning to appear about surrealism—some on the movement, others about Breton himself.[20]

Two literary men of a younger generation, who had indeed been too young to participate in the surrealist movement in its activist years, had written books about André Breton shortly after his return to France. One was Julien Gracq. In a book that demonstrates how far his own sensibilities were awakened by contact with Breton's power to love and to illuminate, Julien Gracq says: "The only truly adventurous work of our epoch is perhaps before us in the books of Breton." [21] He himself, on the eve of World War II, had written a novel that Breton could accept as truly "surrealist." Breton wrote a letter to Léon-Pierre Quint [22] to ask what he thought of Gracq's *Au Château d'Argol*, and added that "for my part I find this work magnificent."

The other was Claude Mauriac, the son of François Mauriac, a giant among traditional French novelists. Sons rebel against their fathers; no filial rebellion could have been more dramatic than that of the son of the devoutly Catholic Mauriac abandoning his father's tradition and following in the path of one who was the antithesis of his father. Claude Mauriac, son of the eminent, world-renowned, richly rewarded novelist, had gravitated toward the Lucifer of the literary world, the poet free of all honors and recognitions, who seduced other men's sons away from respectable literary circles. From the regionalist father and his closed-circuit world of fiction centering on Bordeaux, Claude had moved to the open world of the Montmartre poet for whom reality was more fantastic than fiction. "There is in our epoch undoubtedly no enterprise more exalting nor more fecund than the one attempted by Breton," he wrote in 1949.[23] Claude Mauriac has since become a well-known novelist and a leader of the "new novel"; but he has never written anything so discerning of the qualities of human sensitivity, so aware of the nature of human love as in his study of the work of André Breton.

Actually his book was not as alien to the spirit of his father as he or his father may have thought. For there was indeed a common ground, incongruous as it may seem, on the surface, in the intellectual position that the elder Mauriac and Breton occupied in postwar France. Whatever their differences in spiritual ideology, they were both deeply committed to their faith and were more concerned with the destiny of man, the individual, than with collective behavior and regimentation. They had both rejected the cult of self, the narcissism of the age of anxiety; for both, literature had been an ethical issue and a channel for the liberation of the mind rather than an escapist cult, as part of life in full stream rather than a substitute for it. Claude Mauriac had clearly sensed the moral quality of Breton's writings when he said: "Surrealism would not have had this importance, it could not have marked too profoundly our epoch if Breton had not placed it from the beginning and forever more on a moral plane." [24] Above all, Mauriac and Breton resembled each other, though on different ends of the literary spectrum, because they were both passionate men, even if their passions were expressed in diametrically opposite directions. The novelist's son was in a good position to value the poet's measure of dedication.

Two subsequent studies—Michel Carrouges' *André Breton et les données fondamentales du surréalisme* and Victor Crastre's *André Breton* —were less involved with the personality of Breton but highlighted the fundamental qualities of Breton over and above the ostentatious drama of the surrealist group manifestations—which was the way Paris liked to remember her surrealists. Carrouges—who to Breton's dismay turned out to be a devout Catholic—viewed Breton's work from the point of view of its gnostic influences and contributed to surrealist magazines illuminating articles on the nature of automatic writing and its spiritual import. Crastre declared that surrealism was "the capital fact of literary history between 1924 and 1940." [25] He also had noticed that in the immediate postwar era, despite new literary movements and new intellectual leadership, "Breton has not been outstripped by the following generation." "Perhaps," he says, "in the thirtieth century they will come to view the work of André Breton as revealing the true portrait of the man of our time." [26]

Perhaps the most cogent of all the studies on Breton is Ferdinand Alquié's *Philosophy of Surrealism*, a product of the Sorbonne and of a professor—facts that under normal circumstances Breton would have viewed with suspicion, for like Mallarmé before him, he entertained little sympathy for the academic mind and its systematized procedures. But Alquié had the advantage of having in his youth participated in surrealist activities, as a sympathizer if not an actual member of the group. His study had the double advantage of first-hand observation and an organized mind that could bring to the phenomenon of surrealism more than admiration or centrifugal impressions. Alquié was able to place surrealism as an intellectual movement in relation to other, earlier philosophies such as Descartes' classicism, and to extract, in terms of resemblances and differences, the essential from the temporal and the circumstantial.

In the years between 1945 and 1955 Breton was not receiving official honors or medals—which he would have rejected if they had been offered to him; but he nonetheless was attracting the attention of some of the most keen intelligences among French critics. A book of essays celebrating his return, *Essais et témoignages*, was published in 1950 as a testimonial of approval of his function in the world of French letters; it was such as would make a man feel he was reading his obituary before his death. Breton's prestige among those who really mattered to him was solid as the Rock of Percé. He had been used to being a center of attention from his earliest days as a writer; but now the esteem with which he was increasingly regarded was involved less with the destiny of surrealism than with the impact of the man who had created surrealism.

These writings also created the impression that Breton's own literary work had reached a finality that would allow a total view and appraisal. It is significant that whereas Breton protested against the notion of a historical study of surrealism, he had no quarrel with those who felt his own work had come to an end. He was the first to admit that he had said what he had to say in terms of the poetic idiom that was closest to his heart; in fact the title *Arcane 17* had given internal evidence of the final attainment of what Mallarmé had called *"le Livre."*

Breton's literary communication from the time of his return to Paris to the time of his death, twenty years later, consisted primarily of critical pieces and philosophical essays. Except as examples of his personal tastes in literature and his concept of human destiny, in style these writings do not bear the surrealist signet. They are in form and vocabulary closer to the writings of the last years of André Gide, Mauriac, Malraux, Bachelard, and Unamuno than to those of the surrealists. They betray the poet perhaps by the breadth of a sentence, the architectonic alliance of thought to thought, and the easy injection of a metaphor into the heart of abstract thought, there to glow like a jewel and like a magnet to draw all other sequential ideas to itself. This form of the critical and philosophical essay is generally expected of men much older than Breton was in his last twenty years. Apparently the poet in him died young—or perhaps it is truer to say that as he grew older, he gradually abandoned the rhetorical implication of the word "poet." In the quieting effect of the lasting love of and for Elisa there was no longer the turbulence of new images to describe new sensualities. Poetry had permeated his life so wholly that a visit from a young friend, or an encounter with an old one in the flea market, or the opening of a new work by or about a poet, or a protest against a flagrant defamation of a work of art, or an exposition of paintings, or the discovery of a new artist—these were all forms of the poetic art for the poet of the Rue Fontaine.

XV

THE LITERARY
CRITIC

"La Lampe dans l'horloge"
—*La Clé des champs*

From the beginning of his career much of Breton's prose writing had been in the context of criticism; in his last years his critical work became dominant. Breton was following a poetic tradition as critic. Baudelaire, Mallarmé, and Valéry had demonstrated that intelligence was a basic faculty in the creation of the metaphoric device, which more than rhyme and rhythm distinguished the writer of poetry. Breton, like T. S. Eliot and Yeats, demonstrated the hypotheses of Baudelaire, Mallarmé, and Valéry, that the poet in modern times is a thinker rather than a singer, that the poetic imagination can proceed to critical intelligence of the work—although it does not necessarily follow that the critical mind is in turn gifted with poetic imagination. It was perhaps Edgar Allan Poe more than anyone else who had instilled in his French admirers the notion that the poetic principle was nurtured by a mind aware of its structure, of its mechanism, and functioning, which in turn would understand better than any other the genesis of the work of art of a fellow artist.

Literary criticism serves two distinct purposes: it gives us insight into the author studied or into the author of the criticism. A critic may be subservient to the author he is examining; this is particularly true of scholar critics and of reviewers of current works. On the other hand criticism may serve merely as a pretext for an author to highlight his own thinking, to find an alter ego to confront with his own; much of "new" criticism falls in this category and makes the reader suspect that the critic would have preferred to write a philosophical essay but felt insecure or unreadable in the bold stance of his naked thought; it would appear that he needed the support of the "other," as an instrument on which to play his own tune. Today it seems easier to discuss freely such notions as time, space, reality, and exteriorization of the ego in relation to a particular book by someone else than as a purely philosophical meditation; and often the critic in this context comes out a stronger, more resourceful mind than the subject of his so-called criticism.

This was certainly the case with Baudelaire, whose articles on Delacroix, Gautier, Hugo, Banville, and Wagner revealed more about his own concepts of art, reality, and the evocative power of words than about the artists with whom he was allegedly preoccupied. Baudelaire surely had an ulterior motive. He was not well known as a poet at the time he wrote these critical works, and it is doubtful that anyone would have paid much attention to the isolated aesthetic notions of a relatively unknown writer. On the other hand, the authors and artists he was dealing with were famous names, and whoever wrote of them was likely to be read for the sake of the subjects of his writing. In his meditations about them Baudelaire has told us a great deal about his own sensibilities, aesthetic tastes and aspirations.

This was true to a certain extent of André Breton's earlier articles on Gide, Apollinaire, and Lautréamont. He did not exactly inject his own aesthetic into his analysis of their writing or character; but he thrust upon the reader's consciousness the originality of thought or structure that he had perceived in an author (who was accepted in some other way than his own understanding) or he promoted authors who, in his opinion, had been grossly neglected. The objects of his criticism were discoveries in the surrealist sense: he used them more to define the burgeoning concepts of surrealism than to give a balanced insight into a particular work or author that he scrutinized. These subjects were actually objects of illustration. Breton was not alone in this activity: a number of his young poet colleagues were doing the same thing—Aragon, Soupault, Michel de Leiris, Marcel Jean, Maurice Heine, etc. They succeeded in salvaging from literary oblivion writers such as Sade, Lautréamont, Jarry, Roussel, even as Baudelaire, Mallarmé, and Valéry had recovered for French literature (if not for American) the significance of Edgar Allan Poe.

Breton went further than any of his colleagues in this direction and actually managed to reshuffle the hierarchies of French literary history. He was a prodigious reader, and in discovering a writer, he was like a geologist unearthing a precious stone. His choice was of writers who had contributed to the libertarian spirit of mankind by their sense of beauty, a disturbing kind of beauty, by their intimacy with the subterranean workings of nature, and most of all by the "mechanism of intellectual subversion" [1] that they had manifested. To these spirits, Breton was happy to be subservient, and his criticism was not a vehicle of his thought but a constant defense and illustration of the manifestation of freedom as the basic and inalienable quality of the artist in the all-inclusive sense of the word.

From the beginning, literary criticism had been for Breton part of his rejection of the static structure of society. For if institutions and establishments needed purging, a reconstruction of the hierarchy of literary values seemed equally important. He had noticed early in life the marginal, underground character of a whole series of writings, rich nourishment for the modern mind yet excluded by or rapidly disposed of in manuals of literary history, which he thought as officially bigoted as all other forms of history. He made this quite clear in his lecture in Barcelona, which preceded the surrealist manifestoes, on November 17, 1922:

> Through a great number of productions, some completely deprived of personality, others which appeared to have as little to recommend them as possible, . . . I had thought that I distinguished a minimum of common affirmation and I was burning to draw from them for myself the law of a trend.[2]

Somewhat later he came to the conclusion, revealed in the Second Manifesto, that there was a subterreanean continuity among certain writers, unrelated in style and personality, who had a common metaphysical orientation—from the English Gothic novel and the poetry of William Blake to the German romanticists, and through Nerval, Rimbaud, Germain Nouveau, the older Hugo, Raymond Roussel, and others to the twentieth century. Some of them were not noted primarily for their metaphysical propensities, but were unconsciously linked to a *sub rosa* tradition; they were imbued with occult, gnostic preoccupations, and their frame of reference was largely the symbols of the ancient religious heresies. Just as established Catholicism bypassed or minimized the heretic rebellion of the Albigenses in the South of France and the heretical language of symbols engraved in the sculpture on the mightiest cathedrals, so literary history had been wont to deprive these hermetic authors and their lineage of their due and allocated to them a marginal place in its recorded annals and in academic programs.

> All truly qualified critics of our time have been led to establish that the poets whose influence has been shown to be the most relevant today, whose action on modern sensibility had made itself felt [Hugo, Nerval, Baudelaire, Rimbaud, Lautréamont, Mallarmé, Jarry] have been more or less marked by this tradition.[3]

In discussing such authors Breton is no more technical in his literary vocabulary than in his art criticism. In fact he lifts the poets he names from their artistic context to judge them as men, and he measures their human values in terms of their degree of protest and their power to stir and arouse the imaginative faculty and the spirit of rebellion in the reader, to bring him to a state where the desire to change becomes acute and compelling. Breton's critical activity consists in effect of selecting from the great body of literature the visionary writers; his definition of "visionary" as it emerges from his critical writings is that quality of a writer that, without necessarily driving the reader to action, creates an almost chemical change in his mind, makes him aware of the dynamic character of the universe and thus unsettles his established mental classifications of arts and institutions. In Breton's view it is as much through this "critical" activity as with their own particular writing that the surrealists reshaped modern sensibility.[4] This view of literature identifying the critic's motivation with that of the author he is discussing, belies the sheltered stance of the self-contained artist. It also explains his disappointment in the Rimbaud of the last years: as a trader, he revealed in his letters a constricted consciousness of life, whereas in his child-poet phase he had given such promise of an expanded sensibility and of the potential for untangling some of the snags of the human labyrinth.

Although all his life Breton maintained an attitude of high suspicion in regard to the academic approach to literary criticism, there was from the beginning in him the quality of the teacher, just as in the case of Mallarmé. His broad range of reading included contemporary works which he probed with the same intense interest as a rare volume, or a long and seemingly tedious documentary study in whose dark corners he might discover something luminous and exciting, and which he was immediately compelled to impart and for which he spontaneously communicated his enthusiasm. As Elisa said of him, he had a constant, unflinching curiosity —for books, for people, for objects, for stones. He himself suggested that his contribution in the field of criticism was one of discovery. Giving the credit to surrealism as a whole, rather than taking it for himself, he says: "think of all the figures of the past whom surrealism lifted out of the shadows and who are today recognized as *torchbearers*, and of all the false torchbearers that it returned to obscurity." [5]

Breton's social subversiveness is, then, closely affiliated with his literary iconoclasm; all this is entrenched in his adamant rejection of the Greek and Latin culture which had so long been the groundwork of French culture. The search for new myths—such as the Celtic and those of the Germanic North and the meridional gnostic South—is the basis of his literary predilections. In an early essay, "Le Merveilleux contre le Mystère," he highlighted a "splendid nineteenth century" and found only the fourteenth century its equal: the first for the great impact of the Germanic mystique, the other for the forces of the gnostics. Both these unorthodox forms of mysticism are matched in his opinion only by the Gothic spirit of eighteenth-century England. "It is enough to say to what point we are anxious to see gnosticism put in its true place, after having been so long decried as a Christian heresy." [6]

In viewing individual authors, then, his motivation for literary criticism is neither in the field of pure asthetics nor, as in the case of Sartre in relation to Baudelaire and Flaubert, a preoccupation with biographical data that aids in comprehending the personality and indirectly draws moral or philosophical conclusions from them. Except in the case of Jacques Vaché, whose life rather than writings (since there were none) was the poem for Breton, all his other subjects of literary study attracted Breton through their works rather than their characters—unless he wished to point out the incongruity of the work with the life of the author. "Their tribulations in the course of their lives, as we can retrace them approximately, are of infinitesimal interest in contrast to their message and bring to its deciphering only a derisible contribution." [7]

In general, then, Breton searches in the authors to whom he is drawn for messages to support his own convictions or visions. It is difficult to tell which comes first: the intuitive interest or the spiritual inclination that seeks affinities and in the magnetic fields of criticism becomes polarized. The fact is that his criticism is illustrative of an idea and leans heavily on internal evidences for the concepts or attitudes Breton extracts from the writers in question.

This power of scrutiny, undistracted by peripheral data, stood him well in the Rimbaud affair, which caused Breton to write a monograph, *Flagrant Délit*. The journalistic world and a number of university scholars had hailed the discovery of Rimbaud's legendary lost manuscript, *La Chasse spirituelle*, and thus accepted what was perhaps the biggest literary hoax of the century. Breton read the text, published by no less prestigious a publishing house than the Mercure de France. Instead of using as supporting evidence the obvious imitations of known Rimbaud images, he identified the structures and choices of alliances of words that, from his intimate knowledge of the work of Rimbaud, he knew to be incompatible with Rimbaud's taste or syntax. In the analysis of Rimbaud in this essay, we can see one of the earliest "structuralist" approaches to literary texts before the trend that was to revolutionize French critical attitudes of the 1960's. Owing to his long-standing knowledge of phenomenology and to his eye trained in the recognition of patterns and organizations in painting, Breton had developed a manner of studying writing that enabled him to grasp the intimate rapports between language and its multifaceted, shifting meanings, its power not merely to express but also to create meaning.

This very important essay on Rimbaud contains Breton's usual acrimonious comments against limited views of the role of critic and of the self-interest that his eye caught so fast in the seemingly innocuous comments of the promoters of the Rimbaud manuscript. Breton as poet takes his reader into the creative process and, in demonstrating what poetry entails in the modern world, gives an insight into the evolution of poetry that is prophetic of subsequent mutations in poetic structure. Specifically Breton states that it was not necessary to go into a long study of Rimbaud's handwriting and his use of certain words in certain of his writings to establish internal evidence that would reverse the accepted chronology of *Une Saison en Enfer* and *Les Illuminations*. As Breton views that problem in chronology, the significant thing is that in the metamorphosis of the poetic idiom Rimbaud illustrates dramatically the progression "from verse to prose" [8] and once the gap is bridged, a poet can never go back to a fixed prosody. It is inconceivable to Breton that Rimbaud would ever again have written even in free verse once he had realized that within the structure of what is known as prose, there can be created certain associations of words and images that effect stricter and more binding alliance and groupings than ever imposed by the superficial dictums of versification. In explaining the prosody and techniques of Rimbaud, Breton has the scientific and linguistic precision of a scholar, and this essay is a far cry from the easy, spontaneous, somewhat disorganized critical writings of Mallarmé and Valéry.

The question of inner structure had been earlier developed in a brief and somewhat unnoticed piece, which appears in *La Clé des champs* and is entitled "Silence d'or." The true poet, according to Breton, is directed not by the visual appearance of words, not by *a priori* rules of an external harmony but by an interior music, most like the composer's, who hears internally the composition he transcribes.

Language for the writer has a greater auditory character than a visual one. The true poet is sensitive to acoustical dimensions, rhythm, degrees of intensity and *timbre* which preclude the possibility of harboring "pure thought." The ensuing musicalities of exterior speech and the visions that they may create are effects—that is, results of the mental activity that has *occurred*—rather than intended objectives. When Breton comes to the astounding conclusion that great poets are great auditories rather than visionaries, he means that words are never put together because of the visual or auditory harmony they might create for a reader or speaker of the text. The words on paper are merely a transcription of what happened in the mind of the signifier, and the visionary power of the signified (the words themselves) depends not on how they look or sound (form) but on the degree of evocative power they contain to enlarge for the reader the scope of the signified (the things or feelings they represent). To say it another way, in his silence the poet has caught what for him is true harmony—that is, words attuned to his concept, and the manner and the pattern in which the words emerge on the sheet of paper is far less significant than the degree of concordance between their inner disposition in regard to each other and the degree of representative value they achieve of the sensibility of the writer. He is poet not according to exterior form, disposed as it were according to a visually motivated pattern, but in keeping with a structure that transcribes the auditory image of inner speech. It is in discerning this inner auditory pattern of Rimbaud's poetry and the evolutionary process through which it passed in a few brief years that Breton was able to recognize the real thing from the artificially contrived patterns of Pascal Pia's sensational pastiche.

An anthology is also a critical statement; choice is value judgment, and in publishing an anthology of black humour on the eve of World War II, Breton had completed a book of extracts from a wide, international range of authors, and prefaced in concise terms the significance of each selection. The extent to which an anthology can reflect the power of judgment is evidenced by the fact that this anthology was one of the books banned by the invading German government. The idea of such an anthology was not Breton's but Edouard Roditi's, the future translator of Breton's only collection of poems to appear in English. As editors of Sagittaire and long and faithful friends of Breton's, publishers of his manifestoes, Roditi and Léon Pierre-Quint had suggested the idea some years earlier more as a source of income for Breton, who was in particularly dire straits just after the birth of his daughter, than for any other reason. Léon Pierre-Quint had himself magnificently defined the subversive and metaphysical nature of dark humor as ingrained in Lautréamont's work.[9] The idea was genial, as it implied—like the streak of gnosticism Breton had sensed in the history of literature—a signet identifiable not in sundry authors but in an uninterrupted stream overcoming time and geographical boundaries, making the Word a weapon of rebellion. As early as 1928, Léon Pierre-Quint had brought to light this vein in the work of Lautréamont, the patron saint of the surrealists, and had hinted that it was a major current in world literature. Breton went along with the notion of continuity by insisting that his notes preface each text rather than be gathered in an appendix at the end of the book.[10] As a result these introductions are a running commentary, which the excerpts appear almost to illustrate, and they give the book a critical unity. From Swift, Lewis Carroll, Sade, Lautréamont, all the way to Jarry, the texts Breton chose were of uneven literary value, some were no more than letters, but they had in common that very quality which Breton placed above all others in literature, and quite independent of the merits of style: it was the disturbing effect of verbal protest that used humor in its sarcastic sense as a weapon without participating in the derisive effects achieved. As Breton describes it early in the anthology, dark humor becomes "the superior rebellion of the mind." [11] The author, in his noninvolvement in the wounds he inflicts, avoids, in the pressing of moral issues, the state of sentimentality—incompatible, as Breton thought, with the modern spirit. From the point of view of literary criticism, what is significant and applicable to future criticism by Breton is the fact that those numerous authors are not put in historical context; but they are assessed rather from the point of view of what they contribute to the modern spirit of freedom and justice. Again the analysis has an illustrative intention already noted in Breton's criticism in earlier writings.

In Lewis Carroll's apparent fantasies he recognizes the sense of revolt that makes him a fitting master of student rebels. Breton's notion of dark humor is broad and flexible enough to include De Quincey for his "profound compassion for human misery." To the poet Germain Nouveau, a contemporary and friend of Rimbaud, Breton is attracted for his "absolute nonconformism and absence of moderation." Another much neglected poet, a contemporary of the Symbolists but independent of all coteries, was Charles Cros, whom Breton extols for his "prodigious mental adventure." Raymond Roussel, too difficult to appeal to the general public, is for the type of reader Breton projects in a transformed society as "the greatest magnetizer of modern times." Breton admires Roussel's ability to reconstruct the world solely on the basis of his individual thought independent of his time or place. He sees in Roussel the same audacity of perspective and rejection of tradition that in the plastic arts he noted and admired in Marcel Duchamp. Literary value, then, becomes identified with a system of ethics even as in other instances it is permeated with metaphysics or linguistic rebellions. An author who uses the device of dark humor, according to Breton's introductory observations, has built himself a defense mechanism against the vulnerable condition of human existence and thereby found a channel of release. That is why he considers his handpicked nonnational gallery of writers particularly free in spirit and possessed of a contagious power to stir subversion in the conscience of their readers.

In fine, Breton put his pen to the service of anyone who through writing awakened sensibilities, sharpened the imagination, stirred rebellion or caused restlessness, whether or not he maintained the established norms of literary values. On the other hand, he had no indulgence for brooding, egocentric writers, regardless of their prestige or literary achievements. Static meditation, however representative of the age or of the delicacy of feeling of its author, had a festered character that was not appealing to Breton. Therefore, many luminaries of the time are absent from his critical evaluations. For instance, Breton was attracted to Gide during the First World War when he "incarnated nonconformism in all its forms" but when later Gide seemed to have lost his intransigence as he assumed the posture of a famous literary figure, Breton had no more use for him. Similarly, the Valéry he admires is the creator of M. Teste and not the poet of the meticulously composed neosymbolist poems, which made him famous in the latter part of his career. By caring for an author merely for part of that author's lifetime, Breton demonstrates how wrong it is to make critical generalizations about the human mind or personality, which are not static structures but are in constant flux and receptive to the atmospheric pressures of society or human contacts. Such is the case with Valéry and Gide, whom he approves in their earlier years and with whose so-called mature capacities he is disappointed.

Breton's predilections had global dimensions and encompassed authors of various ages: his choices range from budding poets like the child, Gisèle Prassinos, to the septagenarian Maurice Fourré. Of Henry Miller, whom he admired for his guts, he said with a generous measure of his own dark humor, that his lack of popularity among Americans had made it obvious that Miller was like the atomic bomb earmarked for foreign consumption.[12] He was particularly partial to indigenous talents of faraway places, unspoiled by European influences. In Aimé Césaire he admired the "capacity for refusal" and said that his speech was "beautiful as a fresh supply of oxygen."[13] In the Haitian poet Magloire-Saint-Aude he saw passion like "the wheel of anguish as it is geared with ecstasy."[14] In Malcolm de Chazal he applauded the definition of volupté as the resolution of the physical and mental in that sort of unity so akin to his own concept of the universe.

It was particularly in the last decades of his life that Breton seized every occasion to signalize the free spirit in men of letters. In fact what Breton was seeking from Paris to remote Oceania, from the annals of occult philosophies to the artwork of the inmates of insane asylums, was "a reservoir of moral health."[15]

He was drawn to writers who like himself achieved a mystical intimacy with nature, who were easily aroused to wonder by simple manifestations of the dynamism of the physical world, who gave love and sensuality a high place in their existence, and who had been able to deliver themselves from the self-torture of an inherited code of sins, who loved the immediacy of life and in the name of liberty were not afraid to use the pen as others used the sword. Convulsive beauty, which he had defined early in his writing career, led to the discovery of convulsive literature, which was the fundamental excuse of the work of art, as Breton believed and evidenced in the long series of critical writings that are an important and integral part of his work. It was on the basis of their common frame of reference that Breton had used "La Lampe dans l'horloge" as the title of an article in 1948 whose central subject was the work of Malcolm de Chazal, and that a year later in a letter addressed to Breton, Chazal summed up Breton's particular place in the world of letters and of human thought by identifying him with the symbol: "You have the rigor of a Novalis or Rilke . . . , with your mental arrow aimed at the Orient . . . the lamp always burning in the clock of Divine Knowledge . . . a true mind cannot be patriated to any particular land." [16] Since Breton's article was full of references to Fulcanelli's *Les Demeures philosophales* although with no precise reference to the lamp image, it is evident that Fulcanelli's explanation would clarify the compliments that Breton and Chazal exchanged. Fulcanelli explains that in the hand of the statue of the figure called Temperance at the foot of the tomb of François I in the Cathedral of Nantes, one can detect a clock with a lantern inside of it. In the "profound signification of the symbol" Fulcanelli points out that "the meaning of *lantern* completes that of *clock*. In fact, if the lantern illuminates because it contains light, the clock appears as the dispenser of that light, which is not received in one shot but little by little, progressively, in the course of the years and with the aid of time. . . . Time, sole master of wisdom" [17]: the message of the tribute to Breton is evident. Would not his wisdom—Chazal was implying—be the more acutely understood as time charged and recharged its luminosity?

XVI

TOWARD
A NEW
HUMANISM

"Where there is no fire there is nothing left"
—*Entretiens*

Whereas André Breton had many fervent affiliates in his audacious literary reforms and co-travelers in his early political orientations, his aspiration to emancipate the human intelligence had left him virtually alone. As his friend Pierre de Massot, who observed him closely at the end of his life, said: "The fate of such a man, even when surrounded, is to remain alone." [1] In the long dialectics of his *Entretiens* of 1952, he constantly proposed to subordinate his personality and assume the role primarily of narrator and chronicler of the various phases of the surrealist movement: "In view of the fact that I was invited to give an account of the chronological unfolding of a spiritual adventure which had been and still remains a collective venture, I should relatively efface myself." [2] Yet if his last essays collected in *La Clé des champs* are read as a whole, rather than as occasional pieces, they maintain an ideological consistency. Breton is the first to admit this, not as a token of sincerity, but as a conscious pursuit of a goal in keeping with a well-defined concept of the purpose of life. Although there will no doubt be many surrealist poets and artists to leave their names and their mark on the literature and art of the century, André Breton's philosophy has remained uniquely his own; and as he grew older it became more and more his basic concern whether he was viewing a new painting, discovering a new writer, or contemplating the political scene. Although modestly he searched for a spiritual genealogy among philosophers of the past, from the gnostics to the nineteenth-century phenomenologist, if indeed his thought had affinities with the occultist tradition as we have noted, if it has roots in Hegel and has derived inspiration from Charcot, Janet, and Freud—nonetheless it is distinct, original, and unshared in its particular comprehension of the chain of events, free will, love, liberty, destiny, and eternity. It has suggested a climate totally foreign to both nineteenth-century attitudes and to twentieth-century prolongations of them. As in his last years he elaborated on them and found their confirmation in his life experience in the ensuing years, Breton modified the notions of humanism prevalent in European literature for a millennium.

In the fourth issue of *La Révolution surréaliste*, Breton had proclaimed, "we wish, we shall have the beyond here and now." As we view his work at the end of his career and juxtapose it with that of his early colleagues, it would almost appear as if his "we" were an editorial one, and that as he defined and illustrated his notion of the "beyond here and now" in both his life and his writings, he came closer to some modern theologians and philosophers of science than to most literary men.

When the world was proclaiming "liberation"—Breton had heard of the liberation of Paris while writing *Arcane 17*—his exhilaration had been somewhat mitigated by his far broader notion of liberty. He suggested that when men and nations have left their prisons and broken their shackles, they will not necessarily become free. They will be like people who are passing the crisis of a serious illness; but when the crisis is passed, they have not necessarily recovered. It may simply be, as he says, the "remission of the ailment." With all his optimism in regard to the inherent nature of man, Breton viewed the end of World War II with pessimism as far as man's immediate ethical and political future was concerned. The end of the hostilities had given him no reason to alter his notion that the destiny of man was in a state of crisis and that we were witnessing what he had called in an article on Marcel Duchamp "a civilization that is ending." [3] Throughout the rest of his life he sought an awareness of this fact on the part of latter-day humanists; he espoused the firm conviction that what Marcel Duchamp had done in the field of art by radical surgery of the notion of art, had to occur in the drastic revision of the notion of humanism itself.

Liberty from any specific disaster was to him of no consequence unless there were forces in movement to effect the ethical transformation of man, to make true social liberty a viable state. That ethical change involved a state of constant vigilance, a refusal of all escapism in the face of troubling realities. Breton shared Descartes' faith in the human mind, but for Breton the mind was something more varied, more subtle, more powerful than Cartesian reason, equal to the problems it had to face but not fully aware of its own potential. Rationalism leads to despair; the true exercise of imagination, of which he gave so many illustrations in the various facets of his work, leads to a greater comprehension of reality. "The imaginary is what tends to become real," as he had said early in the development of his surrealist concept in *Il y aura une fois*.

In "Second Arche" (1947) as he envisages the indubitable transition that must occur between a "finishing civilization and the civilization of the future," he sees the dangers of calling by new names the intolerances, the vilifications of the human spirit that were symptomatic of the old. Breton was particularly suspicious that the word "decadent" was being used in Communist countries to qualify those elements of the West that were actually the heritage of liberty; this sense of liberty had somehow survived in the hands of individuals, who passed it as a torch to each other despite the defaults of the group. For Breton, the libertarian attitude is incompatible with political commitments or indoctrinations. If it is in the nature of human society as with the physical universe to be in a constant state of flux, then the libertarian is the one who, whether artist or humanist or even physicist, is in a constant state of search and discovery, ever on the alert to recognize the symptoms that indicate that the sign has survived the thing that was signified by it, which is the point, Breton thought, "where dogmas end." [4]

In the article "Comète surréaliste," where he was ostensibly speaking about art and the surrealist exposition of 1947, he concluded his meditation about art with a statement on the three integral needs of humanity to which the artist must dedicate himself: "(1) to seek the social liberation of man, (2) to work without respite for the integral *encrusting* of mores, (3) to remake human intelligence." [5] The French expression, hard to translate into English, is "*l'entendement humain*," which means more than "understanding." It encompasses that enormous human reservoir of experience, which we have neither probed fully nor really understood because we have established another of those untrue contradictions in creating an antithesis between the conscious and the subconscious. Breton believes psychic distance involves various strata, going from the bright or intense consciousness to the penumbras of the subconscious—a series of modulations, all equally vital to the recognition of human reality. Judging from the number of times Breton returns in his last essays to a review of the explanations of psychic automatism, it becomes apparent that surrealist investigations into the psyche have been, as he thought, grossly misunderstood. The exploration of the lower depths of consciousness was neither a game, as some would have us believe, nor a desire to find causative explanations for the aberrations and abnormalities, as is the case with Freudian psychology. Rather, it was an attempt to reclaim for the creative mind the unused resources of human consciousness, which are deemed part of the normal attributes. In his study of Nadja, in his investigations of dreams and of the spontaneous imagery of automatic writing, Breton was not after disorder for disorder's sake but searching for the tracks of man's natural but lost heritage, symbolically identifiable with the ancient search for the Philosopher's Stone. His search is poetically evocative of *l'age d'or*. Even in the period when with his colleagues he engaged in automatic writing, hypnotic slumber, séances in the guise of medium interrogations, simulations of insanity, and dialogues concerning erotic experiences, Breton was wary of excess and very vigilant lest the experimenter lose control of his experiment. He was from the beginning preoccupied with the dangers and affected by considerations of mental hygiene. One of the basic reasons for much of the conflict between Breton and his surrealist comrades had been his efforts to exercise on their activities the intellectual controls of the man of science, whereas so many of the others went into automatic writing and hypnotic states for personal hallucinatory kicks. In *Entretiens* Breton explains the confrontations in no uncertain terms:

> The "slumbers" . . . developed in certain of the sleeping subjects an impulsive activity in which one could fear for the worst. I remember, in particular, one séance grouping about thirty guests at the house of a friend of Picabia's, Mme de la Hire. A vast house, discreet lighting: despite everything we did to prevent it a dozen persons, men and women, who were far from being acquainted with each other, had fallen asleep at the same time. As they came and went, vaticinated and gesticulated competing with each other, the spectacle was not very different from that of the convulsive patients of Saint-Menard. Around two o'clock in the morning, worried about the disappearance of several of them, I finally discovered them in the obscure antechamber, where as if by common consent and having procured the necessary cord, they were trying to hang themselves from the coat-rack. . . . Crevel, who was of their number, seemed to have persuaded them. They had to be awakened rather harshly. Another time after a dinner at Eluard's in a suburb of Paris, several of us had to control Desnos who, in a sleeping state, was brandishing a knife, in hot pursuit of Eluard in the garden. As you can see the suicidal ideas which existed in Crevel in a latent state, the silent hatred of Desnos for Eluard, took under these conditions an extremely active and critical turn. . . . The aggravation of my fears on the subject of what could menace the mental equilibrium of Desnos made me become determined to take all possible measures to avoid future incidents. It goes without saying that our relations became profoundly affected.[6]

This type of apprehension proved the basis of Breton's break not only with Desnos but with many other surrealists, who in the long view of things, appear to have been more interested in the "games" than in the search for psychic truth. Objective observations of subjective experiences prove difficult to achieve. Breton had grave misgivings about deviations prolonged beyond the experiment, such as the use of artificial stimulants and narcotics as aids to the artistic creative impulse. Baudelaire in his *Les Paradis artificiels* had warned against the same problems connected with the distinction between observation of mental and sensual aberrations and uncontrolled participation in them. It is in this context that one can understand Breton's total lack of sympathy for all forms of deep-rooted narcissism including homosexuality. When he states in "L'Art des fous" that there is a "reservoir of moral health in the mentally sick," [7] he does not mean that the insane person is thereby an artist, nor does he confuse the destiny of the explorer who dives lucidly into the reservoir with that of the mentally ill person who has been overpowered by these very resources of the psyche. For Breton the exploration of the psyche does not entail the disturbance of the psychic balance of man, and it is not necessarily a narcissist cult of the ego. It is more akin to Apollinaire's idiom and ideal embodied in that line of "Les Collines" in which he expresses the hope that as a result of man's ever-increasing knowledge of the human condition he would become "more pure more live more learned." The cult of *being* is directed toward a loss of self-consciousness in reaction to the intense egotism it becomes in so many writers.

In "La Lampe dans l'horloge," which is the key essay of his later years, André Breton views the position of modern humanity as one in high and imminent danger and is aware of an "immediate peril" menacing the human species, caused primarily by the disappearance of the sense of responsibility. Characteristically he makes a distinction between the human condition per se and the abject *situations* that man has created for himself. In keeping with his consistent philosophical position of some thirty years, he can be pessimistic about the situations without extending the condemnation to the essential human state.

After World War II he had seen no reason to wave flags, and he asserted in *Entretiens* the need to redefine the social problem. "La Lampe dans l'horloge" starts with the most severe indictment of the human situation: "From the end of this pestilential corridor where contemporary man has placed himself it becomes morally almost impossible to begin to breathe again." [8] It has been proved to him conclusively that the transformation of the world can occur only on a moral basis. If defaults such as moral license, the pursuit of personal gain, and the gratuitous existence geared to routine tasks continue to possess man, he can never recuperate his human heritage.

> From the throes of the frightful physical and moral misery of our time, we are awaiting, this side of despair, for the untamed energies of rebellion to return to the premises of the task of emancipating man.

Though not despairing, Breton scrutinizes with apprehension systems that under the deceiving banners of social change may engulf man even more deeply in the old, demagogical bondages.

On the other hand, he found himself in a constant state of retaliation against "end of the world" attitudes of his politically noncommitted contemporaries who were proclaiming the end of Western humanism, equating the transient character of certain facets with the total mortality that has beset other past civilizations. André Malraux sought solace from the evanescent character of vanished civilizations in the survival of the work of art as a token, the eloquent museum that outlasts its creators, granting man a vicarious immortality. Breton's interest in ancient myths and civilizations is quite different. It is not the object or relic that interests him per se, as a static if beautiful reminder of the dead past; rather, he sees in the object the survival of the spirit of man's inventive imagination, and for him this spirit is not an ephemeral, intangible asset but is as persistent as the gene that is transmitted from one mortal body to another, effecting the continuity of civilizations and resisting definitive extinction. Just as we have seen him search for common bases beyond national divisions, so Breton looks for links between what are for him not successive civilizations but intermittent waves of the notion of civilization. His search for the spark that survives the old flame and lights up a new one, is at the basis of his sustained interest in primitive civilizations, of the intense stimulation he drew out his visits to Mexico and the American Far West, in the discovery of Indian folklore, and the uninhibited forms of pre-Christian myth and cultures.

Breton was not really quite ready to call the millennium, for he could detect in man's abject state some reversible signs. "La Lampe dans l'horloge" has the structure of most of Breton's essays: the point of departure is a recent book or human contact, and around the immediate object of his meditation Breton develops the broader implications and repercussions that justify his choice. In this case the target is Malcolm de Chazal, and the title "La Lampe dans l'horloge" is used in the hermetic sense of the image explained in the previous chapter. In his essay Breton searches in contemporary society for such minds as carry the true wisdom of the human heritage and combat the almost overwhelming forces that may be able to reverse the sign so that man "may cease to live on the bank of a mined hill like a leaf of grass ashamed that its seed has been blown there by the wind. He will recapture a taste for seeing himself as a being conceived for a purpose determinable by himself alone and whereby he is not duplicated by anyone else. This is not vanity."

Breton was seeking out not men of good will but the modern equivalents of saints, who would bridge the abyss from "anguish to ecstasy" in the words remembered and borrowed from his old teacher, Dr. Pierre Janet, as a fitting designation for the true mystic. According to Breton the modern mystic is one who learns to fuse man's mental and sensual experiences into what Malcolm de Chazal had called *volupté*, the junction between the physical and the mental. Is there a paradox or contradiction between the desire for knowledge and the desire for spontaneous, sensual pleasure? Not really for the modern man, says Breton; for the aesthetic and the scientific are facets of the same total stimulus of the mind which, as he defined it earlier, produces a convulsive sense of the beauty of existence. Man's default as a human stems not from his mortality but from his failure to scratch beyond the surface of his perceptions, from his unawareness of the dynamism of the natural world, from his inability to fathom the scope of his innate liberty. Nature, according to Breton, does not reveal its creator but aids man in discovering his own powers and thereby intensifying his satisfaction with existence here and now. In "Fronton-Virage," another essay of the last collection of prose, Breton gives a tangible illustration of this in the incident of the Mexican beans, which has been told by others as well as by Breton but not quite with the slant he gives the story. It seems that psychologist Jacques Lacan and anthropologist-critic Roger Caillois were visiting André Breton, and the three of them were observing the jumping of the Mexican beans. His friends were amused at his childish fascination with what seemed some kind of miracle, and at his delay in opening the beans to see what caused the apparent magic. Breton explained that his hesitancy was not due to any superstitious beliefs in magic, for he was well aware of the physical cause of the movement (a parasitical insect lodged in the bean), but the sense of wonder was as necessary to his well-being as the knowledge and evidence of the logical cause. "Beauty demands that most often one should enjoy before understanding." [9]

The repression of the sense of magic in human life was for André Breton a narrowing or impoverishment of the scope of the inherent human condition. The weakened or vanishing power of religious ecstasy should be rechanneled, he thought, and applied to the sacralization of life itself. It is in this light that he viewed Chazal's *Sens Plastique II* as it referred to notions of *volupté* that sounded very much like the premises on which Breton had been building his own philosophy of life:

> Penetrating with eyes banded in this super laboratory of the senses I try . . . to delabyrinthize this mixed sensation . . . in view of discovering the relation of "volupté" with the symbolic language of nature, and how beyond this language it is linked to Universal Joy, to form this unity of which we have the most perfect example in this sensation of incorporating with the world of things, much like the paroxysm of happiness experienced by lovers.[10]

In the case of Malcolm de Chazal, as in other subjects of his essays, Breton proceeds from the particular to the general. The exceptional being is a source of optimism, where the norm is often depressing. Each illuminator of the human spirit or inner human adventure is an index for him, a sign, a light in the human labyrinth. The windows have bars, but they are nonetheless windows, an indication that through individual efforts the "capacity of our tomorrows" may yet be pierced. "La Lampe dans l'horloge" is at the same time the most pessimistic and the most optimistic essay of Breton's, as it juxtaposes his images of light and darkness, in correspondence with the interplay of destructive and constructive forces that haunt modern man.

Basically Breton's philosophy is not one of accommodation such as we find in Camus and Sartre, but a *table rase*, even more radical than that of Descartes' three centuries before. A world has simply died with its loss of the basic sense of civilization, and a new one is about to be born in this "epoch of inhumanism." It is not conceived as the end of a world, but as an *interruption*: the cessation of one system of codes and a need to reactivate the ethical mechanism which in itself is continuous. His *table rase* involves not a humanistic attitude but a physio-psychic readjustment of man's nature to a non-anthropocentric view of the universe. If we go back to Sartre's definition of humanism, we see how different is Breton's. In "L'Existentialisme est-il un humanisme?" Sartre says: "Man is not emprisoned in himself but always present in a human universe." In rejecting otherworldly transcendence, Breton refuses the social surpassing of self as well. If man does not need a "beyond" to fulfill himself, neither will he necessarily improve his state by becoming involved in collective social action, for the collectivity will be as meagerly creative and even more constraining than his solitude if it consists of a solidarity of solitudes that have proved by themselves ineffective agents in defining the nature of man. The social entity will simply vilify the personal one so much the more. It would seem indeed, as we superficially view Breton's criticism of society, on which his rebellion was based from the beginning, that the attack is suicidal, since it bears on the mores that have come out of that society and on the constant return of man to the same frame of reference of that society. But the fact is that as with the passage of time Breton lost the early assiduity of his active protest with its revolver symbol and became increasingly skeptical of existing political formats that aimed to restructure society, he became a more fervent defender of *individualism*, and his work became a reservoir of future revolutions and a preparation for future humanisms. To him there came the realization that each man can transform *his world* according to his desire outside the undeniably unjust political formats of the day. He envisaged surrealist activity more and more as "the interior experience and adventure." [11] Just as for Descartes the greatest liberty was an inner liberty, so for Breton the power of transcendence of social mores became not an outer but distinctly an inner battle, belying the early exhibitions of revolt. Unlike the existentialists, Breton did not consider the notion of *becoming* distinct from the search for essence. Involvement in life is not necessarily manifest in outer action but in the search for a fuller sense of being. Paradoxically, if there is something almost neoclassical in Breton's interest in universal man, in qualities latent in all men, rather than in individual eccentricities, the success of the spiritual exploration depends on the initiative of the individual man, not on a *superman* but on an *alerted* one. In *La Philosophie du surréalisme*, Ferdinand Alquié has said: "surrealism represents in the history of humanism the most daring, the most total project that has ever been conceived to restore to man all his right to happiness and the free deployment of his passions." [12] But Alquié asks: "Can one, however, save man without finding recourse beyond man?" The answer may well be that what seems impossible to the philosopher appears more feasible to the artist; perhaps to a certain extent in self-delusion the poet in Breton thought it possible to satisfy his own yearning for the "beyond" through the medium he knew best how to utilize, the metaphor in verbal form; it could be manifest, he thought, in other channels as well.

In rejecting humanisms that place man at the center of the universe, Breton established a broader correspondence between the physical forms of our earth and found the ancient alchemists' notion of "metamorphosis" closer to the philosophies of modern sciences. He refuted precepts of Occidental culture that have made humanism a specific product of the West:

There cannot be any question of a new humanism until history, re-
written after having been agreed upon among all peoples and limited
to a single version, will consent to take as its subject man as a whole,
from as far back as documents permit, and to give an account in complete objectivity of his past facts and gestures without special regard
to the country that this one or that one inhabits and to the language
he speaks.[13]

Any future humanism must have a broader base and a richer sense of the
worth of individual life and of the beauty of its perishable nature. Only
then will "man come out of the labyrinth having groped and found in
the night the lost thread." [14]

Breton's philosophy did not prove popular in his lifetime. For one
thing, his constant emphasis on the role of the individual as the basis of
any new humanism, and the degree of liberty he attributed to the individual was incompatible with the leveling tendencies of the various types of
collectivism that constitute society today. The championship of the
unexploitable qualities of the essential man as opposed to the exploitable
ones of men reduced to norms was completely out of tune with the
processes of regimentation of work, study, play, and war. His very optimism
irritated his philosopher contemporaries; for instead of confronting man
with burdens of responsibility toward other men or toward God, Breton's
table rase left everything wide open, and therefore man remained free
not merely to *choose* his destiny but to create it. If you declare the world
"absurd" and deprive it of any significance, you give man a nonpersonal
excuse for stagnation. But as Victor Crastre says in his distinction between
Dadaism and surrealism, "Breton and his friends ventured to give significance to the world—or to create a world which might at last have a
significance." [15] By this presumption Breton made himself vulnerable and
his philosophy forbidding. For him even the meaning of the word "absurd"
was quite different from its later use. Life is absurd not in the nauseating
sense of the word but so far as "absurd" designates the forces that out-
distance the narrow limits of logic and gravitate toward the wondrous. To
lull oneself in lyrical transcendence with the illusion that man must
find his dignity in the act of suffering is poor comfort, according to Breton.

But man is more receptive to the lyricism of despair than to that of
exuberance. The popularity of dark philosophies is understandable. Tragedy is in its fashion comforting, casting the faults of our insufficiencies on
our own imperfect nature or on the cruelty of the universe and its creator.
Tragedy has its accompanying emotion of despair that purges man of the
sense of default and of the much more devastating pang of regret for

what was attainable but not attained. Society is much more likely to applaud those who commiserate with man's plight than with those who offer constant reminders of his unsurmounted but not unsurmountable shortcomings. That is why Breton in his last years gave the impression of a solitary figure although he was surrounded with successive generations of young people. Among these youths he was careful to distinguish between the large number whose enthusiasms were based on a superficial interest in automatism and the various other techniques of surrealism, and those whose aesthetics was based on a valid code of ethics. His own silence at the end, as he tried to adjust to the notion of old age, was based on the conviction that he had been consistent and had said all that he had to say. If there was a tinge of sadness in the stubborn optimism of his philosophy, it was the awareness of the unfulfillment of the spiritual scope of man's allotted time on earth: "the flagrant disproportion between the breadth of man's aspiration and the individual limits of his life." [16]

XVII

THE LAST
YEARS

—Non c'est vrai tu t'en vas?

—La Terre fait eau de toutes parts la mousse
vit aux dépens des mots d'amour. Ce soir, le
vent porte mes couleurs j'ai laissé la clé sur la
cheminée
—*Tragic, à la manière des "comics"* (1943)

Breton's writing in the last ten years of his life was minimal. Outside
of fragmentary pieces and collaborations with some of the younger colleagues he had attracted around him, he felt that he had completed his
written work; he had no addendas or retouches to make. How contrary to
the Mallarméan concept of the Great Work! Mallarmé, dead prematurely
at the age of fifty-six, failed to accomplish what he had looked forward to
doing: to retire and devote his last twenty years to the Book that would
crystallize the meditations of a lifetime. Not so Breton! Even in his most
active years he had considered writing second to the creation of human
contacts and to the search for the comprehension of the symbols of the
human labyrinth. As he approached seventy * a haunting sense of age had
come over him, and he thought a great deal about the position that an
aging writer should assume in the world, and about the dignity of human
silence. He derided with his famous sarcasm the ludicrous display of de-
bility made by some of his elderly colleagues on television and in sweeping
statements in the press. The probity, which his enemies had identified
with puritanism, became more than ever evident in his desire to be a voice

* My own last interview with Breton in the fall of 1964 was the most informal
I had had, giving me for a moment the sense of affinity with him that so many
others had felt during a life that Breton shaped around human contacts and encounters. Later, in comparing notes with others, I discovered that what I had taken
for my mismanagement of the interview, was really not my fault but the way most
interviews with Breton came out: that one ended up by talking more than he.

d'outre-tombe rather than an anachronism or a broken record. He did not seem to feel his public relevance, and he thought of his ideology as something private, available to a small coterie, effective only in the dim future if a moral transformation should take place in society: "Curious prophet who does not notice that the hour of his prophecy has arrived." [1]

In his study, where books and objects seemed to have standing room only, his mind conveyed a sense of total order, clarity, and serenity, of complete satisfaction with the course taken and the ends achieved. He thought he might live to be eighty, but he seemed to be more curious about the happenings in the world outside of himself and in the minds of those younger than himself than in his own future destiny.

On the eve of his death *Nadja* had finally come back into print and was accessible again in the kiosks of Paris in paperback for a few francs. He was happy that it had become available to a brand-new generation, for his faith in the young had not abated, and what he thought it might do for them was not indoctrinate but serve as that same kind of provocation that so many objects, adventures, and books had been for himself as a young man. Discovery of what goes on in the mind of a young person was for Breton the same type of activity as finding beautiful stones or objects, or a fascinating cave, or some primitive imprint on a piece of wood. It was part of the unraveling of the human mystery: the dawn of a mind like the dawn of the day over the mountain.*

"André"—strange how five generations of young people whom he had befriended or magnetized called him by his first name, not out of disrespect but because, as Robert Benayoun remarked: "Never did the youngest of his friends ever have with him the generation gap. They considered him as one of their own group and confided in him fraternally." He added: "André, let it be known, terrorized only the imbeciles." [2]

His sense of fraternity had become intensified with the years despite many breaks of friendships and disillusionments with those he had called friends. The last years were spent almost exclusively in group activities where he signed his name to tracts and proclamations in alphabetical order along with the others of the group. Jehan Mayoux observed in one of the many tributes after his death: "No one was less anxious than he to impose his thought, to obtain agreement founded on his personal prestige (and

---

* This man, known for his violent outbursts and forbidding demeanor, with what gentleness he questioned my own small daughter, age fourteen, whom I had "cruelly," as he thought, left standing for an hour in the courtyard below while I was talking with him. When on his insistence I had her come up, I had the extraordinary chance of seeing the charm of André Breton operating on the young, as in her hesitant French she freely spoke of her likes and dislikes about French literature under his inquiry and total attention.

his prestige was great) on the authority of the past; no one was more curious about someone else's thought, more attentive to what each had to say." [3]

Despite a certain mellowness of manner he maintained the sharp character of his moral protest, which incited the exaltations and indignations of those who were attracted to his circle. After the war his attacks had been directed against the return of bourgeois complacency and the palliative accorded to it by dark and fatalistic philosophies. As his friend André Pieyre de Mandiarques observed: "at seventy Breton was still fighting against the scandal of the world." [4]

The last surrealist exposition that Breton initiated was in the form of a retaliation against the one of the rue Saint-Honoré, organized by the museum establishment, which threatened, he thought, to make surrealism an object of pleasure in the hands of the philistines. The counter exhibit, L'Ecart Absolu, as it was called, showed, characteristically, Breton's unwillingness to reminisce about the past but his desire to look rather to the future; judging from the works exhibited by his young friends and postwar artists, Breton was not so much interested in an inventory of past accomplishments of surrealism as in its radiation, its continued verve for discovery, the scientific character of its investigations of the enigma of human nature, of what in Entretiens he had called "the extrareligious sense of the sacred." It was an exposition de combat, which "attacks directly the most intolerable aspects of the society in which we live." [5] In a pamphlet "Tranchons-en," which Breton signed, it becomes obvious that art itself had ceased for Breton and for his latter-day associates to harbor any "aesthetic alibis." The exposition was a form of social criticism against those who, in confining surrealist art to specific dates and hanging the paintings on the museum walls, would act as gravediggers to the movement. There is in this, one of the most significant of the pamphlets, an attempt to determine the essential distinction between surrealism and other avant-garde movements: the purity of its protest which, "contrary to Dada," did not cultivate "negation for negation's sake" and was not attracted to "paroxysms of nihilism." Nor was its power of vaticination simply a "brave new world" attitude, for as Breton had already insisted in Arcane 17, progress and material comforts are not a sign of the transformation of man. The marvelous is not even what science considers its miracles, but a "fulguration" of desire "replenished with each surge of a new generation of youth."

What Breton had established in those last years was a climate of excitement and disinterested collaboration among his young friends as they met in the Café de la Promenade de Vénus. As one of them observed at

Breton's death: "He was the link among men who, without him, would never have met each other." [6] In the wake of Breton's sudden departure from their midst, they were still sitting around the café tables, conversing in quiet tones over a cup of coffee or some short liqueur, their indelible accents of mourning for the absent Breton incompatible with the burning radical passion of the pamphlets and the magazine, *L'Archibras*, which had been planned with Breton and was to appear without him, but whose first number was to be an epitaph to him.*

The group's life together had been an almost daily encounter, continued in the summer months by their frequent visits to Breton's retreat in Saint-Cirq in his fifteen summers there. The young men and women who shared Breton's enthusiasm and subversiveness blended "the revolutionary will and the poetic spirit." [7] In Saint-Cirq they explored for stones and agates, for rare objects in antique shops, and played revelatory games such as *l'un dans l'autre*, which was a way of discovering the endless evidences of the analogies of things in the universe. The summer after his death the friends returned, the activities were still mechanically being performed by a small group searching for shining pebbles under the oppressive heat in the dried-up bed of the Lot River, and his absence was as enormous and as haunting as it had been at the Promenade de Vénus.

In one of his last articles Breton had explained why he looked so piercingly and obstinately for stones. He questioned the stones as he had questioned all things and all phenomena of life. As he said, "the necessity of a quest becomes more and more exigent every day." [8] In Rimbaud's *Les Illuminations* stones play a mysterious and recurring role: they seem to talk or to hide, depending on the psychic awareness of the viewer. The mysticism of stone is cultivated in deeper and more persistent fashion not in Breton's writings but in the human quest which is the core of the poetic search. "One may as well say that in this way one enters in the domain of indices and signs." Questioning the stones was for him a way of transcending a world denuded of sense. The stone carried as the mountain, as the eagle, as the water, "the signature of nature." "The stones . . . continue to speak to those who will listen to them." He saw a strong link between the caprices of nature and those of the arts, and where has nature left as permanent an imprint as on stone? But beyond the message, beyond the intimation of the lost paradise on earth that lies buried in the stone, Breton viewed his agates with an even more significant purpose. The search

* In the year that followed Breton's death, I had occasion to attend several of the meetings of the group at the Promenade de Vénus, and saw a number of his followers in the summer at Saint-Cirq La Popie. In 1969 the group disbanded, seeing no longer a unifying purpose in the association.

for lucidity in the most opaque of all material things is the emblematic gesture of the alchemist in his quest for the Philosopher's Stone; Breton's gold is made of light, whether epitomized in the North Star or in the clarity of the stone polished by the ages. It is the last of the many forms of communication he found with the physical world in the course of his lifetime. In the dark recesses of the cellar of his Saint-Cirq castle there was a mountain heap of agates, glowing harvest of the relentless pursuit of luminosity.

Through the *aubépine de la pluie,* through the flesh of the loved one seen "as one with the snow of the mountain in the rising sun," through the soaring of the eagle and all the other miraculous birds such as the ibis, and finally through the communion with the stone, Breton discovers an ever-widening orbit of reality, which is identified with the living experience in the world of things and beings. The imaginary was the projection of that reality. On the other hand, the metaphysical sense was intensified by the notion that the inert stone shining in the mud of the river Lot held a dynamic potential for revelation.[9]

Saint-Cirq La Popie was ideally suited for the surrealist role it played in the last years of Breton's life. High on a hill was the modest farmhouse, the realization of that mysterious castle that Breton had dreamed of in the days of the First Manifesto, where he had hoped to unite all his friends. The friends of that day were no longer with him, but the later groups enjoyed their visits in the rustic manor. It was both emblematic and paradoxical. The most cosmopolitan of French writers of the first half of the twentieth century had found his roots in the most French section of France, a retreat that was totally unspoiled by foreign or even tourist influences, an anachronism in time, vested with medieval character, completely free of any traces of modern improvements. The gnostic Breton, whose antipathy to established religion had been a running theme in his writings, had found his retreat next door to a church, from whose towers the bells rang regularly to mark the passage of time, to emphasize repeatedly the fact that it dominated the countryside and the hearts of the simple people who tilled the land in that uncomplicated heart of France. Rimbaud has said that he had his ancestors' blue Gallic eyes; Saint-Cirq, in fact the whole department of the Lot of which it is part, appears typical Gallic country, somehow untouched, guarding in its hills the reality of its archeological past.

Almost daily in the summer Breton dined with his family and friends in the only inn on the summit, overlooking the wide panorama of the valley. There the old cashier characterized him as *doux,* and tears filled her eyes. Breton *doux* (gentle and sweet), a friend of the simple and the illiterate, totally devoid of snobbishness except in regard to the conceited and the fatuous; he saw a vast difference between the simplicity of the honest uneducated man and the dishonest pretentiousness of many educated ones; he would sit and smoke his pipe by the hour in the company of a poor peasant woman but would annihilate with a glare and a lion's roar the publicitymonger and the *arriviste*.

As his wife Elisa explained, the hot sun and the steep hills had become harder and harder to take, yet to the last summer he continued the excursions in the company of his young companions. His asthma grew worse, and he disdained medical aid. He avoided doctors as much as possible and did not go to see one until the end. He had been told that he had an allergy to dust, but there was nothing he could do about it, since at the rue Fontaine he had an old-fashioned furnace, no central heating, and took care of the coals himself. When the final crisis came, he was in Saint-Cirq and the local hospital could not take care of him; his daughter Aube believed that when they found out who he was, they were petrified lest they fail to save him and be blamed for their inadequacies. An almost surrealist solution was suggested: that he be taken by ambulance to Paris. It was rather prophetic, for in speaking of his own future death, Breton had said in his First Manifesto that he would want to be taken to the cemetery in a moving van. Instead, in a state of heart failure he was taken on an ambulance ride which lasted ten hours; the giving of oxygen was forbidden because of his asthmatic condition. In his agony he had enough of his dark humor to remark, *"Je fais une mauvaise sortie."* After the long ride he was taken up the four flights of stairs to his apartment, accompanied by his distraught wife. Aube, who was waiting for them, could not find a doctor in the middle of the night. When one finally arrived, Breton was already in a semiconscious condition. Down the long flight of stairs they took him and on to a hospital. He was unconscious when they arrived, but the last person who took care of him was a beautiful woman doctor, and Aube hoped that her father was able to sense that one of those salutary heroines, in whom he had all his life put so much faith, was hovering over him in his moment of agony. As a last attempt to save his life, they did a tracheotomy, but it did no good. He died at 2 A.M. in the arms of his daughter Aube on September 28, 1966.

As he had left no indications in his will about the place of burial, it was decided that he would have wanted to lie near his best friend, Benjamin Péret, in the cemetery of Batignolles. There on the first of October occurred a silent ceremony. His friend Benayoun described the funeral: "waves of young men and young girls often in couples, with arms entwined, had come from unknown parts to give tribute. Some came from the provinces; others from foreign lands, and returned immediately to their homes." [10] His widow and two former wives were there, as well as his daughter and all the young friends that had shared the *coin de table* of the Promenade de Vénus. Love had been a warm and lasting shield to his old age; it was there to lay him in his final resting place, in keeping with the spirit of his own wishes woven into the text of the poem, *Les Etats Généraux:*

> Je ne suis pas comme tant de vivants
> qui prennent les devants pour revenir
> Je suis celui qui va
> On m'épargnera la croix sur ma tombe
> Et l'on me tournera vers l'étoile polaire

> (I am not like so many living men
> who make plans to come back
> I am the one who goes
> They will spare me the cross on my tomb
> And they will turn me toward the polar star)

Toward the North Star! Indeed, strangely enough, the last object he had purchased in Saint-Cirq La Popie was a large stone star. It was to be included in the monument that his artist friend Alexander Calder would fashion for his tomb.

Among the many tributes that poured into Paris in the week that followed, Octavio Paz possibly summed up best the general feeling: "To write of Breton in a language which is not that of passion is impossible." [11] François Mauriac called him his dark brother: "I was the incarnation I suppose of all he despised, although he had sent me a few books. His death moves me, however: we were launched at the same time, we had the same crossing. This dark brother whom I had never seen, he was nonetheless my brother, but who hated what I loved, who loved what I hated— opposition of which he now knows the synthesis." [12]

But in Breton the darkness of anguish was always accompanied by the search for light. He was a solitary man by nature yet loved the gregarious condition of spiritual exchange; he was a nonnationalist as none had been before, yet despite many invitations to lecture all over the world, he remained in Paris for the last twenty years of his life and spent his summers in the most typical rural retreat in the heart of France. He had made a notorious bid for the recuperation of the irrational resources of human personality, yet he was impeccably lucid, had an intelligence strictly controlled, a mind profoundly disciplined. He had been the most notorious protester, the most exalted rebel of his generation of writers, yet there was quiet and serenity in his demeanor, and he was a man of peace, and for peace he would have been willing to sacrifice all the prerogatives of nationalism. He had had tremendous, violent hatreds, yet in his daughter's words "What dominated his life was his force of heart and love for beings and things." [13] He revolutionized poetry, yet for him a beautiful rainbow was a greater poem than all the word imagery in the world. He had combatted religions because he thought that they limited the scope of man's mysticism, yet he lived to the accompaniment of church bells in Saint-Cirq La Popie in the waning summers of his life. He championed the working man, was in easy communication with simple people, though he possessed the most sophisticated form of speech and had the manners of a country gentleman. He was fascinated with painting that broke away from natural lines and ordinary physical properties, yet at the same time he harbored an ever-deepening love for nature and marveled at its metamorphoses. Above all he had made himself essential to an ever-increasing number of tormented, rebellious youths. As one of them, Bernard Caburet, said at his funeral: "With you and the wind we have all we need."

NOTES

(All translations of quotations from the French are mine.)

INTRODUCTION

1. For the most complete and impersonal of such thematic studies, see Clifford Browder, *André Breton Arbiter of Surrealism*, Droz, Geneva, 1967. Less recent and more subjective studies will be discussed in Chapter 14.
2. For controversy about the relative merits and originality of Dada and surrealism and Breton's role in these movements, cf. Michel Sanouillet, *Dada à Paris*, Pauvert, Paris, 1965 and Herbert Gershman, "From Dada to Surrealism," *Books Abroad*, Spring 1969, pp. 175–81. For challenges to Breton as man and thinker, cf. Robert Champigny, "Analyse d'une définition du surréalisme," *PMLA*, March 1966, pp. 139–44 (also included in the author's *Pour une esthétique de l'essai, Lettres modernes,* 1967); also cf. Herbert Gershman, *The Surrealist Revolution in France*, University of Michigan Press, Ann Arbor, 1969.

I THE MAN AND HIS BACKGROUND

1. Malcolm de Chazal, *Almanach surréaliste du demi-siecle*, March–April 1950, Nos. 63–64.
2. Adrienne Monnier, *Rue de l'Odéon*, Albin Michel, Paris, 1960, p. 98.
3. *Nadja*, Gallimard, Paris 1928, pp. 73–74.
4. Aragon, *Anicet*, Gallimard (Livre de Poche), Paris, 1969, p. 114.
5. *Les Champs magnétiques*, Au Sans Pareil, Paris, 1920, p. 15.
6. *Ibid.*, p. 24.
7. *Ibid.*, p. 23.

8. *Ibid.*, p. 81.
9. *Ibid.*, p. 40.
10. *Les Champs magnétiques*, p. 25.

II THE FORMATIVE YEARS

1. *Entretiens*, Gallimard, Paris, 1952, p. 10.
2. *Les Pas perdus*, Gallimard, Paris, 1924, p. 12.
3. *Op. cit.*, p. 10.
4. *Les Pas perdus*, p. 98.
5. From "Caractère de l'évolution moderne et ce qui en participe," in *Les Pas perdus*, p. 186.
6. Ducasse (Lautréamont), *Les Chants de Maldoror* (Viau, Paris, several editions).
7. *Entretiens*, p. 12.
8. *Ibid.*, p. 22.
9. *Ibid.*, p. 21.
10. *Ibid.*, p. 22.
11. *Les Pas perdus*, p. 44.
12. *Ibid.*, p. 203.
13. "Lettres d' Apollinaire à André Breton," *La Revue des lettres modernes*, Nos. 104–7 (1964), p. 20 (December 21, 1915).
14. See *Entretiens*, p. 23.
15. "Lettres d'Apollinaire à André Breton," *op. cit.*, p. 29 (May 20, 1916).
16. Monnier, *op. cit.*, p. 58.
17. "Lettres d' Apollinaire," *op. cit.*, p. 32 (March 24, 1918).
18. "Caractères de l'évolution moderne et ce qui en participe," *Les Pas perdus*, pp. 203–5.
19. Cf. Marguerite Bonnet, "Aux Sources du surréalisme," in *Guillaume Apollinaire*, (*La Revue des lettres modernes*) 1964, on the attitude of Breton toward Apollinaire.
20. *Les Pas perdus*, p. 17.
21. *Ibid.*, p. 18.
22. *Entretiens*, p. 27.
23. *Les Pas perdus*, p. 9.
24. *Ibid.*, (same page).
25. Cf. Apollinaire, "La Petite Auto," *Calligrammes*.
26. *Les Pas perdus*, p. 71.

III   MEDICINE, MAGIC, AND MATHEMATICS

1. *Entretiens*, p. 29.
2. Breton refers to Janet frequently in his writings; cf. the discussion of the limitations of the influence of Freud in A. Balakian's *Surrealism: the Road to the Absolute*, 1959, new edition, Dutton, N.Y. 1970.
3. Pierre Janet, *L'Automatisme psychologique*, Felix Alcan, Paris, 1921 (9th ed.) p. 464.
4. *Ibid.*, p. 2.
5. *Ibid.*, p. 414.
6. *Ibid.*, p. 421.
7. Pierre Janet, *De l'Angoisse à l'extase*, Felix Alcan, Paris, (1926–8 ed.) p. 667. (Originally appeared in *Travaux du labiratoire de psychologie de la salpetrière*, 9–10 Serie.)
8. Pierre Janet, *L'Automatisme psychologique*, p. 421.
9. *Ibid.*, p. 422.
10. *Ibid.*, (same page).
11. Louis Ménard, trans., *Hermes Trismégiste*, Diderot & Cie, Paris, 1867.
12. Cf. A. J. Festugière, *L'Hermétisme*, Lund, CWK, Gleerup, 1948.
13. Cf. A. Balakian, "Les Champs magnétiques à la clé des champs," *Cahiers de l'Association Internationale des Etudes Françaises*, March 1963, No. 15.
14. Abbé Constant (Eliphas Lévi), *Transcendental Magic, Its Doctrine and Ritual*, trans. Arthur Edward Waite, Dutton, N.Y., no date, p. 105.
15. *La Clé des champs*, Sagittaire, Paris, 1953, p. 192.
16. Abbé Constant, *op. cit.*, p. 222.
17. *Ibid.*, p. 79.
18. *Ibid.*, p. 42.
19. *Ibid.*, p. 141.
20. *Ibid.*, p. 79.
21. *Ibid.*, p. 69.
22. *Ibid.*, p. 68.
23. *Ibid.*, p. 93.
24. *Ibid.*, p. 339.
25. *Ibid.*, p. 341.
26. *Ibid.*, p. 97.
27. Cf. Michel Sanouillet, *Dada à Paris*: Documents inédits, "Enquêtes chiffrées de Littérature," p. 595.
28. Abbé Constant, *op. cit.*, p. 39.
29. *Ibid.*, p. 47.
30. *Ibid.*, p. 236.
31. Pierre Vendryes, "Surréalisme et Probabilité," *Medium*, No. 3, p. 6.
32. *Ibid.*, p. 6.
33. *Ibid.*, (same page).
34. See *Entretiens*, p. 248.

35. *Les Pas perdus,* p. 15.
36. *Ibid.,* p. 36.

IV THE YOUNG POET IN PARIS

1. *Entretiens,* p. 50.
2. Letter quoted in Michel Sanouillet, *Dada à Paris,* No. 202 (Proust à Soupault), p. 559.
3. *Op. cit.,* pp. 41–42.
4. Sanouillet, *op. cit.,* No. 10 (September 5, 1919), p. 448; cf. also No. 9, p. 447.
5. *Entretiens,* p. 51.
6. *Ibid.,* p. 39.
7. Aragon, *Anicet,* pp. 237–38.
8. *Ibid.,* p. 119.
9. *Ibid.,* p. 116.
10. *Ibid.,* p. 242.
11. *Entretiens,* p. 39.
12. *Ibid.,* p. 40.
13. Quoted from Sanouillet, *op. cit.,* No. 4, p. 442.
14. Excerpt quoted from Georges Ribemont-Dessaignes: *History of Dada,* trans. Robert Motherwell in *The Dada Painters and Poets,* Schultz, Inc., Wittenborn, 1951, p. 101.
15. *Dada,* No. 3 (pamphlet), 1918.
16. *Ibid.*
17. *Dada* No. 2, in Motherwell, *op. cit.,* p. 106.
18. *Ibid.,* p. 92.
19. "Dada Fragments" (1916–1917), Motherwell, *op. cit.,* p. 51.
20. *Sept Manifestes,* ed. Tristan Tzara, Jean Budry, Paris, 1924, p. 11.
21. Sanouillet, *op. cit.,* No. 1, p. 440.
22. *Ibid.,* No. 5, p. 443.
23. *Ibid.,* No. 9, p. 446.
24. *Entretiens,* p. 58.
25. *Les Pas perdus,* p. 15.
26. Sanouillet, *op. cit.,* No. 8, p. 445.
27. *Entretiens,* p. 59.
28. He describes in *Entretiens* the difficulties he had serving the septuagenarian Jacques Doucet who was very reluctant to buy paintings by young artists. Breton would make earnest pleas on behalf of friends such as Max Ernst and André Masson. Breton was inclined to call him "Ubu protector of the arts," but Doucet was to redeem himself by leaving his collection of arts and letters to the city of Paris in what has come to be called *la bibliothèque Doucet.* As Breton tells the story, "Aragon, like myself, owed his most steady means of livelihood to Doucet, with an assignment to write him two

letters a week on literary subjects. . . . I received a thousand francs a month for this."

29. In *Littérature No. 5*, quoted by Sanouillet, *op. cit.* p. 354.
30. "Clairement," *Les Pas perdus*, p. 136.

V AUTOMATIC WRITING

1. Michel Carrouges, "Ecriture Automatique," *Cahiers GLM*, May 1, 1936, p. 31.
2. Collected in *Point du jour*, Gallimard, Paris, 1934, p. 249.
3. *Ibid.*, p. 250.
4. *Les Pas perdus*, p. 151.
5. *Les Champs magnétiques*, p. 79.
6. *Ibid.*, p. 12.
7. *Ibid.*, p. 82.
8. Cf. the article on Roussel, "Fronton-Virage," in *La Clé des champs*, Sagittaire, Paris, 1953, p. 199.
9. I refer to the edition of *Poisson soluble* in *Manifestes du surréalisme*, Pauvert, Paris, 1962, p. 103.
10. *Ibid.*, p. 134.
11. *Ibid.*, p. 118.

VI THE SURREALIST REBELLION

1. Collected in *Les Pas perdus*.
2. *Entretiens*, p. 70.
3. "Le Message automatique," written after the publication of *Les Champs magnetiques*, is included in the collection *Point du jour*.
4. *Les Pas perdus*, p. 24.
5. He explains this pointedly in "Le Message automatique," *Point du jour*.
6. *Entretiens*, p. 79.
7. Victor Crastre, *Le Drame du surréalisme*, Editions du Temps, Paris, 1963, pp. 43–44.
8. Clara Malraux, *Le Bruit de nos pas*, II, (*Nos Vingt Ans*), Grasset, Paris, 1966.
9. "Discours sur le peu de realité," collected in *Point du jour*.
10. Meanwhile the newly formed group had made its presence felt through a series of public activities; the most flagrant was a scandalous *cadavre* proclamation on the death of Anatole France, a much respected and popular novelist of the time. In indignation Doucet took Breton and Aragon off his payroll. They were truly and totally on their own.

11. Breton refers to the expression from Jules Monnerot's *La Poésie moderne et la sacré* in *Entretiens*, p. 71.
12. See Maurice Nadeau, *The History of Surrealism*, trans. Richard Howard, Collier Books, New York, 1965 and Herbert S. Gershman, *The Surrealist Revolution in France*, University of Michigan Press, Ann Arbor, 1969.
13. Dali, *Journal d'un génie*, Table Ronde, Paris, 1964, p. 25.
14. Crastre, *op. cit.*, p. 65.
15. *Entretiens*, pp. 110–11.
16. Collected in Nadeau, *Documents surrealistes*, Editions du Seuil, Paris, 1948.
17. *Entretiens*, p. 168.

VII   THE SURREALIST MANIFESTOES

1. As there are a number of editions of the Manifestoes in French there will be no page references. The Pauvert edition of 1962 includes other writings of Breton as well; its English translation appeared in 1969: *André Breton, Manifestoes of Surrealism*, translated by Richard Seaver and Helen R. Lane, University of Michigan Press, Ann Arbor, 1969.
2. It must be remembered that the first and only issue of a review called *Surrealism* had appeared on October 1, 1924. Its director, Yvan Goll, had used the word to put the review under the literary aegis of Apollinaire. Under the circumstances it can be better understood why Breton insists so much on taking the emphasis off aesthetic concerns and putting it on a more englobing, psychic level. Cf. Marguerite Bonnet, "*Aux Sources du surréalisme*," in *Guillaume Apollinaire*, (*La Revue des lettres modernes*), 1964.
3. Robert Champigny distinguishes, in his logical and intelligent analysis of Breton's First Manifesto, *op. cit.*, certain contradictions; out of context it may look as if Breton were structuring the irrational forces upon logical premises. But is must be remembered that the surrealist process was a two-step affair: the convocation of the psychic, automatic data, and the utilization of the data in verbal or pictorial expression. The human will was reacting to its own internal evidences, a facet of the subject having become the focal object of himself.

VIII   TOWARD A NEW STRUCTURE OF WRITING: ANALOGICAL PROSE

1. Among the many works appearing concurrently in those years were the surrealist writings of Dali, most of Max Ernst's, and important prose and verse

of Crevel, Desnos, and Eluard, as well as works Breton collaborated on with Eluard: *Ralentir Travaux* (1930) and *L'Immaculée Conception* (1930). Also many diversified writings of the surrealist group were appearing in the six issues of the review *Le Surréalisme au service de la révolution*, which ran from 1930 to 1933.

2. Cf. *Les Vases communicants*, Gallimard, Paris, 1955 ed., p. 23.
3. *Ibid.*, p. 97.
4. *Les Pas perdus*, p. 12.
5. *Les Vases*, p. 148.
6. *Ibid.*, p. 117.
7. *Ibid.*, p. 144.
8. *L'Amour fou*, Gallimard, Paris, 1937, p. 47.
9. *Nadja*, Gallimard, Paris, 1928, p. 74.
10. *Les Vases communicants*, p. 149.
11. Cf. the studies of the problem of reality in *Nadja* in Roger Shattuck's "The Nadja File," *Cahiers Dada surréalisme*, 1966, pp. 49–56; Carlos Lynes, "Surrealism and the Novel: Breton's *Nadja*," *French Studies*, 1966, pp. 366–87; Michel Beaujour, "Qu'est-ce que *Nadja*?" (Hommage à André Breton), *Nouvelle Revue Française*, April 1, 1967, pp. 780–800.
12. *Les Vases*, p. 41.
13. *Nadja*, p. 84; the following unnumbered quotations come from pp. 108, 115, 146, 190, 195, 206, 185, 187, 91, 210–11.
14. *Les Vases communicants*, p. 119; the following unnumbered quotations come from pp. 186, 187, 194, 195.
15. *L'Amour fou*, p. 44; the following unnumbered quotations come: the first two from p. 53 and the next two from p. 134.

IX BRETON THE POET

1. J. H. Matthews justly points out in his essay on Breton that "no assessment of his contribution to surrealism will be complete until his achievements as a poet have been established." *André Breton* (Columbia Essays on Modern Writers), Columbia University Press, N.Y., 1968, p. 6.
2. This is also very much the cabalistic notion that "thought is realized in becoming speech," or that verbal alchemy must be taken literally, as Breton suggested in effect in his *Second Manifesto*.
3. There is in Clifford Browder's book, *André Breton, Arbiter of Surrealism*, a classification of some of the extraordinary vocabulary, both biological and botanical. Relegated to a footnote in Browder's book, the subject of Breton's lexicon deserves thorough exploration not only in terms of Breton's work but as an index to the process of melding literary language with scientific terminology.
4. Fulcanelli, *Les Demeures philosophales*, Pauvert, Paris, 1966, Vol. I, p. 65.

5. *Ibid.*, p. 97.
6. *Ibid.*, Vol. II, p. 90.
7. *Poèmes*, Gallimard, Paris, 1938, p. 33.
8. *Ibid.*, "Hôtel des étincelles," p. 84.
9. *Ibid.*, p. 80.
10. *Ibid.*, "Les Ecrits s'en vont," p. 87.
11. *Ibid.*, p. 92.
12. *La Clé des champs*, p. 192.
13. *Poèmes*, "Le Soleil en laisse," p. 88.
14. *Ibid.*, "Noeud des miroirs," p. 92.
15. *Ibid.*, "Attitudes spectrales," p. 81.
16. *Ibid.*, "Tout paradis n'est pas perdu," p. 43.
17. Fulcanelli, *op. cit.*, Vol. I, p. 24.
18. *Poèmes*, "Sur la route qui monte et descend," p. 79.
19. Abbé Constant, *op. cit.*, p. 79.
20. *Ibid.*, p. 220.
21. *Ibid.* (same page).
22. *Ibid.*, p. 222.
23. Letter of Jacqueline Lamba to me, August 2, 1968.

X   SURREALISM AND PAINTING

1. The edition I refer to is *Le Surréalisme et la Peinture*, Brentano, New York, 1945.
2. *Ibid.*, p. 31.
3. *Ibid.*, p. 24.
4. For references to Chirico see *ibid.*, pp. 44, 41, 47.
5. *Ibid.*, p. 63.
6. *Ibid.*, p. 93.
7. *Point du jour*, p. 250.
8. Claude Lévi-Strauss, *The Savage Mind*, University of Chicago Press, Chicago, 1966, pp. 20 and 28. It is interesting to note that Breton and Lévi- Strauss worked side by side at the Voice of America during World War II. Breton, the older of the two, had an edition of *Le Surréalisme et la Peinture* published by Brentano during his stay in New York, and he had of course used the word *sauvage* in this context before Lévi-Strauss did. It is unlikely that Lévi-Strauss remained unaware of Breton's work. It was also when they were both in the United States that they both developed a great interest in the Hopi Indians. Breton used his observations in a poetic context, while Lévi-Strauss examined them as anthropological data.
9. *Le Surréalisme et la Peinture*, p. 65.
10. *Ibid.*, p. 74.
11. *Entretiens*, p. 139.

12. *Point du jour*, pp. 88–89.
13. *Le Surréalisme et la Peinture*, p. 71.
14. *Ibid.*, pp. 56–57.
15. *Entretiens*, p. 162.
16. *Op. cit.*, pp. 126–27.
17. Cf. Mary Ann Caws's parallel study of the notion of imagination in Breton and Bachelard: *Surrealism and the Literary Imagination*, Mouton & Co., The Hague, 1966.
18. For references to Tanguy, cf. *Le Surréalisme et la Peinture*, pp. 73 and 74.
19. *Ibid.*, p. 93.
20. For references to Matta, cf. *ibid.*, p. 195.
21. *Ibid.*, p. 97.
22. Breton, "L'Introduction à l'oeuvre de Toyen," *Toyen* (co-authors, Jindrich Heisler and Benjamin Péret), Editions Sokolova, Paris, 1953, p. 11.

XI THE POLITICAL ADVENTURE ON TWO CONTINENTS

1. *Entretiens*, p. 92.
2. *Les Manifestes du surréalisme*, Pauvert, Paris, 1962, p. 281 ("Discours au Congrès des écrivains").
3. New edition: Editions Sociales, Paris, 1961.
4. Cf. *ibid.* p. 45.
5. *Les Manifestes*, p. 253.
6. *Ibid.*, p. 253; following quotations from same essay are from pp. 250–61.
7. *Ibid.*, p. 235.
8. Cf. Marx, Engels, *op. cit.*, p. 42.
9. The quotations from "*Du Temps ou les surréalistes avaient raison*," are in *Manifestes*, pp. 285, 280, 281.
10. Salvador Dali, *Journal d'un génie*, Table Ronde, Paris, 1964, p. 87.
11. *Poésie et autre*, Le Club du meilleur livre, Gallimard, Paris, 1960, pp. 159–60.
12. *La Clé des champs*: "Limites non Frontières du surréalisme," p. 15.
13. *Ibid.*, p. 23.
14. *Ibid.*, p. 15.
15. *Entretiens*, p. 178.
16. *La Clé des champs*, "Visite à Léon Trotsky," p. 54.
17. *Entretiens*, p. 194.
18. *La Clé des champs*, p. 74.
19. *Arcane 17*, pp. 74–77.
20. Preface to Pierre Mabille, *Le Miroir du Merveilleux*, Editions de Minuit, Paris, 1962, p. 11.
21. *Entretiens*, p. 244.
22. "Le Surréalisme," *Conjonction*, Jan. 1946, p. 13.

XII   All quotations from the three long poems are from the anthology, *Poèmes*, Gallimard, 1940. They are now also available in Gallimard's *Signe Ascendant*.

XIII   ARCANE 17

1. The title's hermetic meaning substantiates Michel Beaujour's impression that "*Arcane* 17 is the text where the quest of an entire life takes shape, and of which all the others are only fragments." Preface, *Arcane* 17, Pauvert, Paris, 1965, p. 217.
2. In his eulogy of Breton, Armand Hoog gave an exact and at the same time poetic evocation of the Rock as he described its four million tons of natural structure—1565 feet long, 300 feet wide, 200 feet high—pierced by a giant arc. What struck Hoog more than the massive physical presence of the blond and rose conglomeration of fossils that constitutes the Rock were the millions of birds that tossed around it madly. He believed that the Rock immediately took on for Breton the same kind of emblematic significance as had previously the Tour St. Jacques in Paris and the Albigensian Montségur.
3. Cf. Auguste Viatte, *Victor Hugo et les illuminés de son temps*, Editions de l'Arbre, Montreal, 1942.
4. Cf. Michel Beaujour's cogent and detailed interpretations of the applications of the myths in *Arcane* 17 in "André Breton mythographe: *Arcane* 17," *Etudes Françaises*, Montreal, May 1967.
5. Albert Camus, *L'Homme révolté*, Gallimard, Paris, 1951, p. 127.

XIV   THE EXILE'S RETURN

1. Sartre, *Situations III*, Gallimard, Paris, 1949, p. 16.
2. "Libération de l'écrivain de 1947," *Situations II*, Gallimard, Paris, 1948, p. 225.
3. Tristan Tzara, *Le Surréalisme et l'après-guerre*, Nagel, Paris, 1948.
4. *Situations II*, p. 229.
5. *Ibid.*, p. 320.
6. *Ibid.*, p. 322.
7. *Ibid.*, p. 324.
8. Interview with Dominique Arban, *Combat*, May 31, 1947; included in *Entretiens*, p. 253.

9. Albert Camus, *L'Homme révolté*, Gallimard, Paris, 1951, p. 123.
10. "Un grand poète noir," *Hémisphères*, Nos. 2–3, 1943–4, p. 11.
11. Letter from Aube to me, Paris, November 5, 1966.
12. *Entretiens*, p. 217.
13. *Ibid.*, p. 22.
14. *La Clé des champs*, p. 270.
15. The wealth and variety of poetry written under the aegis of surrealism is revealed in J. H. Matthews' *An Anthology of French Surrealist Poetry*, University of Minnesota Press, Minneapolis, 1966.
16. *La Brèche*, No. 5, October 1963, p. 2.
17. *Entretiens*, p. 216.
18. *La Clé des champs*: "Lettre à une petite fille d'Amérique," p. 275.
19. *Entretiens*, p. 253.
20. The earliest of these was Sir Herbert Read's *Surrealism* in England, and Georges LeMaitre's *From Cubism to Surrealism* in America. My own *Literary Origins of Surrealism*, concentrating on the sources of surrealist mysticism, was written during the war and appeared in 1947. Meanwhile in France, Maurice Nadeau had already written a "history" of surrealism in Breton's absence, which greatly angered Breton, because Nadeau had not only buried him alive ("One never saw a more impatient biographer," *Entretiens*, p. 209) but had also determined the historical scope of surrealism and enclosed it in the period of the two world wars. This, Breton protested, ran counter to any comprehension of the essence of surrealism, which he conceived as an ascending awareness of life and art in a new context, liberated from old forms of humanism and the Judeo-Christian tradition. To say that surrealism was finished was tantamount, in Breton's opinion, to saying that there was no hope for the world; for him surrealism was an attitude of total subversion in relation not only to the literature of the past but to its notion of history, to its concepts of morality and sensibility, even to its comprehension of freedom, and as such it was an open road, very much at the beginning of work in progress. To delimit it in a specific era was to say that protest was futile, that it was like the foam of the waves, violent and inconsequential in the ceaseless tides of time. Breton could accept many penalties for having frightened the world with his symbolic and random revolver shot in 1930, but he could not accept a history of surrealism, which was so eager to establish boundaries and to catalogue the intellectual movement he had set in motion. However, even he had to admit that Nadeau did him and surrealism a great service in bringing back into print some of the most important documents of surrealism, and that in the role of historiographer, if not historian, he recorded as accurately as an outsider could the major events of the surrealist phenomenon. In its dissemination of the surrealist story Nadeau's book was to prove effective and provocative of interest in the movement.

    Other books gave Breton more immediate comfort. One such, which appeared at the same time as Nadeau's, and to which Breton was to refer constantly in his future writings, was Jules Monnerot's *La Poésie moderne et le sacré*. Monnerot was a native of the South Pacific French colonies—a fact which made him highly attractive to Breton. With the Martiniquan Aimé Césaire, the African Leopold Senghor, and the Oceanian Malcolm de Chazal, all of whom became close to Breton in this period of his life, Monnerot shared the enviable position of having been brought up in a place where French culture was superimposed on a more primitive culture, which, according to Breton, had closer communion with nature and was therefore more intimately involved with the basic principles of existence, human sensibility, and man's relationship to the rest of creation. Such French subjects as these had, he thought, the advantage of sharing the convenient qualities of French civilization: the language, the literary frame of reference, the spirit of free thought—despite the fact, according to Breton, that free thought had for a long time been waging a losing battle in France. But in addition to those acquisitions from foreign culture, they had kept in tune with the basic ethnic character of their native land, with its more genuine and natural mysticism, which made religion in the primitive sense of the word a part of social reality. To his great joy these concepts were expressed in Monnerot's book, which aimed to demonstrate that the monistic view of existence inherent in surrealism was very akin to the attitudes of the primitive mind (what Lévi-Strauss calls the "savage mind") that accepted the real and the so-called supernatural as a continuum and part of an over-all harmony. Breton's own voyages in the far West of the United States, among the Hopi Indians, in the caves of America's primitive Mexican and Indian cultures, had oriented him more and more toward sociological preoccupations: these held his interest and provided him with many of the answers to problems of human behavior and the functioning of human imagination with which literature had in many respects failed to be concerned.

21. Julien Gracq, *André Breton*, Corti, Paris, 1948, p. 104.
22. Letter of June 2, 1939.
23. Claude Mauriac, *André Breton*, Editions de Flore, Paris, 1949, p. 211.
24. *Ibid.*, p. 97.
25. Victor Crastre, *André Breton*, Arcanes, Paris, 1952, p. 11.
26. *Ibid.*, p. 20.

XV THE LITERARY CRITIC

1. *Anthologie de l'humour noir*, Sagittaire, Paris, 1950, p. 161.
2. *Les Pas perdus*, p. 187.
3. *Flagrant Délit*, Thésee, Paris, 1949, p. 50.
4. See *Entretiens*, p. 216
5. *Ibid.*, (same page).
6. *Flagrant Délit*, p. 51.
7. *Ibid.*, p. 14.

8. *Ibid.*, p. 41.
9. Cf. Léon Pierre-Quint, *Le Comte de Lautréamont et Dieu*, Fasquelle, Paris, 1967.
10. "It would be regrettable in my opinion to assemble the portraits at the beginning or at the end of the volume." Letter to Léon Pierre-Quint, April 29, 1940.
11. *Anthologie de l'humour noir*, p. 11; the following unnumbered quotations come from pp. 67, 167, 130, 232, 205.
12. Cf. *La Clé des champs*, p. 123.
13. *Hémisphères* (Review), Nos. 2–3, p. 11.
14. *La Clé des champs*, p. 110.
15. *Ibid.*, p. 227.
16. 14 December, 1949, collected in *Surrealist Almanach of a Half-Century* (La Nef), Nos. 63–64, March–April 1950.
17. Fulcanelli, *Les Demeures Philosophales*, Vol. II, p. 207.

XVI TOWARD A NEW HUMANISM

1. Pierre de Massot, "Dans le Château étoile," *André Breton, Le Septembriseur*, Eric Losfeld, Paris, 1967.
2. *Entretiens*, p. 213.
3. *View*, Series V, No 1, 1944, p. 13.
4. *La Clé des champs*, pp. 108, 109.
5. *Ibid.*, p. 105.
6. *Entretiens*, pp. 89–91.
7. *La Clé des champs*, p. 277.
8. *Ibid.*, p. 116; the following unnumbered quotations are from the same article pp. 118, 121.
9. *Ibid.*, p. 186.
10. As quoted by Breton from *Sens Plastique II*.
11. *Entretiens*, p. 134.
12. Ferdinand Alquié, *La Philisophie du Surréalisme*, Flammarion, Paris, 1955, p. 211.
13. *Arcane 17*, p. 67.
14. *Entretiens*, p. 278.
15. Victor Crastre, *André Breton*, Arcanes, Paris, 1952, p. 12.
16. *Entretiens*, p. 266.

XVII THE LAST YEARS

1. *Le Monde*, September 29, 1966.
2. *Le Figaro littéraire*, October 20, 1966.

3. *L'Archibras,* No. 1, 1967.
4. *Le Monde,* September 29, 1966.
5. *Entretiens,* p. 282.
6. *L'Archibras,* No. 1, 1967.
7. Georges Neveux, "Un Poète révolutionnaire," *Le Figaro littéraire,* October 6, 1966.
8. "La Langue des pierres," *Le surréalisme même,* No. 3, Autumn 1957, 63.
9. For a perceptive article on the subject, cf. Michel Beaujour, "The Stone Age," *Yale French Studies,* 1964, No. 31.
10. *Le Figaro littéraire,* October 2, 1966.
11. *L'Archibras,* No. 1, 1967.
12. "Le Bloc-Notes," *Le Figaro littéraire,* October 6, 1966.
13. Letter of November 5, 1966.

A SELECTED BIBLIOGRAPHY

The works of André Breton have all been listed chronologically, in their original editions, with indications of later and more available editions. However, articles that have appeared in magazines and have later reappeared in volumes of his collected essays have not been listed separately. Breton collaborated on many pamphlets and tracts, and gave numerous interviews to newspapers. These have not been listed here. A very thorough listing of these short pieces appears in Clifford Browder's *André Breton: Arbiter of Surrealism*.

Until the mid-1960's books and articles on André Breton were few enough so that a high proportion of them could be listed, even in a selected bibliography of secondary sources; however, since Breton's death in 1966 the number has been increasing rapidly. Particularly numerous were the short testimonial articles on the occasion of his death. Most of these have been omitted from this listing.

Of magazine issues devoted exclusively to Surrealism and/or André Breton the following may be of particular interest as critical references:

> *Yale French Studies*, no. 31, 1964.
> *L'Esprit Créateur*, Spring, 1966. Vol. VI, no. 1.
> *La Nouvelle Revue Française*, April 1, 1967.
> *Surréalisme Europe*, November–December 1968.

The most complete bibliography of surrealism to date is that of Herbert Gershman, University of Michigan Press, 1969.

THE WORKS OF ANDRÉ BRETON

Mont de piété. Paris: Au Sans Pareil, 1919.
Les Champs magnétiques (with Philippe Soupault). Paris: Au Sans Pareil, 1920.
Clair de Terre. Paris: Collection Littéraire, 1923.
Les Pas perdus. Paris: Gallimard, 1924, 1949. (Livre de Poche, 1970)
Manifeste du surréalisme, Poisson soluble. Paris: Sagittaire, Simon Kra, 1924.

Nouvelle edition augmentée d'une préface et de la *Lettre aux Voyantes,* 1929.

Légitime défense. Paris: Editions Surréalistes, 1926.

Introduction au discours sur le peu de réalité. Paris: Gallimard, 1927.

Nadja. Paris: Gallimard, 1928; other editions: 1945, '49; revised ed. 1963. English translation by Richard Howard, N.Y.: Grove Press, 1960. (Livre de Poche, 1964)

Le Surréalisme et la Peinture. Paris: Gallimard, 1928; enlarged edition: N.Y.: Brentano's, 1945; enlarged edition, Paris: Gallimard, 1965.

Second Manifeste du surréalisme. Paris: Simon Kra, 1930.

L'Immaculée Conception (with Paul Eluard). Paris: Corti, 1930, Seghers, 1961.

Ralentir Travaux (with René Char and Paul Eluard). Paris: Corti, 1930.

L'Union libre (unsigned). Paris: Editions Surréalistes, 1931. Later included in collection *Poèmes* (1948).

Le Revolver à cheveux blancs. Paris: Editions des Cahiers libres, 1932.

Misère de la poésie. Paris: Editions Surréalistes, 1932.

Les Vases communicants. Paris: Editions des Cahiers libres, 1932; Gallimard, 1955.

L'Air de l'eau. Paris: Cahiers d'Art, 1934.

Qu'est-ce que le surréalisme? Brussels: Henriquez, 1934. Translated by David Gascoyne. London: Faber and Faber, 1936.

Point du jour (collected essays). Paris: Gallimard, 1934.

Du Temps que les surréalistes avaient raison. Paris: Editions Surréalistes, 1935.

Position politique du surréalisme. Paris: Sagittaire, 1935.

Au Lavoir noir. Paris: GLM, 1936.

Notes sur la poésie (with Paul Eluard). Paris: GLM, 1936.

L'Amour fou. Paris: Gallimard, 1937.

Anthologie de l'humour noir. Paris: Sagittaire, 1940; revised and augmented: 1950. (Livre de Poche, 1970)

Fata Morgana. Marseille: Sagittaire, 1941. Buenos Aires: Editions des Lettres Françaises, 1942.

Pleine Marge. N.Y.: Karl Nierendorf, 1943.

Arcane 17. N.Y.: Brentano's, 1945; Paris: Sagittaire, 1947: new edition with article by Michel Beaujour, "André Breton ou la transparence," Paris: Pauvert, 1965.

Situation du surréalisme entre les deux guerres. Paris: Editions de la revue *Fontaine,* 1945.

Young Cherry Trees Secured Against Hares. (First translations of selected poems of André Breton by Edouard Roditi). N.Y.: *View,* 1946; reissued 1970.

Les Manifestes du surréalisme suivi de prolégomènes à un troisième manifeste ou non. Paris: Sagittaire, 1946.

Yves Tanguy. N.Y.: Pierre Matisse, 1946.

Ode à Charles Fourier. Paris: Editions de la revue *Fontaine,* 1947. Ed. Jean Gaulmier, Paris: C. Klincksieck, 1961. (Translation)

Martinique, charmeuse de serpents. Paris: Sagittaire, 1948.

Perspective cavalière. (Posthumous collection of final essays), edited by Marguerite Bonnet, Paris: Gallimard, 1970.

Poèmes. (Collected poems of Breton including "Fata Morgana," "Les Etats généraux," and "Ode à Charles Fourier.") Paris: Gallimard, 1948.

La Lampe dans l'horloge. Paris: Robert Marin, 1948.

Flagrant délit. Paris: Thésée, 1949; Pauvert, 1964.

Almanach surréaliste du demi-siècle (with Benjamin Péret). Sagittaire, 1950.

Entretiens (1913–52). Paris: Gallimard, 1952.

La Clé des champs. Paris: Sagittaire, 1953.

Introduction à l'oeuvre de Toyen (with Jindrich Heisler and Benjamin Péret). Paris: Sokolova, 1953.

Adieu ne plaise. Alès: P.A.B., 1954.

Les Manifestes (additional article: "Le Surréalisme en ses oeuvres vives,") Paris: Sagittaire, 1955.

L'Art magique (with Gérard Legrand). Paris: Club Français du livre, 1957.

Constellations. N.Y.: Pierre Matisse, 1959.

Le La. Alès: P.A.B., 1961.

ANTHOLOGIES

André Breton (Poètes d'aujourd'hui no. 18), Introduction by Jean-Louis Bedouin. Paris: Pierre Seghers, 1950.

Les Manifestes du surréalisme (and other essays). Paris: Pauvert, 1962. English translation by Richard Seaver and Helen R. Lane, Ann Arbor: University of Michigan Press, 1969.

Poésie et autre. Edited by Gérard Legrand. Paris: Le Club du Meilleur Livre, 1960.

Selected Poems. Translated by Kenneth White. London: Cape Editions, 1969.

CRITICAL WORKS ON SURREALISM AND ANDRÉ BRETON

Alexandre, Maxime. *Mémoires d'un surréaliste.* Paris: La Jeune Parque, 1968.

Alquié, Ferdinand. *Philosophie du surréalisme.* Paris: Flammarion, 1955. English translation. Ann Arbor: University of Michigan Press, 1965.

Audoin, Philippe. *Breton.* Paris: Gallimard, 1970.

Balakian, Anna. *Literary Origins of Surrealism.* N.Y.: King's Crown Press, 1947; N.Y.U. Press, 1966.

——. *Surrealism: the Road to the Absolute.* N.Y.: Noonday Press, 1959; Dutton, 1970.

——. "Des Champs magnétiques à la clé des champs," *Cahiers de l'Association Internationale des Etudes Françaises,* March 1963, no. 15.

——. "André Breton as Philosopher," *Yale French Studies,* 1964, 31.

——. "Metaphor and Metamorphosis in André Breton's Poetics," *French Studies,* vol. 19, no. 1, Jan. 1965.

——. "The Significance of the Surrealist Manifestoes," *L'Esprit Créateur*, Spring, 1966.

——. "Mort d'André Breton," *Bulletin de la Société des Professeurs Français en Amérique*, Année 1966.

Baron, Jacques. *L'An I du Surréalisme, Suivi de l'An dernier*, Paris: Denoël, 1969.

Beaujour, Michel. "The Stone Age," *Yale French Studies*, 1964, no. 31.

——. "Qu'est-ce que Nadja," *Nouvelle Revue Française*, April 1, 1967.

——. "André Breton mythographe: 'Arcane 17,' " *Etudes Françaises*, Montreal: May, 1967.

——. "De l'Océan au château: Mythologie surréaliste," *French Review*, Feb. 1969.

Bédouin, Jean-Louis. *Vingt ans de surréalisme*. Paris: Denoël, 1961.

Brodin, Pierre. "André Breton," *Présences contemporaines*. Third edition, Paris: Editions Debrasse, 1956.

Browder, Clifford. *André Breton, Arbiter of Surrealism*. Geneva: Droz, 1967.

Bruno, Jean. "André Breton et la magie quotidienne," *Revue Métaphysique*, Jan.–Feb. 1954, no. 27.

Cardinal, Roger. "André Breton: The Surrealist Sensibility," *Mosaic* 1, 1968.

Carrouges, Michel. "Ecriture automatique," *Cahiers GLM*, May 1, 1936.

——. *André Breton et les données fondamentales du surréalisme*. Paris: Gallimard, 1950. (Idées, 1967.)

Caws, Mary Ann. *Surrealism and the Literary Imagination: a Study of Breton and Bachelard*. The Hague: Mouton, 1966.

——. *The Poetry of Dada and Surrealism*. Princeton: Princeton University Press, 1970.

Champigny, Robert. *Pour une esthétique de l'essai: "Une Définition du surréalisme."* Paris: Lettres Modernes, 1967.

Chazal, Malcolm de. *Almanach surréaliste du demi-siècle*. March–April, 1950, Nos. 63–4.

Crastre, Victor. *André Breton*. Paris: Arcanes, 1952.

——. *Le Drame du surréalisme*. Paris: Edition du Temps, 1963.

Dali, Salvador. *Journal d'un Génie*. Paris: La Table Ronde, 1964.

Dhainaut, Pierre. "André Breton présent," *Cahiers du Sud*, no. 62, 1966.

Duits, Charles. *André Breton a-t-il dit passe*. Paris: Lettres Nouvelles, 1969.

Eigeldinger, Marc. *André Breton: essais et témoignages*. Neuchâtel: La Baconnière, 1949.

Fowlie, Wallace. *Age of Surrealism*. N.Y.: The Swallow Press, 1950.

Fumet, Stanislas. "André Breton ou le défi concerté," *Table Ronde*, no. 226.

Gaulmier, Jean. Critical edition of *Ode à Charles Fourier*. Paris: C. Klincksieck, 1961.

Gershman, Herbert. *The Surrealist Revolution in France*. Ann Arbor: University of Michigan Press, 1969.

——. *A Bibliography of the Surrealist Revolution in France*. Ann Arbor: University of Michigan Press, 1969.

Gracq, Julien. *André Breton*. Paris: Corti, 1948.

Gros, Léon-Gabriel. "André Breton, la leçon du cristal," in *Poètes contempo-rains*. Second Series. Paris: *Cahiers du Sud*, 1951.

Hardré, Jacques. "Present State of Studies on Literary Surrealism," *Yearbook of Comparative and General Literature*. Chapel Hill: University of North Carolina Press, vol. iv, 1960.

Hoog, Armand. "Permanence du surréalisme," *La Nef*, no. 35 (Aug. 1947).

Hubert, J. D. "André Breton et le paradis perdu," *French Review*, Dec. 1963.

Hubert, René Riese. "Miró and Breton," *Yale French Studies*, no. 31, 1964.

——. "The Coherence of Breton's *Nadja*," *Contemporary Literature*, no. 2 (Spring 1969).

Lemaître, Georges. *From Cubism to Surrealism in French Literature*. Cambridge, Mass.: Harvard University Press, 1941; rev. ed., 1947.

Lynes, Carlos. "Surrealism and the Novel: Breton's Nadja," *French Studies*, Vol. XX, no. 4 (Oct. 1966).

Massot, Pierre de. *André Breton: le Septembriseur*. Paris: Eric Losfeld, 1967.

Matthews, J. H. *Introduction to Surrealism*. University Park: Pennsylvania State University Press, 1965.

——. *André Breton* (Columbia Essays on Modern Writers). N.Y.: Columbia University Press, 1967.

——. *Surrealist Poetry in France*. Syracuse: Syracuse University Press, 1969.

Mauriac, Claude. *André Breton*. Paris: Editions de Flore, 1949.

——. "Breton et l'humour noir," in *Hommes et Idées d'aujourd'hui*. Paris: Albin Michel, 1953.

Motherwell, Robert, ed. *The Dada Painters and Poets*. N.Y.: Wittenborn, Schultz, Inc., 1951.

Nadeau, Maurice. *Histoire du Surréalisme*. Paris: Editions du Seuil, 1945.

——. *Documents surréalistes*. 1948, new edition, Paris: Editions du Seuil, 1964.

——. Translations of these works by Richard Howard, N.Y.: Macmillan, 1965.

Nelli, René. "Des Troubadours à André Breton," *Cahiers du Sud*, no. 38, 1951.

Ray, Paul. "Some Notes on Surrealism in the Novel," *Romance Notes*, VII, 1965.

Rougemont, Denis. "André Breton," *Preuves*, no. 189.

Rubin, William. *Dada, Surrealism and Their Heritage*. N.Y.: Museum of Modern Art Catalogue, 1968.

Sanouillet, Michel. *Dada à Paris*. Paris: Pauvert, 1965.

Schuster, Jean. *Archives 57/68*. Paris: Eric Losfeld, 1969.

Shattuck, Roger. "The Nadja File," *Cahiers Dada, Surréalisme*, 1966.

Short, Robert, in Walter Laqueur and George L. Mosse, eds. *The Left-Wing Intellectuals between the Wars*, 1919–1939. N.Y.: Harper and Row, 1966.

Soupault, Philippe. *Le Vrai André Breton*. Liége: Dynamo, 1966.

Tzara, Tristan. *Le Surréalisme et l'après-guerre*. Paris: Nagel, 1948.

Vendryes, Pierre. "Surréalisme et Probabilité," *Medium*, No. 3.

Waldberg, Patrick. *Chemins du surréalisme*. Bruxelles: Editions de la Connaissance, 1965.

RELATED WORKS

Aragon, Louis. *Anicet*. Paris: Gallimard, 1921; Livre de Poche, 1969.

Bonnet, Marguerite. "Aux sources du surréalisme," in *Guillaume Apollinaire* (La Revue des Lettres Modernes), 1964.

Camus, Albert. *L'Homme révolté*. Paris: Gallimard, 1951.

Constant, Abbé (Eliphas Levi). *Transcendental Magic, Its Doctrine and Ritual* (translated by Arthur Edward Waite). N.Y.: Dutton, no date.

Drieu La Rochelle, Pierre. *Sur les Ecrivains*. Paris: Gallimard, 1964.

Festugière, A. J., *L'Hermétisme*. Lund, O.C.K., Gleerup, 1948.

Fulcanelli (no given name indicated). *Les Demeures Philosophales*, vols. I & II. Paris: Pauvert, 1965.

Janet, Pierre. *L'Automatisme psychologique*. Paris: Felix Alcan, 1921. 9th edition.

——. *De l'Angoisse à l'Extase*. Paris: Felix Alcan, 1926. 8th edition.

Jean, Marcel. *Histoire de la peinture surréaliste*. Paris: Editions du Seuil, 1959.

Jean d'Arras. *La Légende de Mélusine* (renouvelé par Jean Marchand). Paris: Boivin and Cie, 1927.

Lévi-Strauss, Claude. *The Savage Mind*. Chicago: University of Chicago Press, 1966.

Mabille, Pierre. *Le Miroir du merveilleux*. Paris: Editions de Minuit, 1962.

Malraux, Clara. *Le Bruit de nos pas*, II (*Nos Vingt Ans*). Paris: Grasset, 1966.

Marx and Engels. *Etudes Philosophiques*. Paris: new ed., Editions Sociales, 1961.

Ménard, Louis. *Hermes Trismégiste*. Paris: Diderot & Cie, 1867.

Monnerot, Jules. *La Poésie moderne et le sacré*. Paris: Gallimard, 1945.

Monnier, Adrienne. *Rue de l'Odéon*. Paris: Albin Michel, 1960.

Myers, F. W. *The Subliminal Consciousness, Sensory Automatism and Induced Hallucination*. 1892.

Pierre-Quint, Léon. *Le Comte de Lautréamont et Dieu*. Paris: Fasquelle, 1967.

Sartre, Jean-Paul. *Situations II, III*. Paris: Gallimard, 1949.

Vaché, Jacques. *Lettres de Guerre*. Paris: Au Sans Pareil, 1919, 1949.

Viatte, Auguste. *Les Sources occultes du romantisme*. 2 vols., Paris: Librairie ancienne Honoré Champion, 1928.

——. *Victor Hugo et les illuminés de son temps*. Montreal: Editions de l'Arbre, 1942.

INDEX

NOTE: pages on which primary discussion occurs are indicated by italics; an asterisk indicates that a term has been defined.